Advanced
Word
Power

Second Edition

Advanced
Word
Power

Second Edition

Beth Johnson
Janet M. Goldstein

Townsend Press Reading Series
Groundwork for College Reading with Phonics
Groundwork for College Reading
Ten Steps to Building College Reading Skills
Ten Steps to Improving College Reading Skills
Ten Steps to Advancing College Reading Skills
Ten Steps to Advanced Reading

Townsend Press Vocabulary Series
Vocabulary Basics
Groundwork for a Better Vocabulary
Building Vocabulary Skills
Building Vocabulary Skills, Short Version
Improving Vocabulary Skills
Improving Vocabulary Skills, Short Version
Advancing Vocabulary Skills
Advancing Vocabulary Skills, Short Version
Advanced Word Power

Supplements Available for Most Books
Instructor's Edition
Instructor's Manual and Test Bank
Online Exercises
PowerPoint Presentations
Blackboard Cartridges

Copyright © 2011 by Townsend Press, Inc.
Printed in the United States of America
9 8 7 6 5 4 3 2 1

ISBN-13 (Student Edition): 978-1-59194-226-9
ISBN-10 (Student Edition): 1-59194-226-8
ISBN-13 (Instructor's Edition): 978-1-59194-227-6
ISBN-10 (Instructor's Edition): 1-59194-227-6

Send book orders and requests for desk copies or supplements to:

Townsend Press Book Center
439 Kelley Drive
West Berlin, New Jersey 08091

For even faster service, contact us in any of the following ways:

By telephone: 1-800-772-6410
By fax: 1-800-225-8894
By e-mail: cs@townsendpress.com
Through our website: www.townsendpress.com

Contents

NOTE: For ease of reference, the title of the selection that closes each chapter is included.

Unit Four

Unit Five

Unit Six

Appendixes

Preface: To the Instructor

The problem is all too familiar: *students just don't know enough words.* Reading, writing, and content teachers agree that many students' vocabularies are inadequate for course demands. Weak vocabularies limit students' understanding of what they read and the clarity and depth of what they write. In addition, students with weak vocabularies do not perform well on either the vocabulary *or* the reading comprehension parts of such standardized tests as the SAT.

The purpose of *Advanced Word Power* and the other books in the Townsend Press vocabulary series is to provide a solid, workable answer to the vocabulary problem. In the course of 30 chapters, *Advanced Word Power* teaches 300 important words, all of which are part of a solid college vocabulary and all of which occur with high frequency on standardized college-admission tests. Here are the book's distinctive features:

1 **An intensive words-in-context approach.** Studies show that students learn words best by reading them repeatedly in different contexts, not through rote memorization. The book gives students an intensive in-context experience by presenting each word in **six** different contexts. Each chapter takes students through a productive sequence of steps:

● Students infer the meaning of each word by considering two sentences in which it appears and then choosing from multiple-choice options.
● On the basis of their inferences, students identify each word's meaning in a matching test. They are then in a solid position to deepen their knowledge of a word.
● Finally, they strengthen their understanding of a word by using it three times: in two sentence-length practices and in a passage practice.

Each encounter with a word brings it closer to becoming part of the student's permanent word bank.

2 **Abundant practice.** Along with extensive practice in each chapter, there are a crossword puzzle and a set of unit tests at the end of every five-chapter unit. The puzzle and tests reinforce students' knowledge of the words in each chapter. In addition, Chapters 2 through 30 reuse words from earlier chapters (such repeated words are marked with small circles, like this°), allowing for more reinforcement. Last, there are supplementary tests in the *Instructor's Manual and Test Bank* and the online exercises that accompany the book. All this practice means that students learn in the surest possible way: by working closely and repeatedly with each word.

3 **Controlled feedback.** The opening activity in each chapter gives students three multiple-choice options to help them decide on the meaning of a given word. The multiple-choice options also help students complete the matching exercise that is the second activity of each chapter. A limited answer key at the back of the book then provides answers for the third activity in the chapter. All these features enable students to take an active role in their own learning.

4 **Focus on essential words.** A good deal of time and research went into selecting the 300 words featured in the book. Word frequency lists were consulted, along with lists in a wide range of vocabulary and SAT preparation books. In addition, the authors and editors each prepared their own lists. A computer was used to help in the consolidation of the many word lists. A long process of group discussion then led to final decisions about the words that would be most helpful for students.

5 **Appealing content.** Dull practice materials work against learning. On the other hand, meaningful, lively, and at times even funny sentences and passages can spark students' attention and thus enhance their grasp of the material. For this reason, a great deal of effort was put into creating sentences and passages with both widespread appeal and solid context support. We have tried throughout to make the practice materials truly enjoyable for teachers and students alike. Look, for example, at the selection on page 23 that closes the fourth chapter of this book.

6 Clear format. The book has been designed so that its very format contributes to the learning process. Each chapter consists of two two-page spreads. In the first two-page spread (the first such spread is on pages 8–9), students can easily refer to all ten words in context while working on the matching activity, which provides a clear meaning for each word. In the second two-page spread, students can refer to a box that shows all ten words while they work through the fill-in activities on these pages.

7 Supplementary materials.

   a A convenient *Instructor's Edition* is available at no charge to instructors using the book. It is identical to the student book except that it contains answers to all of the activities and tests.

   b A combined *Instructor's Manual and Test Bank* is also offered at no charge to instructors who have adopted the book. This supplement contains a general vocabulary placement test, along with a pretest and a posttest for the entire book as well as for each of its six units. It also includes teaching guidelines, suggested syllabi, an answer key, and an additional mastery test for each chapter.

   c *PowerPoint presentations and a Blackboard cartridge* are available for the book and may be downloaded from the "Supplements" area for instructors at www.townsendpress.com.

   d *Online exercises,* available in the Online Learning Center at www.townsendpress.com, also accompany the book. These exercises consist of two additional tests for each vocabulary chapter in the book. In addition, they include—at the instructor's option—some of the practice material in the book itself. The program includes a number of user- and instructor-friendly features: brief explanations of answers, a sound option, frequent mention of the user's first name, a running score at the bottom of the screen, a record-keeping file, and actual pronunciation of each word.

   Probably in no other area of reading instruction is the computer more useful than in reinforcing vocabulary. These online exercises take full advantage of the computer's unique capabilities and motivational appeal. Here's how the program works:

   ● Students are tested on the ten words in a chapter, with each word in a sentence context different from any in the book itself.

   ● After students answer each question, they receive immediate feedback: The program states that the answer is right or wrong and why, frequently using the student's first name and providing a running score.

   ● When they complete each test, students receive their scores. If they repeat the test, they then receive a new score, labeled "R" on the scores report, with a number following the "R" indicating how many times they have taken the same test. What is so valuable about this, of course, is that the program gives students immediate additional practice with the words they need to review.

   ● In addition, the online exercise program offers a second, more challenging "Word Definitions" test in which students must identify the meanings of the chapter words without the benefit of context. This test is a final check that students have really learned the words. And, again, there is the option of a retest, with its own score.

   ● Finally, if the instructor so chooses, the online program will provide the student with two of the exercises in the book—Sentence Check 2 and the Final Check. Students can take these exercises online and receive immediate feedback and the option of a retest.

   Once students complete these exercises, their knowledge of each word in the chapter will have been carefully reinforced. And this reinforcement will be even more effective for having occurred in an electronic medium that especially engages today's students.

To obtain a copy of either the *Instructor's Edition* or the *Instructor's Manual and Test Bank*, instructors may contact Customer Service at 1-800-772-6410 or at cs@townsendpress.com.

8 **Realistic pricing.** As with the previous edition, the goal has been to offer the highest possible quality at the lowest possible price. While *Advanced Word Power* is comprehensive enough to serve as a primary text, its modest price also makes it an inexpensive supplement.

9 **One in a sequence of books.** The most fundamental book in the Townsend Press vocabulary series is *Vocabulary Basics*. It is followed by *Groundwork for a Better Vocabulary* (a slightly more advanced basic text) and then by the three main books in the series: *Building Vocabulary Skills* (also a basic text), *Improving Vocabulary Skills* (an intermediate text), and *Advancing Vocabulary Skills* (a more advanced text). The most advanced book in the Townsend Press vocabulary series is *Advanced Word Power*. There are also short versions of the *Building*, *Improving*, and *Advancing* books. Suggested grade levels for the books are included in the *Instructor's Manual.* Together, the books can help create a vocabulary foundation that will make any student a better reader, writer, and thinker.

Notes on the Second Edition

A number of changes have been made in the second edition of *Advanced Word Power:*

- **A full-color design.** Color has been carefully used throughout, not as window dressing but to add clarity and readability to the different parts of each chapter and the different sections of the book.

- **Discussion topics and writing assignments.** A new section, "Topics for Discussion and Writing," provides five high-interest items for each of the vocabulary chapters. Each item uses one or more of the vocabulary words in the chapter in a brief scenario suitable for class or small-group discussion, writing, or both.

- **Additional multicultural names and repeated words.** To broaden both the appeal and the effectiveness of the practice materials, ethnic names have been used more frequently, and more than twice as many vocabulary words have been repeated in the Sentence Checks and Final Checks.

- **Revised and updated practice items.** Most of the practice items throughout the book have been revised or updated to ensure that each item works as clearly and effectively with students as possible.

Acknowledgments

We are grateful to the teachers and editors who helped us determine the final list of words for *Advanced Word Power:* Donald J. Goodman, John Langan, Paul Langan, Carole Mohr, and Sherrie L. Nist. In particular, we would like to thank Susan Gamer for her extensive work on the first edition. We would also like to thank Kathryn Bernstein, Denton Cairnes, and Rick Moore for design, editing, and proofreading assistance with the second edition. Finally, we much appreciate the skills of designer extraordinaire Barbara Solot, whose full-color text design is as clear as it is inviting. The result of her artistry is a strikingly attractive book that both students and teachers will enjoy. All of these talented colleagues have helped us make *Advanced Word Power* even more effective and user-friendly than before.

Beth Johnson   *Janet M. Goldstein*

Introduction

Why Vocabulary Development Counts

You have probably often heard it said, "Building vocabulary is important." Maybe you've politely nodded in agreement and then forgotten the matter. But it would be fair for you to ask, "*Why* is vocabulary development important? Provide some evidence." Here are four compelling kinds of evidence.

1 Common sense tells you what many research studies have shown as well: vocabulary is a basic part of reading comprehension. Simply put, if you don't know enough words, you are going to have trouble understanding what you read. An occasional word may not stop you, but if there are too many words you don't know, comprehension will suffer. The content of textbooks is often challenge enough; you don't want to work as well on understanding the words that express that content.

2 Vocabulary is a major part of almost every standardized test, including reading achievement tests, college entrance exams, and armed forces and vocational placement tests. Test developers know that vocabulary is a key measure of both one's learning and one's ability to learn. It is for this reason that they include a separate vocabulary section as well as a reading comprehension section. The more words you know, then, the better you are likely to do on such important tests.

3 Studies have indicated that students with strong vocabularies are more successful in school. And one widely known study found that a good vocabulary, more than any other factor, was common to people enjoying successful careers in life. Words are in fact the tools not just of better reading, but of better writing, speaking, listening, and thinking as well. The more words you have at your command, the more effective your communication can be, and the more influence you can have on the people around you.

4 In today's world, a good vocabulary counts more than ever. Far fewer people work on farms or in factories. Far more are in jobs that provide services or process information. More than ever, words are the tools of our trade: words we use in reading, writing, listening, and speaking. Furthermore, experts say that tomorrow's workers will be called on to change jobs and learn new skills at an ever-increasing pace. The keys to survival and success will be the abilities to communicate skillfully and learn quickly. A solid vocabulary is essential for both of these skills.

Clearly, the evidence is overwhelming that building vocabulary is crucial. The question then becomes, "What is the best way of going about it?"

Words in Context: The Key to Vocabulary Development

Memorizing lists of words is a traditional method of vocabulary development. However, you are likely to forget such memorized lists quickly. Studies show that to master a word, you must see and use it in various contexts. By working actively and repeatedly with a word, you greatly increase the chance of really learning it.

The following activity will make clear how this book is organized and how it uses a words-in-context approach. Answer the questions or fill in the missing words in the spaces provided.

Inside Front Cover and Contents

Turn to the inside front cover.

●   The inside front cover provides a _____ that will help you pronounce all the vocabulary words in the book.

Now turn to the table of contents on pages v–vi.

●   How many chapters are in the book? _____

●   What two sections conclude each unit? _____

●   Four sections follow the last chapter. The first of these sections provides a limited answer key, the

second gives helpful information on using _____, the third contains

_____, and the fourth is a list of the 300 words in the

book.

Vocabulary Chapters

Turn to Chapter 1 on pages 8–11. This chapter, like all the others, consists of five parts:

●   The *first part* of the chapter, on pages 8–9, is titled _____.

The left-hand column lists the ten words. Under each **boldfaced** word is its _____

(in parentheses). For example, the pronunciation of *affinity* is _____. For a guide

to pronunciation, see the inside front cover as well as "Dictionary Use" on page 179.

Below the pronunciation guide for each word is its part of speech. The part of speech shown for

affinity is _____. The vocabulary words in this book are mostly nouns, adjectives, and verbs.
Nouns are words used to name something—a person, place, thing, or idea. Familiar nouns include
boyfriend, city, hat, and *truth*. **Adjectives** are words that describe nouns, as in the following word pairs:
former boyfriend, *large* city, *red* hat, *whole* truth. All of the **verbs** in this book express an action of some
sort. They tell what someone or something is doing. Common verbs include *sing, separate, support,* and
imagine.

To the right of each word are two sentences that will help you understand its meaning. In each
sentence, the **context**—the words surrounding the boldfaced word—provides clues you can use to figure
out the definition. There are four common types of context clues: examples, synonyms, antonyms, and the
general sense of the sentence. Each is briefly described below.

1 Examples

A sentence may include examples that reveal what an unfamiliar word means. For instance, take a
look at the following sentence from Chapter 1 for the word *incessant*:

The children nearly drove their parents crazy on the long car trip with their **incessant** questions: "Where are we going?" "Are we there yet?" "When can we get out of the car?"

The sentence provides three examples of incessant questions: "Where are we going?" "Are we there yet?" and "When can we get out of the car?" What do these three examples have in common? The answer to that question will tell you what *incessant* means. Look at the answer choices below, and in the answer space provided, write the letter of the one you feel is correct.

____ *Incessant* means   A. silent.   B. wise.   C. nonstop.

All of the examples given in the sentence are questions that young children on car trips ask over and over. So if you wrote *C*, you chose the correct answer.

2 Synonyms

Synonyms are words that mean the same or almost the same as another word. For example, the words *joyful, happy,* and *delighted* are synonyms—they all mean about the same thing. Synonyms serve as context clues by providing the meaning of an unknown word that is nearby. The sentence below from Chapter 2 provides a synonym clue for *dispassionate*.

> The surgeon's voice was **dispassionate** when he told the patient's family that the operation had failed, but despite his calm tone, his eyes looked very sad.

Instead of using *dispassionate* twice, the author used a synonym in the second part of the sentence. Find that synonym, and then choose the letter of the correct answer from the choices below.

____ *Dispassionate* means   A. unreasonable.   B. unemotional.   C. disturbing.

The author uses two terms to describe the surgeon's tone of voice: *dispassionate* and *calm.* Therefore, *dispassionate* must be another way of saying "calm." (The author could have written, "The surgeon's voice was calm.") Since *calm* can also mean "unemotional," the correct answer is *B*.

3 Antonyms

Antonyms are words with opposite meanings. For example, *help* and *harm* are antonyms, as are *work* and *rest.* Antonyms serve as context clues by providing the opposite meaning of an unknown word. For instance, the sentence below from Chapter 1 provides an antonym clue for the word *opulence.*

> The **opulence** of the magnificent, luxurious resort was in stark contrast to the poverty of the little fishing village at its gates.

The author is contrasting the resort and the fishing village, so we can assume that *opulence* and *poverty* have opposite, or contrasting, meanings. Using that contrast as a clue, write the letter of the answer that you think best defines *opulence.*

____ *Opulence* means   A. closeness.   B. riches.   C. permanence.

The correct answer is *B*. Because *opulence* is the opposite of *poverty,* it must mean "riches."

4 General Sense of the Sentence

Even when there is no example, synonym, or antonym clue in a sentence, most of the time you can still figure out the meaning of an unfamiliar word. For example, look at the sentence from Chapter 1 for the word *affinity.*

> My cat has an **affinity** for small, dark hiding places—I've often found her asleep in my dresser drawer, under the footstool, and inside my suitcase.

After studying the context carefully, you should be able to figure out the connection between the cat and small, dark hiding places. That will be the meaning of *affinity.* Write the letter of your choice.

____ *Affinity* means   A. a preference.   B. a fear.   C. ignorance.

Since the sentence says that the cat is often found in these places, it is logical to conclude that the cat has a preference for them. Thus answer *A* is correct.

By looking closely at the pair of sentences provided for each word, as well as the answer choices, you should be able to decide on the meaning of a word. As you figure out each meaning, you are working actively with the word. You are creating the groundwork you need to understand and to remember the word. *Getting involved with the word and developing a feel for it, based upon its use in context, is the key to word mastery.*

It is with good reason, then, that the directions at the top of page 8 tell you to use the context to figure out each word's _____. Doing so deepens your sense of the word and prepares you for the next activity.

● The *second part* of the chapter, on page 9, is titled _____.

According to research, it is not enough to see a word in context. At a certain point, it is helpful as well to see the meaning of a word. The matching activity provides that meaning, but it also makes you look for and think about that meaning. In other words, it continues the active learning that is your surest route to learning and remembering a word.

Note the caution that follows the activity. Do not proceed any further until you are sure that you know the correct meaning of each word as used in context.

Keep in mind that a word may have more than one meaning. In fact, some words have quite a few meanings. (If you doubt it, try looking up the word *make* or *draw* in a dictionary.) In this book, you will focus on one common meaning for each vocabulary word. However, many of the words have additional meanings. For example, in Chapter 1, you will learn that *fledgling* is an adjective meaning "inexperienced," as in the sentence "Myra and her sisters are excited about their fledgling catering service." If you then look up *fledgling* in the dictionary, you will discover that it has another meaning as a noun—"a young bird that has recently acquired its flight feathers," as in "We watched a robin giving flying lessons to her three fledglings." After you learn one common meaning of a word, you will find yourself gradually learning its other meanings in the course of your school and personal reading.

● The *third part* of the chapter, on page 10, is titled _____.

Here are ten sentences that give you an opportunity to apply your understanding of the ten words. After inserting the words, check your answers in the limited answer key at the back of the book. Be sure to use the answer key as a learning tool only. Doing so will help you to master the words and to prepare for the last two activities and the unit tests, for which answers are not provided.

● The *fourth and fifth parts* of the chapter, on pages 10–11, are titled _____ and _____.

Each practice tests you on all ten words, giving you two more chances to deepen your mastery. In the fifth part, you have the context of an entire passage in which you can practice applying the words.

At the bottom of the last page of this chapter is a box where you can enter your score for the final two checks. These scores should also be entered into the vocabulary performance chart located on the inside back cover of the book. To get your score, count the number of items that you answered correctly in each section. Then add a zero. For example, if you got seven answers right in Sentence Check 2, you would write "70" on the first line in the score box.

You now know, in a nutshell, how to proceed with the words in each chapter. Make sure that you do each page very carefully. *Remember that as you work through the activities, you are learning the words.*

How many times in all will you use each word? If you look, you'll see that each chapter gives you the opportunity to work with each word six times. Each "impression" adds to the likelihood that the word will become part of your active vocabulary. You will have further opportunities to use the word in the crossword puzzle and tests that end each unit and in the online exercises available at www.townsendpress.com.

In addition, many of the words are repeated in context in later chapters of the book. Such repeated words are marked with a small circle (°). For example, which words from Chapter 1 are repeated in the Final Check on page 15 of Chapter 2?

_____   _____   _____   _____

A Final Thought

The facts are in. A strong vocabulary is a source of power. Words can make you a better reader, writer, speaker, thinker, and learner. They can dramatically increase your chances of success in school and in your job.

But words will not come automatically. They must be learned in a program of regular study. If you commit yourself to learning words, and you work actively and honestly with the chapters in this book, you will not only enrich your vocabulary—you will enrich your life as well.

Unit One

Chapter 1

affinity	proximity
fledgling	sagacious
hackneyed	supplant
incessant	unassailable
opulence	voluminous

Chapter 2

brusque	morose
dispassionate	nonchalance
effervescent	progeny
indefatigable	stoic
misanthrope	voracious

Chapter 3

coalesce	insolvent
decadence	parsimonious
exemplary	prodigal
exuberance	surreptitious
incidental	writhe

Chapter 4

brevity	querulous
clemency	reproach
frivolous	respite
heist	torpor
lampoon	unscathed

Chapter 5

copious	meander
dearth	peripheral
eloquent	substantiate
jargon	unobtrusive
levity	vacillate

affinity	proximity
fledgling	sagacious
hackneyed	supplant
incessant	unassailable
opulence	voluminous

Ten Words in Context

In the space provided, write the letter of the meaning closest to that of each **boldfaced** word. Use the context of the sentences to help you figure out each word's meaning.

1 affinity
(ə-fĭn′ĭ-tē)
- *noun*

- It is hard for someone with an **affinity** for warm weather to be happy living in Alaska.
- My cat has an **affinity** for small, dark hiding places—I've often found her asleep in my dresser drawer, under the footstool, and inside my suitcase.

___ *Affinity* means   A. a preference.   B. a fear.   C. ignorance.

2 fledgling
(flĕj′lĭng)
- *adjective*

- The short-story class is full of **fledgling** writers. They're all enthusiastic, but since they're beginners, they're shy about sharing their work.
- Myra and her sisters are excited about their **fledgling** catering service, which was booked for three parties during its first week of business.

___ *Fledgling* means   A. old.   B. new.   C. different.

3 hackneyed
(hăk′nēd)
- *adjective*

- The **hackneyed** phrase "Have a nice day!" is heard so often that it has become almost meaningless.
- The worst part of our family reunions is hearing my uncle's **hackneyed** jokes—the ones he's been telling since about 1980.

___ *Hackneyed* means   A. worn-out.   B. insulting.   C. funny.

4 incessant
(ĭn-sĕs′ənt)
- *adjective*

- Mrs. Soto finally insisted that her husband see a doctor about his **incessant** snoring. It didn't bother him, but she wasn't getting any sleep.
- The children nearly drove their parents crazy on the long car trip with their **incessant** questions: "Where are we going?" "Are we there yet?" "When can we get out of the car?"

___ *Incessant* means   A. silent.   B. wise.   C. nonstop.

5 opulence
(ŏp′yə-ləns)
- *noun*

- The **opulence** of the magnificent, luxurious resort was in stark contrast to the poverty of the little fishing village at its gates.
- The writer Thoreau had no liking for **opulence**. He wrote in his journal, "That man is richest whose pleasures are the cheapest."

___ *Opulence* means   A. closeness.   B. riches.   C. permanence.

6 proximity
(prŏk-sĭm′ĭ-tē)
- *noun*

- The **proximity** of the railroad tracks worries neighborhood parents when their children play outside.
- My brother doesn't drive a car, so when he was apartment hunting, he had to consider the **proximity** of public transportation.

___ *Proximity* means   A. similarity.   B. contrast.   C. nearness.

7 sagacious
(sə-gā′shəs)
- *adjective*

● The Bible tells the story of King Solomon, who was so **sagacious** that he knew what to do when two women came to him, both claiming to be the mother of the same child.

● Often when you are faced with a difficult situation, the most **sagacious** response is to do nothing right away, but wait to see what happens.

__ *Sagacious* means   A. silly.   B. intelligent.   C. strong.

8 supplant
(sə-plănt′)
- *verb*

● The Acme Company fired its entire accounting staff today. It intends to **supplant** these employees with part-time workers.

● An idealistic young revolutionary overthrew the dictator and set up a democratic government. But he too was soon **supplanted** when a military strongman seized power.

__ *Supplant* means   A. to replace.   B. to restore.   C. to support.

not attack / Capable

9 unassailable
(ŭn′ə-sā′lə-bəl)
- *adjective* accent

● The Bradleys' claim that their house is the oldest in town is **unassailable**. They have a deed dated 1804, and a copy was filed in the county courthouse that same year.

● "My opponent may try to attack me," said the candidate, "but my record is **unassailable**. On every issue, I've voted for the benefit of this city."

__ *Unassailable* means   A. untrue.   B. undeniable.   C. unimportant.

10 voluminous
(və-lōō′mə-nəs)
- *adjective*

● Denise chose a wedding dress in a "Southern belle" style, with a long, **voluminous** skirt. Now she's worried she'll trip over all those yards of material.

● In the weeks before Christmas, each issue of our newspaper is **voluminous**, swollen enormously by all the ads. After the holidays, the paper shrinks back to its normal size.

__ *Voluminous* means   A. valuable.   B. cut short.   C. large.

Matching Words with Definitions

Following are definitions of the ten words. Clearly write or print each word next to its definition. The sentences above and on the previous page will help you decide on the meaning of each word.

1. ~~Opulence~~ Fledgling   New and untried; inexperienced
2. Opulence   Luxury; great wealth
3. Proximity   Closeness
4. Hackneyed   Overused; stale; trite
5. unassailable   Impossible to deny or disprove
6. Voluminous   Big; bulky
7. Supplant   To take the place of
8. Affinity   A natural attraction or liking
9. Sagacious   Wise; sensible
10. incessant   Constant; without stopping

CAUTION: Do not go any further until you are sure the above answers are correct. Then you can use the definitions to help you in the following practices. Your goal is eventually to know the words well enough so that you don't need to check the definitions at all.

Sentence Check 1

Using the answer line provided, complete each item below with the correct word from the box. Use each word once.

A. **affinity**	B. **fledgling**	C. **hackneyed**	D. **incessant**	E. **opulence**
F. **proximity**	G. **sagacious**	H. **supplant**	I. **unassailable**	J. **voluminous**

* Exact form the Quiz

Opulence 1. Irene knew her roommate's family was <u>wealthy</u>, but nothing had prepared her for the ___ of their home—it was like a <u>palace</u>.

Unassailable 2. During the 1960s, the Beatles held a(n) ___ position as the world's most <u>popular</u> rock group. They sold more records and won more fame than any other band.

Voluminous 3. In her ___ tote bag, my mother carries money, credit cards, photos, makeup, a mirror, running shoes, and an amazing quantity of other stuff.

Sagacious 4. It would not be ___ to go out today without an umbrella—look at those black clouds!

Affinity 5. Crows have a(n) ___ for bright, shiny things, so they sometimes pick up bits of mirrors, metal, or jewelry and carry them back to their nests.

Supplant 6. "You'll always be my best friend," Christy told Keisha when Keisha moved away. "I may have other friends, but no one will ever ___ you in my heart."

Incessant 7. Mr. Engelhardt finally told his daughter to stop running in place in her upstairs bedroom; the ___ <u>pounding noise was giving him a headache</u>.

Proximity 8. While visiting Hollywood, Sayda was excited by the ___ of movie stars. "You could be <u>standing right beside one</u> and never know it!" she said.

Fledgling 9. I get my hair done cheaply by going to a beauty school, where ___ hairdressers do cuts and coloring for half of what more experienced beauticians charge.

hackneyed 10. Allie has decided to stop saying the ___ word "<u>Hello!</u>" when she answers the phone. Instead, she says "<u>Greetings!</u>"

NOTE: Now check your answers to these items by turning to page 175. Going over the answers carefully will help you prepare for the next two practices, for which answers are not given.

Sentence Check 2

Using the answer lines provided, complete each item below with **two** words from the box. Use each word once.

Affinity
hackneyed 1–2. The instructor told me, "You have an unfortunate ___ for ___ phrases. To improve your writing, you'll need to get over your <u>fondness for stale</u>, worn-out expressions." *overused*

Fledgling
Sagacious 3–4. Though only a(n) ___ politician, our <u>new young</u> senator made very ___ decisions during her <u>first year</u> in office. Her <u>wisdom</u> suggests that she has a promising future.

Proximity
Opulence 5–6. The luxury hotel stands in close ___ to a shabby, run-down housing project, and the ___ of the one is a <u>striking</u> contrast to the <u>poverty of the other</u>.

_____Voluminous_____   7–8. The report on child abuse was ___—over a thousand pages—and filled with
_____unassiable_____   ___ evidence that child abuse is a widespread problem today.

_____Incessant_____   9–10. After receiving ___ complaints for weeks that its telephone operators were
_____Supplant_____   rude and careless, the mail-order company decided to ___ them with a
                                  computerized ordering system.

Final Check: *Blue Jeans*

Here is a final opportunity for you to strengthen your knowledge of the ten words. First read the following selection carefully. Then fill in each blank with a word from the box at the top of the previous page. (Context clues will help you figure out which word goes in which blank.) Use each word once.

"An American classic" is a(n) (1)___hackneyed___ phrase, overused to describe everything from meatloaf to the latest hairstyle. But at least one thing has a(n) (2)___unassiable___ right to be called an American classic. Blue jeans were born in the United States during the great California gold rush of 1849. They were created by Levi Strauss, a German who sold dry goods to the cowboys and gold miners of San Francisco. Strauss realized that the (3)___proximity___ of all those workingmen created an opportunity for him. He considered what all those miners and cowboys would be likely to buy, and he was (4)___sagacious___ enough to realize that they needed tough, inexpensive pants. He founded the Levi Strauss Company to manufacture what he called "waist trousers." At first, the (5)___fledgling___ company did make a few mistakes. For instance, it placed a copper rivet at the jeans' crotch, where the main seams came together. When cowboys wearing the jeans sat around the campfire, that copper rivet heated up, making getting back into the saddle a painful experience. But such mistakes were few, and Levi Strauss's pants became so popular that they soon (6)___supplant___(e)d almost every other kind of pants among the workingmen of the West. Strauss was able to retire and live in (7)___opulence___. Since then, the general public has developed such a(n) (8)___affinity___ for blue jeans that they have never gone out of style. However, they have been constantly changed by the (9)___incessant___, never-ending tides of fashion. During the 1950s, teenagers wore them straight and tight. In the 1960s, the look was (10)___voluminous___ bell-bottoms that swept the ground. Since then jeans have been tie-dyed, acid-washed, ripped, cut off, and made of every imaginable material. Still, they all have a common ancestor: the tough "waist trousers" invented by Strauss a century and a half ago.

| Scores | Sentence Check 2 _____% | Final Check _____% |

brusque	morose
dispassionate	nonchalance
effervescent	progeny
indefatigable	stoic
misanthrope	voracious

Ten Words in Context

In the space provided, write the letter of the meaning closest to that of each **boldfaced** word. Use the context of the sentences to help you figure out each word's meaning.

1 brusque
(brŭsk)
- *adjective*

- Rose lost her job as a receptionist because she was so **brusque** with people who called. The office replaced her with someone who spoke more politely.
- Although Maria seems **brusque** when you first meet her, she's really just shy with people she doesn't know well. After you talk with her awhile, she becomes more relaxed and friendly.

___ *Brusque* means   A. blunt.   B. admirable.   C. silly.

2 dispassionate
(dĭs-păsh′ə-nĭt)
- *adjective*

- The surgeon's voice was **dispassionate** when he told the patient's family that the operation had failed, but despite his calm tone, his eyes looked very sad.
- "Historians are supposed to be **dispassionate**," the speaker apologized, "but when my topic is the horrors of slavery, I find it difficult to keep my feelings hidden."

___ *Dispassionate* means   A. unreasonable.   B. unemotional.   C. disturbing.

3 effervescent
(ĕf′ər-vĕs′ənt)
- *adjective*

- The instructor could hardly be described as **effervescent**. She droned on about the Federal Reserve in a dreary voice, never looking up from her notes.
- Marnie is on the way to stardom. When her play opened last night, the critics raved about her "**effervescent** charm," saying that she "lit up the stage."

___ *Effervescent* means   A. hard-working.   B. nervous.   C. lively.

4 indefatigable
(ĭn′dĭ-făt′ĭ-gə-bəl)
- *adjective*

- When Mona and her friend Patty get together, they are **indefatigable** talkers. They talk endlessly and tirelessly about everything.
- The great athlete seemed **indefatigable**. After running a marathon, swimming for miles, and biking up steep hills, she was still full of energy.

___ *Indefatigable* means   A. easily tired.   B. never getting tired.   C. depressed.

5 misanthrope
(mĭs′ən-thrōp′)
- *noun*

- Molière's play *The Misanthrope* is about a man named Alceste who is enraged and disgusted by his fellow humans. To put it briefly, Alceste hates everyone.
- One of our neighbors is a true **misanthrope**. She hasn't a friend in the world; in fact, she looks on everyone as an enemy.

___ *Misanthrope* means   A. an antisocial person.   B. a criminal.   C. a lunatic.

6 morose
(mə-rōs′)
- *adjective*

- On the first workday of the year, everyone at the office seemed **morose**. No wonder they felt low; after the holidays, it's always a letdown to get back to work.
- Miguel always becomes **morose** after he sees a sad movie. Since "tearjerkers" make him feel so dreary and depressed, you'd think he'd stop going to them.

___ *Morose* means   A. confused.   B. frantic.   C. gloomy.

7 nonchalance
(nŏn′shə-läns′)
- *noun*

- **Nonchalance** is not appropriate behind the wheel of a car. An automobile is not a toy to be played with casually—it is a dangerous machine to be handled with concentration.
- Trying to create an impression of **nonchalance** despite his nervousness, Hollis strolled to the speaker's stand, smiling and whistling a little tune.

__ *Nonchalance* means   A. uneasiness.   B. lack of concern.   C. lack of awareness.

8 progeny
(prŏj′ə-nē)
- *noun*

- In the wonderful children's book *Charlotte's Web*, Charlotte, the spider, dies, but several of her **progeny** stay to befriend Charlotte's beloved Wilbur, the pig.
- Grandfather worked at two jobs in order to provide food and clothing for his many **progeny**—three sons and six daughters.

__ *Progeny* means   A. enemies.   B. leaders.   C. offspring.

9 stoic
(stō′ĭk)
- *adjective*

- My dog's reaction to getting his yearly shots is hardly **stoic**. It takes the vet and two assistants to hold him down, and he howls as if he's being torn to pieces.
- "Some patients' **stoic** response to illness or injury is truly amazing," the doctor said. "No matter what happens, they remain calm and courageous."

__ *Stoic* means   A. emotional.   B. showing no distress.   C. planned.

10 voracious
(vô-rā′shəs)
- *adjective*

- Beagles are **voracious** eaters—their owners say they will eat anything that's not nailed down—so they tend to become fat unless they get enough exercise.
- Ginny has a **voracious** appetite for news. She gets a morning and an evening newspaper, listens to an "all news, all the time" radio station, and watches a TV newscast every night.

__ *Voracious* means   A. greedy.   B. small.   C. unconcerned.

Matching Words with Definitions

Following are definitions of the ten words. Clearly write or print each word next to its definition. The sentences above and on the previous page will help you decide on the meaning of each word.

1. __misanthrope__   A person who hates or distrusts humankind
2. __Progeny__   Children; descendants
3. __effervescent__   Bubbling with high spirits; exhilarated
4. __dispassionate__   Not influenced by emotion; impartial
5. __brusque__   Rudely abrupt; curt
6. __nonchalance__   Casual indifference; lack of concern
7. __indefatigable__   Untiring
8. __Stoic__   Seemingly unaffected by pain or discomfort
9. __Voracious__   Consuming or eager to consume large amounts; insatiable; ravenous
10. __Morose__   Very gloomy; ill-tempered

CAUTION: Do not go any further until you are sure the above answers are correct. Then you can use the definitions to help you in the following practices. Your goal is eventually to know the words well enough so that you don't need to check the definitions at all.

Sentence Check 1

Using the answer line provided, complete each item below with the correct word from the box. Use each word once.

A. **brusque**	B. **dispassionate**	C. **effervescent**	D. **indefatigable**	E. **misanthrope**
F. **morose**	G. **nonchalance**	H. **progeny**	I. **stoic**	J. **voracious**

Brusque 1. It's difficult to ask Mr. Henderson a question. His typical response is a(n) ___ "What? What kind of question is that?"

indefatigable 2. Dad was a(n) ___ walker. He could hike for mile after mile, never seeming to get <u>weary</u>.

nonchalance 3. When they feel <u>nervous and ill at ease</u>, many people try to achieve an air of ___ by putting their hands in their pockets and humming.

morose 4. The kids were <u>sulky</u> and ___ on the first day of school. They <u>hated to face the fact that summer had ended</u>.

stoic 5. "I intend to bear this with ___ courage," Serena vowed as she set forth for the dentist's office. "And also with plenty of Novocain."

effervescent 6. At the end of the day, the second-graders were as ___ as they had been when it began, telling jokes and giggling. Their teacher envied their <u>high spirits</u>.

Progeny 7. Famous ___ of famous parents include Miley Cyrus, daughter of country music star Billy Ray Cyrus; Kate Hudson, daughter of actress Goldie Hawn; and Colin Hanks, son of actor Tom Hanks.

Voracious 8. Although they are small, most rodents are ___ eaters. Mice, gerbils, and hamsters nibble almost constantly.

misanthrope 9. Humorist and author Will Rogers was the exact opposite of a(n) ___. He once said, "I never met a man I didn't like."

dispassionate 10. I find this editorial convincing, partly because it is so ___. I like it when a writer reasons with readers, rather than trying to manipulate their feelings.

NOTE: Now check your answers to these items by turning to page 175. Going over the answers carefully will help you prepare for the next two practices, for which answers are not given.

Sentence Check 2

Using the answer lines provided, complete each item below with **two** words from the box. Use each word once.

dispassionate
stoic   1–2. Judge Gonzalez has the reputation of being ___, showing <u>no emotion</u> as she listens to testimony. But even she could not be ___ when the jury was shown photographs of a badly abused child—<u>she clearly had tears in her eyes</u>.

effervescent
Brusque   3–4. Simon, who is enthusiastic and ___, was brimming over with excitement as he presented his idea in class. But the teacher, a blunt, curt type, gave it a(n) ___ one-word dismissal: "Wrong."

_____morose_____

_____misanthrope_____

_____voracious_____

_____indefatigable_____

_____nonchalance_____

_____progeny_____

5–6. Our ___, gloomy uncle is utterly friendless, but he insists he is not a(n) ___. "I don't hate people," he claims. "I just haven't met any that I like."

7–8. Jill is a sensation-seeker who has a(n) ___ appetite for excitement and is ___ in looking for it. She is tireless in her quest for thrilling, risky experiences.

9–10. Marian approached parenthood with a certain ___, taking it all lightly. But her husband, who was awed by the thought of having ___, felt very solemn about it.

Final Check: *Do Opposites Attract?*

Here is a final opportunity for you to strengthen your knowledge of the ten words. First read the following selection carefully. Then fill in each blank with a word from the box at the top of the previous page. (Context clues will help you figure out which word goes in which blank.) Use each word once.

With regard to romance, it is widely believed that "opposites attract," but psychologists tell us that lovers usually resemble each other in many ways. Let us hope the psychologists are right, because it seems likely that a marriage between opposites would be a bumpy road.

If Joe is (1)___indefatigable___, ready to jog a few miles after sawing a cord of firewood, while Ann needs to lie down and rest for an hour after dusting the piano, how happy can they be together? If Jordan has a(n) (2)___voracious___ appetite while Amber "eats like a bird," imagine a typical meal: he's on his third helping before she has even taken a bite. If Julio is sad and (3)___morose___ while Anita is bubbly, bouncy, and (4)___effervescent___, how long can it be before one of them starts to get on the other's nerves? What about Jamal, who takes to his bed with the sniffles while his (5)___stoic___ wife Aisha bravely hobbles off to work on a broken leg? What about (6)___dispassionate___ Jin, whose attitude toward life is one of casual (7)___nonchalance___, and his wife Aiko, who is intensely committed to every cause from AIDS to humane zoos?

No, the outlook is not bright for these couples. And what of their (8)___progeny___? Children are supposed to "take after" their parents, but that would be a problem for someone whose father is a(n) (9)___misanthrope___ and whose mother "loves everyone," or for the offspring of a(n) (10)___brusque___, blunt, no-nonsense mother and an easygoing, soft-spoken father.

Opposites may attract, then, but, despite their affinity° for each other, it might not be sagacious° for opposites to marry. After a few years (or even months!) of proximity°, they might be more than ready to supplant° that "opposite" spouse with someone more like themselves.

| Scores | Sentence Check 2 _____% | Final Check _____% |

coalesce	insolvent
decadence	parsimonious
exemplary	prodigal
exuberance	surreptitious
incidental	writhe

Ten Words in Context

In the space provided, write the letter of the meaning closest to that of each **boldfaced** word. Use the context of the sentences to help you figure out each word's meaning.

1 coalesce
(kō′ə-lĕs′)
- *verb*

● Four block associations in our neighborhood will **coalesce** to form a single task force.

● When I got caught in a rainstorm, I learned that the dyes in my new shirt weren't waterproof. The red and blue stripes ran and **coalesced** into purple smears.

___ *Coalesce* means   A. to join.   B. to produce.   C. to prevent.

2 decadence
(dĕk′ə-dəns)
- *noun*

● The older generation always seems to see **decadence** among young people, groaning that "kids today" are spoiled, lazy, and extravagant.

● Grandfather considers the internal combustion engine a sign of the **decadence** of Western civilization. "Stop the decay before it's too late!" he says. "Get out of your cars, get on your feet, and walk!"

___ *Decadence* means   A. a disappointment.   B. a decline.   C. disapproval.

3 exemplary
(ĭg-zĕm′plə-rē)
- *adjective*

● Christine has a glowing letter of recommendation from her former boss, in which he says, "She is an **exemplary** employee who always does more than is asked."

● This year, the "Teacher of the Year" award was given to not one but two **exemplary** educators.

___ *Exemplary* means   A. excellent.   B. extra.   C. exotic.

4 exuberance
(ĭg-zōō′bər-əns)
- *noun*

● Justine called all her friends, shrieking with **exuberance** over being accepted at her first-choice college.

● Students may believe they are the only ones who are happy to see summer vacation arrive, but their teachers feel some **exuberance**, too!

___ *Exuberance* means   A. fear.   B. boredom.   C. joy.

5 incidental
(ĭn′sĭ-dĕn′tl)
- *adjective*

● Selma chose her college because it has such a good nursing program, but an **incidental** reason was that it is located in a beautiful town.

● Although Rita and Zhen moved in together so they could split the rent, they later discovered an **incidental** effect: they can borrow each other's clothes.

___ *Incidental* means   A. secondary.   B. incorrect.   C. secret.

6 insolvent
(ĭn-sŏl′vənt)
- *adjective*

● Barry lost his head when he got his first credit card. He went on a spending spree, couldn't pay his bills, and ended up **insolvent**.

● Compulsive gamblers often lose so much money that they become **insolvent**. Because they can't control their urge to gamble, their debt keeps growing.

___ *Insolvent* means   A. without money.   B. without friends.   C. without goals.

7 parsimonious
(pär′sə-mō′nē-əs)
- *adjective*

- The boss, a **parsimonious** man, insists that all employees save their old memos and letters so they can use the backs of the pages as notepaper.
- Elena is a **parsimonious** cook. She creates cheap meals from old cheese rinds, stale bread, and wilted vegetables. They taste awful.

___ *Parsimonious* means   A. stingy.   B. mischievous.   C. talented.

8 prodigal
(prŏd′ĭ-gəl)
- *adjective*

- Mary and Kim both make decent salaries. They could live comfortably on what they make if they weren't such **prodigal** spenders.
- I don't think it's **prodigal** to spend some extra money to get well-made shoes. Cheap ones fall apart so fast that you soon end up buying another pair.

___ *Prodigal* means   A. useful.   B. extravagant.   C. careful.

9 surreptitious
(sŭr′əp-tĭsh′əs)
- *adjective*

- Students naturally want to know what will be covered on a test. Instead of trying to find out by **surreptitious** means, it is better simply to ask the instructor, who is often willing to provide at least a rough idea.
- As the wedding reception ended, several guests made **surreptitious** trips to the parking lot, where they tied tin cans and crepe paper to the newlyweds' car.

___ *Surreptitious* means   A. straightforward.   B. useless.   C. secret.

10 writhe
(rīth)
- *verb*

- My great-uncle remembers the scratchy long underwear he wore to school in the winter: "It was so itchy that I would **writhe** and wriggle at my desk all day long."
- The children **writhed** with impatience as they waited in line to board the plane. "Stop fidgeting before you drive me nuts," their weary father begged them.

___ *Writhe* means   A. freeze.   B. squeeze.   C. squirm.

Matching Words with Definitions

Following are definitions of the ten words. Clearly write or print each word next to its definition. The sentences above and on the previous page will help you decide on the meaning of each word.

1. _Parsimonious_   Too thrifty; stingy; miserly
2. _Prodigal_   Wasteful and reckless with money
3. _Exuberance_   High-spirited enthusiasm
4. _Writhe_   To twist and turn, as in pain or discomfort; to move with a twisting motion
5. _Decadence_   A condition of moral deterioration; decay
6. _Exemplary_   Worthy of imitation; praiseworthy
7. _Insolvent_   Unable to pay debts; penniless
8. _Coalesce_   To merge together to form one whole; unite; combine
9. _Surreptitious_   Done in a secret or sly way; stealthy
10. _Incidental_   Occurring as a minor consequence of something more important

CAUTION: Do not go any further until you are sure the above answers are correct. Then you can use the definitions to help you in the following practices. Your goal is eventually to know the words well enough so that you don't need to check the definitions at all.

Sentence Check 1

Using the answer line provided, complete each item below with the correct word from the box. Use each word once.

| A. coalesce | B. decadence | C. exemplary | D. exuberance | E. incidental |
| F. insolvent | G. parsimonious | H. prodigal | I. surreptitious | J. writhe |

Coalesce   1. Three high schools in the county have ___(e)d to create a centralized "magnet" school.

exemplary   2. Although the local newspaper is small, it has an excellent reputation. In fact, every year it wins statewide awards for its ___ reporting.

incidental   3. "Stopping smoking can save your life," said the doctor. "And there are some ___ benefits as well: you won't have stained teeth, yellow fingers, or bad breath."

parsimonious   4. The school's ___ administration decided to save money by dimming all the lights. The students, who could barely see to read, protested angrily.

decadence   5. "When the rich get richer and the poor get poorer," the economist warned, "that is a sign of ___: the society is starting to weaken."

Surreptitious   6. Cell phone use is officially banned at school, but many students make ___ calls when they think no one is looking.

Writhe   7. Trying to scratch an itchy spot on its back, the pig ___(e)d and twisted as it rubbed against the fence.

Prodigal   8. When stories came out about the senator's luxurious offices, his many trips to upscale resorts, and his huge staff of underworked employees, taxpayers complained about such a(n) ___ waste of their money.

insolvent   9. The shelter for the homeless has made an urgent appeal for donations. Without more contributions to pay its bills, it will soon be ___.

exuberance   10. As soon as Tony walked into the room, I knew he had good news. His ___ showed all over his face.

NOTE: Now check your answers to these items by turning to page 175. Going over the answers carefully will help you prepare for the next two practices, for which answers are not given.

Sentence Check 2

Using the answer lines provided, complete each item below with **two** words from the box. Use each word once.

Surreptitious   *Coalesce*   1–2. When it comes to food, most of us have some private, ___ pleasures. For example, Liz stirs honey and mashed potatoes together until they ___, then eats the goo with a spoon.

exuberance   *Writhe*   3–4. In their ___ over knowing a secret, children often blurt it out—"My daddy's hair comes *off!*"—while their parents ___ with embarrassment.

insolvent
Parsimonious
Prodigal
decadence

5–6. Vann will never end up ___; he's far too ___ ever to overspend. On Halloween, he gave each trick-or-treater a penny.

7–8. ___ spending is sometimes considered a sign of ___. People who love opulence° and fling their money around senselessly are seen as deteriorating morally.

exemplary
incidental

9–10. "Virtue is its own reward," is an old saying, meaning that ___ behavior is valuable for its own sake. Other benefits, such as praise, are merely ___.

Final Check: *What Are You Stingy About?*

Here is a final opportunity for you to strengthen your knowledge of the ten words. First read the following selection carefully. Then fill in each blank with a word from the box at the top of the previous page. (Context clues will help you figure out which word goes in which blank.) Use each word once.

Few people like to think of themselves as cheap, but almost everyone seems to be (1)_Parsimonious_ about something. Even rich, extravagant people who are (2)_Prodigal_ in most ways are likely to be thrifty about, say, toothpaste. My father, who has taken business trips with many fat-cat executives, reports that even they will squeeze the last little bit out of a tube of toothpaste by shutting a window or a door on it, rather than throw it away. Many of us are stingy with soap, using a bar until it is reduced to a tiny sliver and then squeezing a few of the soap fragments together in the hope they will (3)_coalesce_. Nearly anyone will (4)_writhe_ and crawl to get a dropped nickel out from under the bed.

I fold and save used aluminum foil to reuse again and again. And when a bottle of shampoo is nearly empty, I add water to get a few more washes out of it. Countless people reuse tea bags. My sagacious° mother-in-law taught us a thrifty trick: When a bottle of beer or soda looks empty, lay it on its side for a while—a few drinkable drops will soon collect.

Why do we do these things? We aren't really afraid that taking out a new tea bag or tearing off a new piece of foil is a sign of moral (5)_decadence_, or that it will make us (6)_insolvent_. Nor do we think our thrift is (7)_exemplary_ because it's often (8)_surreptitious_; we do it on the sly rather than holding ourselves up as a model. Since the actual saving is so small, it must be (9)_incidental_ to the main benefit: the feeling of satisfaction we get. This is like the (10)_exuberance_ we feel when we find a dime or a quarter on the street—or even a penny, if it's heads up.

Scores   Sentence Check 2 _____%   Final Check _____%

Enter your scores above and in the **Vocabulary Performance Chart** on the inside back cover of the book.

brevity	querulous
clemency	reproach
frivolous	respite
heist	torpor
lampoon	unscathed

Ten Words in Context

In the space provided, write the letter of the meaning closest to that of each **boldfaced** word. Use the context of the sentences to help you figure out each word's meaning.

1 brevity
(brĕv′ĭ-tē)
- *noun*

● Everyone was surprised by the **brevity** of the principal's speech at graduation. He spoke for less than five minutes.

● President Calvin Coolidge was famous for the **brevity** of his remarks. When a woman told him, "I have a bet that I can get you to say three words to me!" his response was, "You lose."

___ *Brevity* means   A. strength.   B. intelligence.   C. briefness.

2 clemency
(klĕm′ən-sē)
- *noun*

● A good teacher knows when to show **clemency**. For instance, if a student has been working very hard but does poorly on one quiz, the teacher might offer not to count that score.

● The convicted murderer was executed, even though religious leaders asked the court to show **clemency** and reduce his sentence to life in prison.

___ *Clemency* means   A. mercy.   B. haste.   C. strength.

3 frivolous
(frĭv′ə-ləs)
- *adjective*

● Do you feel like seeing a serious movie, or one that's more **frivolous**?

● We were laughing over some ridiculous joke when the news of our friend's injury put an end to our **frivolous** mood.

___ *Frivolous* means   A. lighthearted.   B. cold-hearted.   C. brokenhearted.

4 heist
(hīst)
- *noun*

● Hollywood loves making **heist** movies. A few of the robbery-themed movies of recent years include *Ocean's Eleven, Catch Me If You Can,* and *Snatch.*

● The police believe three people were involved in the jewelry-store **heist**: the lookout, the thief, and the driver of the getaway car.

___ *Heist* means   A. a purchase.   B. an imitation.   C. a theft.

5 lampoon
(lăm-pōōn′)
- *verb*

● Someone in our office **lampooned** all our paperwork by circulating a six-page form to be submitted, in triplicate, by anyone who wanted a pencil. Several humorless employees actually filled it out.

● The funny movie *Tropic Thunder* **lampoons** a number of targets: the washed-up action star, the rapper-turned-actor, and the obnoxious Hollywood agent.

___ *Lampoon* means   A. to summarize.   B. to make fun of.   C. to praise.

6 querulous
(kwĕr′ə-ləs)
- *adjective*

● Although Mr. Hackman frequently says, "I don't like to complain," his conversation is full of **querulous** comments about all the things that upset him.

● The spoiled little boy looked at his pile of birthday presents and said in a **querulous** voice, "There aren't very many of them, are there?"

___ *Querulous* means   A. shaky.   B. dishonest.   C. discontented.

7 reproach
(rĭ-prōch′)
- *noun*

- The kids deserve some words of **reproach** for making such a mess of the house while their parents were away.
- During the campaign, both candidates drew **reproach** from the newspapers for making untruthful statements and generally behaving very badly.

___ *Reproach* means   A. thanks.   B. disapproval.   C. respect.

8 respite
(rĕs′pĭt)
- *noun*

- Emergency-room doctors work long shifts. Their only **respite** is a short nap on a couch.
- Twice a week, a nurse spends an afternoon at the Hendersons' house, so that Mrs. Henderson can have some **respite** from caring for her sick husband.

___ *Respite* means   A. time off.   B. a salary.   C. a mark of respect.

9 torpor
(tôr′pər)
- *noun*

- When Brendan took a midwinter vacation in Florida, the unaccustomed heat drained his energy. His **torpor** was so overwhelming that all he wanted to do was lie in a hammock.
- The sleepy little town seemed to doze peacefully through the summer afternoon. It looked as if nothing could rouse it from its **torpor**.

___ *Torpor* means   A. hostility.   B. curiosity.   C. drowsiness.

10 unscathed
(ŭn-skāthd′)
- *adjective*

- "Thanks to my seat belt," said Jermaine, "I was able to walk away from the collision **unscathed**. Without it, I would probably have been badly injured."
- When her best friend began dating her ex-boyfriend, Mimi lamented, "I wish I could say that this has left me **unscathed**. But the truth is I feel hurt and betrayed."

___ *Unscathed* means   A. strengthened.   B. angry.   C. unhurt.

Matching Words with Definitions

Following are definitions of the ten words. Clearly write or print each word next to its definition. The sentences above and on the previous page will help you decide on the meaning of each word.

1. _Querulous_   Complaining; whining
2. _lampoon_   To attack or ridicule through humorous imitation; spoof
3. _Reproach_   Blame; a rebuke
4. _Brevity_   Briefness; shortness of duration
5. _torpor_   A state of mental or physical inactivity; sluggishness
6. _Heist_   An act of stealing; robbery
7. _frivolous_   Not sensible; not properly serious; silly
8. _Clemency_   Mercy in judging; leniency
9. _unscathed_   Not harmed or injured
10. _Respite_   A short period of rest or relief; time out

CAUTION: Do not go any further until you are sure the above answers are correct. Then you can use the definitions to help you in the following practices. Your goal is eventually to know the words well enough so that you don't need to check the definitions at all.

Sentence Check 1

Using the answer line provided, complete each item below with the correct word from the box. Use each word once.

A. **brevity**	B. **clemency**	C. **frivolous**	D. **heist**	E. **lampoon**
F. **querulous**	G. **reproach**	H. **respite**	I. **torpor**	J. **unscathed**

frivolous   1. Feeling ___ on a sunny Saturday morning, I treated myself to a manicure rather than doing the housework that was waiting for me.

Heist   2. In the action movie, the attempted ___ of a famous painting, Leonardo da Vinci's *Mona Lisa*, was prevented by a beautiful young art student and a quick-thinking security guard.

Clemency   3. Since the shoplifting incident was James's first such offense, the court showed ___ and only fined him, rather than sending him to jail.

Brevity   4. That teacher's classes are famous for their ___. He frequently runs out of material halfway through the class and, with a brusque° "That's all for today," lets his students leave early.

querulous   5. At a restaurant last night, I could not help overhearing the incredibly ___ man at the next table. He complained to the waiter that the napkins were too thin, the soup was too hot, the ice cubes were too small, and the holes in the salt shaker were too large.

torpor   6. After a snake eats, it generally falls into a state of ___ for a day or more, barely moving or even breathing.

unscathed   7. Our cat fell out of an attic window but walked away ___.

lampoon   8. The very funny online *Onion News Network* ___s 24-hour news networks with absurd stories like "NASCAR Coach Reveals Winning Strategy: 'Drive Fast.'"

Respite   9. I spend Thursday mornings at my sister's house, giving her some ___ from her very active two-year-old twins.

reproach   10. Charisse is a very forgiving person. Although she had every right to be angry at me for what I did, she accepted my apology without a word of ___.

NOTE: Now check your answers to these items by turning to page 175. Going over the answers carefully will help you prepare for the next two practices, for which answers are not given.

Sentence Check 2

Using the answer lines provided, complete each item below with **two** words from the box. Use each word once.

lampoon / *Frivolous*   1–2. Political cartoons ___ public figures, but this ridicule is not ___; rather than being merely funny, it is meant to reveal and comment on social problems and wrongdoing.

Unscathed / *Respite*   3–4. Caring for a loved one during a long illness does not leave even an exemplary° caregiver ___. In fact, "burnout" is very likely if the caregiver does not have a(n) ___ from time to time.

Brevity / *Reproach*   5–6. According to Shakespeare, "___ is the soul of wit." If so, the one-line joke is beyond ___, since it could hardly be briefer.

Heist

Clemency

Torpor

Querulous

7–8. The thief who was responsible for the ___ pleaded for ___, claiming that he was a modern-day Robin Hood. "I steal from the rich and give to the poor," he said.

9–10. In the first days after his heart surgery, Grandfather drifted in and out of ___, because the medications he took made him sleepy. As he became more alert, he grew ___, complaining about his pain and the inconvenience of being in the hospital.

Final Check: *Loony but True*

Here is a final opportunity for you to strengthen your knowledge of the ten words. First read the following selection carefully. Then fill in each blank with a word from the box at the top of the previous page. (Context clues will help you figure out which word goes in which blank.) Use each word once.

One reason why people watch TV and movies is to laugh at fictional characters and the goofy things they do. But guess what, folks—real people are every bit as silly, and just as easy to (1) _lampoon_. Here are some stories from the files of "Incredible but True . . ."

An insolvent° homeless man walked into a bank in Michigan and asked a teller for fifty cents. She didn't understand what he'd said and thought he was trying to rob her. So she handed over all the cash in her drawer—about $1,300. He thanked her and left. When the police caught up with the man, they didn't charge him with a crime. They had to show (2) _Clemency_, they said, because he hadn't done anything illegal or surreptitious°—he had just openly asked for money.

A real bank robber was captured within a few minutes of his (3) _Heist_. The (4) _brevity_ of his freedom was easily explained. He had written his holdup note on the back of his own pay stub, complete with his name and address. When he got home, the cops were already there, waiting for him.

When police in Florida noticed a car weaving in and out of its lane, they pulled it over. Imagine their surprise when they found a three-and-a-half-foot-long iguana at the wheel. The large lizard was sitting on the lap of its sleeping owner, who was taking a short (5) _respite_ from driving. Fortunately, he and the lizard were both (6) _unscathed_; of the two, however, the lizard made out better. It got a nice new home, while the man went to jail for drunk driving. The judge didn't pay much attention to the man's (7) _querulous_ complaint that it was the iguana who had actually been driving.

A fishing ship in the Sea of Japan sank, and its crew claimed it had been struck by a cow that had fallen out of the sky. Everyone assumed that the sailors had made up this (8) _frivolous_ story to escape (9) _reproach_ for some mistake of their own. But then the crew of a Russian cargo plane admitted they had stolen a cow they'd found wandering on an airfield and put it aboard the plane. Now, cows are generally quiet animals, famous for their nonchalance°. But cruising at 30,000 feet shook even a calm cow out of her usual (10) _torpor_. The terrified animal panicked, dived out of the plane, and, well, there was the ship. . . .

Scores	Sentence Check 2 _____ %	Final Check _____ %

Enter your scores above and in the **Vocabulary Performance Chart** on the inside back cover of the book.

copious	meander
dearth	peripheral
eloquent	substantiate
jargon	unobtrusive
levity	vacillate

Ten Words in Context

In the space provided, write the letter of the meaning closest to that of each **boldfaced** word. Use the context of the sentences to help you figure out each word's meaning.

1 copious
(kō′pē-əs)
- *adjective*

● The food at the party was too **copious**; the guests stuffed themselves, but there were still platters and bowls of food left over.

● Weeds are **copious** in Charlene's garden, but flowers are few.

___ *Copious* means   A. of poor quality.   (B.) plentiful.   C. persuasive.

2 dearth
(dûrth)
- *noun*

● The director of the Class Night show said gloomily, "We have a **dearth** of talent this year. Not one of these acts is worth putting on stage."

● The **dearth** of snow this winter disappointed the children. They had received new sleds for Christmas but never got a chance to use them.

___ *Dearth* means   A. a surplus.   B. a sufficient amount.   (C.) a shortage.

3 eloquent
(ĕl′ə-kwənt)
- *adjective*

● Lincoln's Gettysburg Address is considered one of the most **eloquent** speeches of all time, but on the day he gave it, many in the audience were insulted. They thought it was too short.

● The director of the shelter for battered women wrote an **eloquent** letter to the newspapers, movingly describing the victims' plight and pleading for donations.

___ *Eloquent* means   (A.) stirring.   B. confusing.   C. simple.

4 jargon
(jär′gən)
- *noun*

● "It's essential that you learn the vocabulary of this subject," the teacher warned us, "or the **jargon**, if you prefer. Whatever you call it, it will be on the test."

● Bernice wanted to make a home-cooked meal for her friends but was puzzled by all the **jargon** in the cookbook. What did *braise* mean? Or *sauté*? Or *mince*?

___ *Jargon* means   A. grammatical errors.   (B.) technical language.   C. humor.

5 levity
(lĕv′ĭ-tē)
- *noun*

● The playwright George Bernard Shaw once remarked that his method was to say very serious things, but with "the utmost **levity**." He wanted to convey weighty ideas through wit and humor.

● The guidance counselor thought Kirk's attitude showed too much **levity**. "You should laugh less and spend more time thinking about serious things," she said.

___ *Levity* means   A. seriousness.   B. surprise.   (C.) lightheartedness.

6 meander
(mē-ăn′dər)
- *verb*

● "Come straight home from school," Mom always said to us. "Don't **meander**."

● The brook **meandered** through the valley, disappearing into the underbrush, then coming into view again, and here and there even turning back on itself.

___ *Meander* means   (A.) to wander.   B. to hurry.   C. to fall.

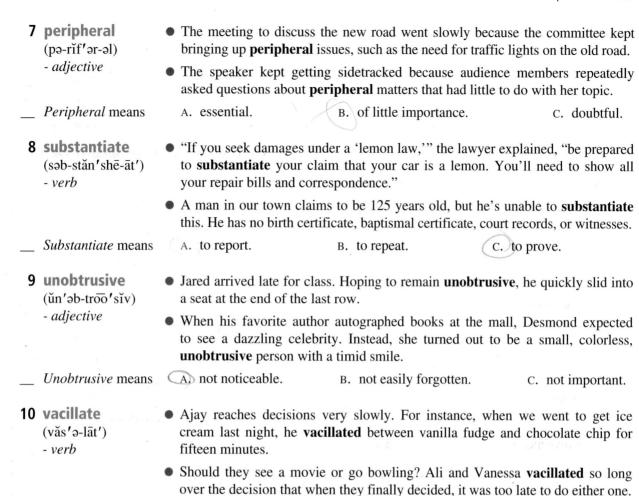

7 peripheral
(pə-rĭf′ər-əl)
- *adjective*

● The meeting to discuss the new road went slowly because the committee kept bringing up **peripheral** issues, such as the need for traffic lights on the old road.

● The speaker kept getting sidetracked because audience members repeatedly asked questions about **peripheral** matters that had little to do with her topic.

___ *Peripheral* means   A. essential.   B. of little importance.   C. doubtful.

8 substantiate
(səb-stăn′shē-āt′)
- *verb*

● "If you seek damages under a 'lemon law,'" the lawyer explained, "be prepared to **substantiate** your claim that your car is a lemon. You'll need to show all your repair bills and correspondence."

● A man in our town claims to be 125 years old, but he's unable to **substantiate** this. He has no birth certificate, baptismal certificate, court records, or witnesses.

___ *Substantiate* means   A. to report.   B. to repeat.   C. to prove.

9 unobtrusive
(ŭn′əb-trōō′sĭv)
- *adjective*

● Jared arrived late for class. Hoping to remain **unobtrusive**, he quickly slid into a seat at the end of the last row.

● When his favorite author autographed books at the mall, Desmond expected to see a dazzling celebrity. Instead, she turned out to be a small, colorless, **unobtrusive** person with a timid smile.

___ *Unobtrusive* means   A. not noticeable.   B. not easily forgotten.   C. not important.

10 vacillate
(văs′ə-lāt′)
- *verb*

● Ajay reaches decisions very slowly. For instance, when we went to get ice cream last night, he **vacillated** between vanilla fudge and chocolate chip for fifteen minutes.

● Should they see a movie or go bowling? Ali and Vanessa **vacillated** so long over the decision that when they finally decided, it was too late to do either one.

___ *Vacillate* means   A. to speak.   B. to hesitate.   C. to select.

Matching Words with Definitions

Following are definitions of the ten words. Clearly write or print each word next to its definition. The sentences above and on the previous page will help you decide on the meaning of each word.

1. ___levity___   Lightness of manner or speech; humor; silliness
2. ___meander___   To move aimlessly; wander lazily; move along a winding course
3. ___peripheral___   Of minor importance; only slightly connected with what is essential; irrelevant
4. ___vacillate___   To go back forth, mentally, from one alternative to another; hesitate
5. ___eloquent___   Extremely expressive and persuasive
6. ___unobtrusive___   Not readily noticeable or eye-catching; inconspicuous
7. ___jargon___   The specialized language of people in the same profession
8. ___substantiate___   To prove the truth of; confirm; verify
9. ___dearth___   A scarcity; lack
10. ___copious___   Abundant; in plentiful supply

CAUTION: Do not go any further until you are sure the above answers are correct. Then you can use the definitions to help you in the following practices. Your goal is eventually to know the words well enough so that you don't need to check the definitions at all.

Sentence Check 1

Using the answer line provided, complete each item below with the correct word from the box. Use each word once.

A. copious	B. dearth	C. eloquent	D. jargon	E. levity
F. meander	G. peripheral	H. substantiate	I. unobtrusive	J. vacillate

Jargon 1. It took Andre all night to put together the wagon he had bought for his daughter. The instructions were written in a strange ___, such as "Attach flange B to sprocket C and secure with Permacaps."

Levity 2. Isabel got an unfortunate case of the giggles during the boss's speech. "This is no time for ___," a colleague hissed at her.

Substantiate 3. "Can you ___ your story that the dog ate your homework?" the teacher asked Kay. "Yes!" Kay said, and showed her the veterinarian's x-rays.

Eloquent 4. The defense attorney's closing argument seemed both ___ and convincing, but the jury convicted his client anyway.

Peripheral 5. "We're supposed to be discussing the death penalty," the moderator reminded the panel. "Let's not get into ___ issues like conditions in prisons."

Vacillate 6. As she thought about what to wear to her job interview, Amy ___(e)d between a conservative navy-blue suit and a more stylish floral dress.

Dearth 7. Remy's vegetable garden yielded an uneven crop. There was a(n) ___ of tomatoes—three, to be exact—and about a ton of zucchini.

Meander 8. During the final exam, the instructor ___(e)d through the room, up and down the aisles, left and then right, apparently with no particular purpose—but the students knew she was keeping a sharp eye on them.

Unobtrusive 9. "The costumes must be ___," the playwright urged. "I want the audience to focus on what the actors are saying, not what they're wearing."

Copious 10. Ved took ___ notes—they filled three notebooks—but they were so badly organized that they didn't do him much good.

NOTE: Now check your answers to these items by turning to page 175. Going over the answers carefully will help you prepare for the next two practices, for which answers are not given.

Sentence Check 2

Using the answer lines provided, complete each item below with **two** words from the box. Use each word once.

Copious
Dearth 1–2. "I'm hearing ___ complaints here," said Mom at our family meeting, "but there's a(n) ___ of constructive ideas. For the next few minutes, I'd like everyone to keep quiet unless you have something sagacious° to say."

Jargon
Eloquent 3–4. Some of the most ___ language is also the simplest. For example, Martin Luther King's famous "I Have a Dream" speech, free of elaborate language or technical ___, is something a child could understand.

_____Meander_____ 5–6. After our picnic, we ___(e)d lazily through the woods, taking delight in the tiny ___ wildflowers that we found half-hidden under the dead leaves.

_____

_____Levity_____ 7–8. "Alice's Restaurant" is a great song by folksinger Arlo Guthrie. It begins with Guthrie and his friends having Thanksgiving dinner, then veers off into a very funny ___ story about being arrested for littering. Despite its ___, it ends up making a serious statement about the absurdity of war.

_____Peripheral_____

_____Substantiate_____ 9–10. Although the suspect said he could ___ his story about being out of town on the night of the crime, he was not very convincing, as he continued to ___ about whether he'd been in Maine or Georgia at the time.

_____Vacillate_____

Final Check: *Writing a Better Paper*

Here is a final opportunity for you to strengthen your knowledge of the ten words. First read the following selection carefully. Then fill in each blank with a word from the box at the top of the previous page. (Context clues will help you figure out which word goes in which blank.) Use each word once.

Many students know enough about grammar and spelling to write a paper that's reasonably correct, but they may need some additional guidelines to produce a paper that will be above average—perhaps even (1)__eloquent__. Here are three rules that can help.

First, choose your topic with care. If a general topic has already been assigned (such as baseball), choose with care what aspect of it you will discuss (watching it? playing it? hating it? loving it?). You may assume that topics are scarce, but in fact it's just the opposite. There's no (2)__dearth__ of potential topics: your problem is to select, from the (3)__copious__ possibilities, the one that's best for your purpose.

Second, decide what tone you will use, and stick to it. If your subject is technical, it's fine to use (4)__jargon__. If your subject lends itself to (5)__levity__, then you can be witty. Decide whether you're going to write in your own voice or remain in the background, (6)__unobtrusive__ and dispassionate°. Be sure your tone is appropriate for your topic: if you're discussing suicide, say, or capital punishment, don't try to be funny or frivolous°. Whatever tone you decide on, be consistent: don't (7)__vacillate__ between tones. Don't be effervescent° or slangy in one sentence but formal in the next—your paper will sound awkward and inconsistent.

Third, decide what your point is, support it, and stick to it. You need to (8)__substantiate__ your point with solid, unassailable° evidence. And don't (9)__meander__ along, wandering off into (10)__peripheral__ issues. You may think that throwing in some incidental° information or a few additional topics will fascinate your readers, but it's more likely to confuse them.

So if you want to produce an exemplary° paper, focus on your topic, your tone, and your point.

Scores	Sentence Check 2 _____%	Final Check _____%

Christina Cano

UNIT ONE: Review

The box at the right lists twenty-five words from Unit One. Using the clues at the bottom of the page, fill in these words to complete the puzzle that follows.

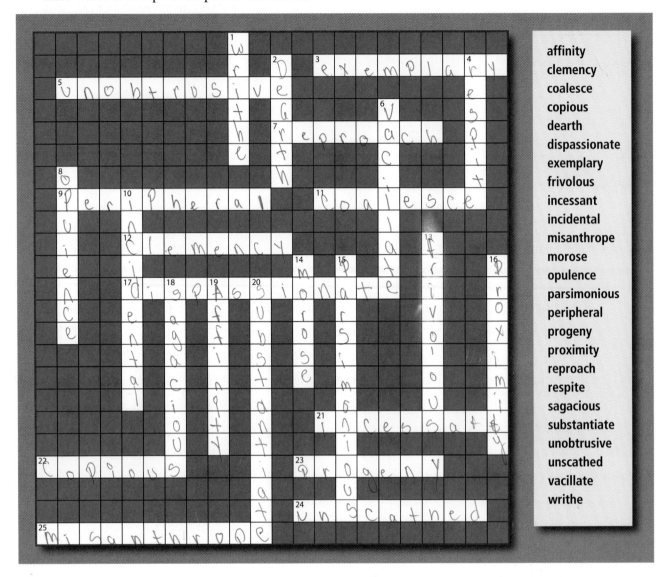

affinity
clemency
coalesce
copious
dearth
dispassionate
exemplary
frivolous
incessant
incidental
misanthrope
morose
opulence
parsimonious
peripheral
progeny
proximity
reproach
respite
sagacious
substantiate
unobtrusive
unscathed
vacillate
writhe

ACROSS

3. Worthy of imitation or praise
5. Not readily noticeable
7. Blame; a rebuke
9. Of minor importance or relevance
11. To merge together to form one whole
12. Mercy in judging
17. Not influenced by emotion; impartial
21. Constant; without stopping
22. Abundant; in plentiful supply
23. Descendants
24. Not harmed or injured
25. A person who hates or distrusts humankind

DOWN

1. To twist and turn, as in pain or discomfort
2. A scarcity; lack
4. A short period of rest or relief
6. To go back and forth, mentally, from one alternative to another
8. Luxury; great wealth
10. Occurring as a minor consequence of something more important
13. Silly
14. Very gloomy; ill-tempered
15. Stingy
16. Closeness
18. Wise; sensible
19. A natural attraction or liking
20. To prove; confirm

28

PART A

Choose the word that best completes each item and write it in the space provided.

_____ 1. When taxpayers fill out their income tax forms, they shouldn't put in any jokes or insults. That is called filing a(n) ___ return, and it can get them in trouble.

     A. unobtrusive   B. incessant   C. frivolous   D. voracious

_____ 2. A heat wave makes most of us feel drowsy and lazy. But did you know that people who freeze to death are also overcome by ___?

     A. jargon   B. torpor   C. clemency   D. affinity

_____ 3. ___ is a factor in friendship and romance. We are most likely to form a relationship with someone who lives next door, sits next to us in class, or works in the next cubicle.

     A. Decadence   B. Levity   C. Opulence   D. Proximity

_____ 4. Do you think juvenile offenders should receive ___ because they are so young? Or should they be punished as harshly as adult lawbreakers?

     A. decadence   B. levity   C. progeny   D. clemency

_____ 5. A teenage boy often has a ___ appetite. He may drink half a gallon of milk a day, and after he raids the refrigerator, there's usually not a crumb left.

     A. voracious   B. sagacious   C. peripheral   D. brusque

_____ 6. "Gloomy Gus" is a traditional name for a(n) ___ person.

     A. sagacious   B. eloquent   C. morose   D. effervescent

_____ 7. "___" music is another term for background music in a play or movie. It isn't a direct result of the plot but is just a minor element to set the mood.

     A. Querulous   B. Insolvent   C. Incidental   D. Indefatigable

_____ 8. Robert feels that the old traditional "Welcome" mat is ___. So on his doorstep, he has a mat that says "Go Away."

     A. stoic   B. hackneyed   C. brusque   D. copious

_____ 9. The ___ of high-wire walkers never fails to astonish me. How in the world can they act relaxed and unconcerned when they're on a skinny wire hundreds of feet in the air?

     A. nonchalance   B. decadence   C. brevity   D. torpor

_____ 10. The verb "to ___" comes from the actual name of a river in Greece, famous for its winding course.

     A. supplant   B. meander   C. lampoon   D. substantiate

(Continues on next page)

_____ 11. The striking workers say that their main demand is higher pay. The other issues, such as working conditions and hours, are just ___.

      A. voluminous   B. unscathed   C. incessant   (D.) peripheral

_____ 12. Dion bore his toothache in ___ silence for a week before he gave in and went to the dentist.

      A. voracious   B. copious   C. frivolous   (D.) stoic

_____ 13. "Swear to me," whispered Juliet, "that no one else will ever ___ me in your heart." Romeo said, "Er, um, well . . ."

      (A.) supplant   B. meander   C. substantiate   D. lampoon

PART B

Write **C** if the italicized word is used **correctly**. Write **I** if the word is used **incorrectly**.

_C_ 14. Tired of the same old writing assignments, Pia decided to *lampoon* the whole idea of the student essay. Her title was "Ten Ways to Produce a Paper without Saying Anything."

_C_ 15. Grandfather needs home health care, but six nurses have quit because he is so *querulous*. He never stops complaining and making demands.

_I_ 16. As Marina's wedding gifts started to arrive, her mother reminded her, "Be sure to send everyone a note of *reproach*."

_I_ 17. Belinda was *unscathed* [unhurt] by the tragedy that struck her family. She became more and more despondent and eventually committed suicide.

_I_ 18. Food was so *copious* in the war-torn, ravaged city that the people were reduced to eating rats and boiled shoe leather.

_I_ 19. "Our fine library," the college catalogue boasted, "offers a *dearth* of material on every important subject." [lack]

_C_ 20. In theater *jargon*, "to fly" means to pull scenery up into the fly loft, the area above the stage.

_I_ 21. The speaker at the funeral said, "I am so overwhelmed by the *levity* of this sad occasion that I cannot find words to express my grief."

_C_ 22. The airline lost Vera's suitcase, but she had thrown away her baggage check, so she could not *substantiate* her claim.

_C_ 23. Denise wanted a rock band to play at her wedding, but her husband-to-be insisted on soft, *unobtrusive* music so that the guests could talk without shouting.

_I_ 24. As he arrived at "Frosty Feast—1,001 Fabulous Flavors," Alex *vacillated*. He strode up to the counter and said firmly, "Vanilla, please."

_C_ 25. The *decadence* of the pioneer settlement was striking. Every man, woman, and child worked long and hard to build a new community in the wilderness.

(handwritten note at item 19: to express too much pride)

Score	(Number correct) _____ x 4 = _____%

PART A

On the answer line, write the word from the box that completes each item below. Use each word once.

A. **affinity**	B. **brevity**	C. **brusque**	D. **coalesce**	E. **eloquent**
F. **heist**	G. **incessant**	H. **opulence**	I. **parsimonious**	J. **prodigal**
K. **progeny**	L. **respite**	M. **writhe**		

_____ 1. Some writers have a(n) ___ for long, unusual words. They love to send the reader scurrying to the dictionary every few lines.

_____ 2. It's good sense to check the bill in a restaurant, to be sure you haven't been overcharged. But many people are embarrassed to do this because they don't want to look ___.

_____ 3. The "___ son" in the Bible recklessly squanders his entire fortune and then limps back to his father's home, penniless, ragged, and starving.

_____ 4. The novelist had no children. When asked if this saddened her, she said no and pointed to a shelf full of her books. "These are my ___," she said.

_____ 5. That boss likes to come across as a hardheaded, tough, ___, no-nonsense type. As a result, many of his employees are afraid of him.

_____ 6. In the limbo, a dance from the West Indies, the dancers must ___ and bend over backward to get under a low pole.

_____ 7. After an afternoon of hearing his kids' nonstop quarrels, Matt yelled, "Stop that ___ squabbling before I go out of my mind!"

_____ 8. The ___ of the theater lobby took our breath away. We were surrounded by gold draperies, crystal chandeliers, gleaming mirrors, velvet carpeting, and marble pillars.

_____ 9. A famous author once apologized for sending a friend a very long letter, saying that the reason was "I didn't have time to write a short one." This suggests that ___ requires considerable work.

_____ 10. Julia was innocently shopping when the store was robbed. But the police suspected that she had taken part in the ___ and arrested her along with the real thieves.

_____ 11. Some elementary schools no longer have recess. This troubles many parents and teachers, who feel that children need a(n) ___ during the school day.

_____ 12. The speaker's appeal for the victims of the famine was so ___ that it moved the audience to tears—and to donate generously.

_____ 13. "Hiding the children's Easter basket behind the radiator was not a good idea," Lee Ann admitted. "I should have realized that all the jellybeans would ___ into one sticky lump."

(Continues on next page)

PART B

Write **C** if the italicized word is used **correctly**. Write **I** if the word is used **incorrectly**.

_____ 14. "Your essay is *exemplary*," the professor told Cara. "With your permission, I would like to include it in the next edition of my textbook, as a model research paper."

_____ 15. The *exuberance* of the children in the hospital was sad to see. Thin, pale, and exhausted, many were too weak even to look up as visitors arrived.

_____ 16. "I've won the million-dollar lottery!" Felice shrieked with joy. "I'm rich! I'll never be *insolvent* again!"

_____ 17. Roy, who was supposed to be on a diet, kept making *surreptitious* trips to the kitchen to nibble on this and that, whenever he thought no one would notice.

_____ 18. The *fledgling* company has an excellent reputation—which is understandable, since it's been in business for twenty years and has thousands of satisfied customers.

_____ 19. Ty made the *sagacious* decision to walk out on his job before he'd gotten a new one. Now he can't find work and can't pay his rent.

_____ 20. "We have an *unassailable* defense," Enrique's lawyer said, "so I advise you to plead guilty and throw yourself on the mercy of the court."

_____ 21. One model in a high-fashion show wore a hat so *voluminous* that it had to be supported with four poles carried by four attendants.

_____ 22. The author took a *dispassionate* approach to the topic. He presented both sides of the issue evenhandedly and did not let his own feelings intrude.

_____ 23. The symphony's second movement—slow, mournful, and *effervescent*—is based on a funeral march.

_____ 24. Reba is *indefatigable*. She can't walk a block without having to stop and rest awhile, and after climbing one flight of stairs, she has to lie down to recover.

_____ 25. The story is about a kindly, generous, cheerful *misanthrope* who loves and is loved by everyone.

Score   (Number correct) _____   x   4 = _____%

Enter your score above and in the **Vocabulary Performance Chart** on the inside back cover of the book.

PART A: Synonyms

In the space provided, write the letter of the choice that is most nearly the **same** in meaning as the **boldfaced** word.

_____ 1. **brusque**	A. gruff	B. bright	C. brainy	D. polite	
_____ 2. **clemency**	A. hopelessness	B. unhappiness	C. cleverness	D. forgiveness	
_____ 3. **decadence**	A. decency	B. corruption	C. confidence	D. defense	
_____ 4. **eloquent**	A. moving	B. boring	C. frightening	D. disappointing	
_____ 5. **exemplary**	A. excellent	B. extinct	C. excessive	D. external	
_____ 6. **fledgling**	A. flying	B. needed	C. new	D. failing	
_____ 7. **heist**	A. a robbery	B. a charity	C. a mistake	D. an imitation	
_____ 8. **incessant**	A. incompetent	B. ceaseless	C. careless	D. rare	
_____ 9. **incidental**	A. major	B. minor	C. memorable	D. incredible	
_____ 10. **indefatigable**	A. satisfied	B. dishonest	C. uncaring	D. untiring	
_____ 11. **jargon**	A. humor	B. specialized language	C. history	D. drama	
_____ 12. **lampoon**	A. to learn	B. to teach	C. to spoof	D. to admire	
_____ 13. **levity**	A. merriness	B. weariness	C. sickness	D. envy	
_____ 14. **misanthrope**	A. a hater	B. a lover	C. a wanderer	D. an entertainer	
_____ 15. **nonchalance**	A. passion	B. coolness	C. nonexistence	D. stupidity	
_____ 16. **progeny**	A. friends	B. enemies	C. defendants	D. descendants	
_____ 17. **querulous**	A. cheery	B. complaining	C. shy	D. helpful	
_____ 18. **reproach**	A. disapproval	B. praise	C. deceit	D. imitation	
_____ 19. **respite**	A. an assignment	B. a vacation	C. a career	D. a skill	
_____ 20. **stoic**	A. insane	B. irresponsible	C. self-controlled	D. disrespectful	
_____ 21. **substantiate**	A. to support	B. to attack	C. to conceal	D. to ignore	
_____ 22. **supplant**	A. to displace	B. to summarize	C. to supervise	D. to dislike	
_____ 23. **vacillate**	A. to leave	B. to return	C. to hesitate	D. to understand	
_____ 24. **voracious**	A. tired	B. hungry	C. busy	D. cautious	
_____ 25. **writhe**	A. to twist	B. to blend	C. to carry	D. to wear	

PART B: Antonyms

In the space provided, write the letter of the choice that is most nearly **opposite** in meaning to the **boldfaced** word.

_____ 26. **affinity**   A. fondness   B. happiness   C. satisfaction   D. dislike

_____ 27. **brevity**   A. length   B. shortness   C. knowledge   D. fame

_____ 28. **coalesce**   A. to come back   B. to come home   C. to come apart   D. to come between

_____ 29. **copious**   A. abundant   B. cooperative   C. uncooperative   D. few

_____ 30. **dearth**   A. abundance   B. pleasure   C. sadness   D. fear

_____ 31. **dispassionate**   A. prejudiced   B. disappointing   C. disastrous   D. predictable

_____ 32. **effervescent**   A. evil   B. eager   C. bouncy   D. dull

_____ 33. **exuberance**   A. apathy   B. excitement   C. wealth   D. poverty

_____ 34. **frivolous**   A. amused   B. witty   C. silly   D. serious

_____ 35. **hackneyed**   A. original   B. true   C. false   D. predictable

_____ 36. **insolvent**   A. healthy   B. wealthy   C. wise   D. handsome

_____ 37. **meander**   A. to go slowly   B. to go directly   C. to stop   D. to start

_____ 38. **morose**   A. happy   B. puzzled   C. depressed   D. bereaved

_____ 39. **opulence**   A. affluence   B. influence   C. poverty   D. obedience

_____ 40. **parsimonious**   A. skillful   B. patient   C. generous   D. impatient

_____ 41. **peripheral**   A. central   B. untrue   C. numerous   D. few

_____ 42. **prodigal**   A. angry   B. sleepy   C. thrifty   D. lonely

_____ 43. **proximity**   A. pronunciation   B. process   C. appearance   D. distance

_____ 44. **sagacious**   A. sensible   B. sensory   C. foolish   D. fearless

_____ 45. **surreptitious**   A. straightforward   B. secret   C. superfluous   D. inadequate

_____ 46. **torpor**   A. relevance   B. irrelevance   C. energy   D. money

_____ 47. **unassailable**   A. strong   B. weak   C. rare   D. common

_____ 48. **unobtrusive**   A. obvious   B. obscure   C. subtle   D. dim

_____ 49. **unscathed**   A. wrong   B. wounded   C. unarmed   D. unharmed

_____ 50. **voluminous**   A. constant   B. towering   C. variable   D. tiny

Score   (Number correct) _____   x 2 = _____ %

Enter your score above and in the **Vocabulary Performance Chart** on the inside back cover of the book.

Unit Two

appall	kindle
cognizant	lavish
commiserate	ludicrous
expedient	negligent
hindrance	scrutinize

Ten Words in Context

In the space provided, write the letter of the meaning closest to that of each **boldfaced** word. Use the context of the sentences to help you figure out each word's meaning.

1 appall
(ə-pôl′)
- *verb*

● At the end of World War II, the facts that emerged about the Nazi concentration camps and death camps **appalled** the entire world.

● "When the facts about this awful crime are disclosed," said the prosecutor, "they will **appall** you and show clearly that the defendant is a monster."

___ *Appall* means   A. to appeal to.   B. to shock.   C. to bore.

2 cognizant *Thinking*
(kŏg′nĭ-zənt)
- *adjective*

● After a picnic in the woods, Shawn found a tick on his ankle and then developed a rash. **Cognizant** of the risk of Lyme disease, he saw his doctor right away.

● Many Americans have diabetes without being **cognizant** of their condition.

___ *Cognizant* means   A. confused by.   B. conscious of.   C. careless about.

3 commiserate
(kə-mĭz′ə-rāt′)
- *verb*

● Mom was disappointed with the widows' support group. The members just wanted to **commiserate** with each other, but she wanted to learn about positive steps to take, not just get sympathy.

● When my dog died, my friends tried to **commiserate** with me, but they didn't really understand how I was feeling.

___ *Commiserate* means   A. to express sorrow.   B. to draw a comparison.   C. to complain.

4 expedient
(ĭk-spē′dē-ənt)
- *adjective*

● Marty's interest in Elaine seems entirely **expedient**; he knows she has money, and he wants to marry someone wealthy who will support him.

● In order to sell his old car for the highest possible price, Jim did the **expedient** thing: he slapped a new coat of paint on it and didn't mention that it needed new brakes and a new exhaust system.

___ *Expedient* means   A. unbelievable.   B. admirable.   C. self-interested.

5 hindrance
(hĭn′drəns)
- *noun*

● Some people seem perfectly willing to lie if the truth would be a **hindrance** to getting what they want.

● Her tendency to faint at the sight of blood will be a **hindrance** to Tonya's plan to become a nurse.

___ *Hindrance* means   A. a cause.   B. an effect.   C. a barrier.

6 kindle
(kĭn′dl)
- *verb*

● Before Tyrone joined the navy, Callie had thought of him as "just a friend." But his warm, affectionate letters began to **kindle** her love for him.

● The senator's lifelong devotion to politics was **kindled** early, when she was elected president of her high-school senior class.

___ *Kindle* means   A. to stop.   B. to inspire.   C. to change.

7 lavish
(lăv′ĭsh)
- *adjective*

● The **lavish** new offices looked very impressive, but behind all that splendor, the company was going broke.

● Avery celebrated his promotion by taking his friends out for a **lavish** dinner. "The best of everything!" he told the waiter. "And it's all on me."

___ *Lavish* means   (A.) overly luxurious.   B. subtle.   C. amusing.

8 ludicrous
(loo′dĭ-krəs)
- *adjective*

● Struggling in the wind and rain with my umbrella, which had turned inside out, while my dog tugged wildly at his leash and my bag of groceries burst and spilled, I must have been a **ludicrous** sight.

● "Diet Tips from Space Aliens"; "Five-Year-Old Gives Birth to Basketball Team"; "Florida Floating Out to Sea"—no idea seems too **ludicrous** to be reported in the supermarket tabloids.

___ *Ludicrous* means   A. horrifying.   (B.) ridiculous.   C. inspiring.

9 negligent
(nĕg′lĭ-jənt)
- *adjective*

● While Hester may be a **negligent** housekeeper—her apartment is dusty and untidy—she makes up for it by being a loving, conscientious mother.

● It's not surprising that Rich flunked out of college. His attitude toward studying has always been **negligent**.

___ *Negligent* means   A. anxious.   B. amusing.   (C.) careless.

10 scrutinize
(skroot′n-īz′)
- *verb*

● The detectives **scrutinized** the crime scene for fingerprints and other clues.

● Before handing in his report, Dan was told to **scrutinize** it for misspellings and other errors.

___ *Scrutinize* means   (A.) to inspect.   B. to describe.   C. to add to.

Matching Words with Definitions

Following are definitions of the ten words. Clearly write or print each word next to its definition. The sentences above and on the previous page will help you decide on the meaning of each word.

1. ____hindrance____ An obstacle; impediment

2. ____Cognizant____ Aware

3. ____expedient____ Self-serving; convenient

4. ____lavish____ Extravagant

5. ____Negligent____ Careless; irresponsible; casual

6. ____Scrutinize____ To examine carefully

7. ____kindle____ To stir up; arouse

8. ____appall____ To horrify; dismay

9. ____ludicrous____ Laughable

10. ____Commiserate____ To sympathize; express compassion

CAUTION: Do not go any further until you are sure the above answers are correct. Then you can use the definitions to help you in the following practices. Your goal is eventually to know the words well enough so that you don't need to check the definitions at all.

Sentence Check 1

Using the answer line provided, complete each item below with the correct word from the box. Use each word once.

A. appall	B. cognizant	C. commiserate	D. expedient	E. hindrance
F. kindle	G. lavish	H. ludicrous	I. negligent	J. scrutinize

Cognizant   1. Janna's parents were ___ of her problems at school, but they did not know the cause until a psychologist diagnosed a learning disability.

hindrance   2. It's OK not to have a car in the city, where public transportation is available; but the lack of a car is a real ___ to getting around in the country.

lavish   3. We exclaimed with delight over our ___ hotel room, with its thick rug, brocade curtains, and gorgeous furniture.

appall   4. The amount of food that's wasted in the school cafeteria ___s me—surely there must be some way to share all that extra food with people who need it.

negligent   5. Delia is ___ about nutrition. She eats mostly junk food, when she bothers to eat at all.

Commiserate   6. "Laugh and the world laughs with you; cry and you cry alone" is an old saying. It means that others would rather share your happiness than ___ with you over your sorrows.

Scrutinize   7. Handwriting experts ___ letters, notes, and signatures to identify the writers.

kindle   8. The Mitchells hope that letting their children have a puppy will ___ the children's sense of responsibility and help them develop respect for animals.

expendient   9. It was ___ for James to tell his new girlfriend, "I attended one of the finest colleges in the country," without mentioning that he'd flunked out.

ludicrous   10. The very funny Marx Brothers comedies are full of ___ scenes, such as the one in *A Night at the Opera* in which fifteen people are stuffed into a room the size of a large closet.

NOTE: Now check your answers to these items by turning to page 175. Going over the answers carefully will help you prepare for the next two practices, for which answers are not given.

Sentence Check 2

Using the answer lines provided, complete each item below with **two** words from the box. Use each word once.

lavish
ludicrous   1–2. Milly gave a(n) ___ birthday party for her dog, complete with an expensive cake, candles, and fancy decorations. The poor animal wore a party hat and a huge satin ribbon and looked ___.

expedient
commiserate   3–4. The mayor found it politically ___ to close the school, but then visited it to ___ with the teachers and students. Everyone felt that his expressions of sympathy were phony.

Kindle
hindrance
negligent
scrutinize

Cognizant
appall

5–6. Parents who want to ___ a love of reading in their kids often complain that television is a serious ___. The kids would rather watch TV than open a book.

7–8. "The boss hates ___ work," Rasheed was told on his first day at his new job. "You can expect her to ___ all your letters and memos—and there's no clemency° if she finds careless errors."
mercy

9–10. Explaining her decision to give up smoking, Celia said, "I am ___ of the statistics on smoking and cancer. The facts are unassailable°, and they ___ me."

Final Check: *Bad Translations*

Here is a final opportunity for you to strengthen your knowledge of the ten words. First read the following selection carefully. Then fill in each blank with a word from the box at the top of the previous page. (Context clues will help you figure out which word goes in which blank.) Use each word once.

When a company introduces a product into a new country, it should (1) _Scrutinize_ the promotional materials carefully. Sometimes a company is not (2) _Cognizant_ of how ads will be read in a foreign language. The results can be (3) _ludicrous_, making would-be customers writhe° with laughter—or with shock—instead of making them want to buy the product. Here are a few examples.

When Coca-Cola was introduced in China, the company mounted a(n) (4) _lavish_ advertising campaign that featured thousands of billboards with the Chinese phrase *Ke-kou-ke-la*. Unfortunately, the company had been (5) _negligent_ about learning just what *Ke-kou-ke-la* meant in Chinese. It translated into something like "Bite the wax tadpole." That phrase did not exactly (6) _Kindle_ anyone's desire to buy Coke.

Maybe soft-drink companies tend to have special problems with Chinese. It certainly would have been (7) _expedient_ for the Pepsi company to test-market its slogan before going into China. The translation of the slogan "Come alive with the Pepsi generation" shocked and (8) _appall_ (e)d Chinese shoppers. What it said was, "Pepsi will bring your ancestors back from the dead."

But problems arise with other languages, too. The Chevy Nova didn't sell very well in South America. Finally company officials realized that the (9) _hindrance_ was the car's name. In Spanish, the phrase *No va* means "It won't go."

When the Pope visited Miami, a fledgling° businessman, perhaps counting on beginner's luck, made thousands of T-shirts that were supposed to say in Spanish, "I saw the Pope." You have to (10) _Commiserate_ with the poor guy—he got stuck with a copious° supply of unsold shirts. What the Spanish phrase really said was, "I saw the potato."

Scores   Sentence Check 2 _____%   Final Check _____%

clamor	rescind
contract	stagnant
duplicity	uniform
equivocal	untenable
irresolute	vilify

Ten Words in Context

In the space provided, write the letter of the meaning closest to that of each **boldfaced** word. Use the context of the sentences to help you figure out each word's meaning.

1 clamor
(klăm′ər)
- *noun*

- By the time the basketball game was over, I had an awful headache from the constant **clamor** of the fans as they cheered for their team.
- The hungry parakeets began an excited **clamor** when they saw their owner enter the room.

__ *Clamor* means   A. loud noise.   B. tense silence.   C. whispers.

2 contract
(kən-trăkt′)
- *verb*

A balloon full of air andout

- That company can't seem to decide whether to grow or to **contract**. First it hired a hundred extra workers; then it laid off two hundred.
- The universe is expanding, but scientists do not know whether it will continue to expand or whether it will eventually start to **contract**, becoming more and more dense until it collapses on itself.

__ *Contract* means   A. to become visible.   B. to become smaller.   C. to become weaker.

3 duplicity
(dōō-plĭs′ĭ-tē)
- *noun*

- "I can't tolerate **duplicity**," said the teacher. "If you didn't get around to writing your paper on time, say so. Don't make up some story about death or illness in your family."
- Dogs seem incapable of **duplicity**. If a dog soils the rug, he will slink around guiltily. He won't try to pretend that the cat did it.

__ *Duplicity* means   A. repetition.   B. exaggeration.   C. deceit. *lying*

4 equivocal
(ĭ-kwĭv′ə-kəl)
- *adjective*

- Akira seemed **equivocal** about whether he'd gotten the job or not. First he said it was "a sure thing," but then he added that he had to go back for another interview.
- After her first date with Chris, Karen was **equivocal** about how she felt toward him. She said he was "interesting," which could mean almost anything.

__ *Equivocal* means   A. vague.   B. the same.   C. discouraged.
not the same thing

5 irresolute
(ĭ-rĕz′ə-lōōt′)
- *adjective*

- In *Hamlet,* why doesn't Hamlet kill Claudius sooner? Is it because he is too **irresolute** to act, or because he is prevented from carrying out his purpose?
- Carleton is **irresolute** about marrying Tania. He's sure they are in love, but he's not sure about getting married because they fight all the time.

__ *Irresolute* means   A. unable to decide.   B. lacking self-control.   C. unknowing.

6 rescind
(rĭ-sĭnd′)
- *verb*

- The state can **rescind** the licenses of people arrested for driving while drunk.
- It's very rude to **rescind** your invitation to one person just because you've met someone else you'd prefer to invite.

__ *Rescind* means   A. to renew.   B. to cancel.   C. to abuse.

7 stagnant
(stăg'nənt)
- *adjective*

[handwritten: Body of River, Career]

- At age forty, Ira is considering a midlife career change. He feels that his present career is **stagnant**: he's going nowhere in his job.
- The pond was **stagnant**, and algae and weeds were growing so thickly that they covered the still water underneath.

___ *Stagnant* means   A. out of control.   B. motionless.   C. spread thin.

8 uniform
(yōō'nə-fôrm')
- *adjective*

[handwritten: alike gravestones]

- To give hand-sewing a professional appearance, it's important to make the stitches **uniform**. Take the trouble to make them all the same size—the result will be worth it.
- People whose teeth are unevenly spaced and discolored may benefit from a dental technique called bonding, which makes teeth look more **uniform**.

___ *Uniform* means   A. alike.   B. different.   C. insupportable.

9 untenable
(ŭn-tĕn'ə-bəl)
- *adjective*

- In the exam room, the teacher looked grimly at the math formulas penciled on my T-shirt. "Your story that you don't know how they got there is **untenable**," she said. "You can't expect me to believe you!"
- Jocelyn's theory that the explorers missing at the South Pole had been eaten by polar bears was interesting but **untenable**. Polar bears live at the North Pole.

___ *Untenable* means   A. uninteresting.   B. unable to be defended.   C. unclear.

10 vilify
(vĭl'ə-fī)
- *verb*

[handwritten: Note to Remember — Vile: evil]

- Most of Mr. Jones's students praise him, but a few **vilify** him. It's strange that he should be so respected by some and so harshly criticized by others.
- "I don't think it's fair to **vilify** an entire college just because one fraternity has behaved badly," said Liam. "People should aim their dislike at the right target."

___ *Vilify* means   A. to argue with.   B. to assault physically.   C. to speak evil of.

Matching Words with Definitions

Following are definitions of the ten words. Clearly write or print each word next to its definition. The sentences above and on the previous page will help you decide on the meaning of each word.

1. _____*duplicity*_____   Deliberate deceptiveness; deceit *[handwritten: lying]*
2. _____*equivocal*_____   Open to more than one interpretation and often intended to mislead
3. _____*uniform*_____   All or always the same; without variety
4. _____*contract*_____   To reduce in size; become compressed
5. _____*clamor*_____   A loud outcry; hubbub
6. _____*untenable*_____   Unable to be held or defended; insupportable
7. _____*stagnant*_____   Not moving; not flowing; motionless
8. _____*vilify*_____   To make abusive statements about
9. _____*rescind*_____   To repeal; take back
10. _____*irresolute*_____   Uncertain how to think or act; undecided

CAUTION: Do not go any further until you are sure the above answers are correct. Then you can use the definitions to help you in the following practices. Your goal is eventually to know the words well enough so that you don't need to check the definitions at all.

Sentence Check 1

Using the answer line provided, complete each item below with the correct word from the box. Use each word once.

A. clamor	B. contract	C. duplicity	D. equivocal	E. irresolute
F. rescind	G. stagnant	H. uniform	I. untenable	J. vilify

Irresolute   1. ___ about whether to take the subway or catch a bus, I vacillated° too long and managed to miss both.

Untenable   2. Lenore insisted that she had paid all the rent she owed, but her claim was ___. She was unable to substantiate° it by producing any canceled checks or receipts.

Contract   3. Bodily movement results when our muscles first ___ and then relax.

Vilify   4. The candidate's voice shook as he showed reporters an ugly cartoon attacking his wife. "___ me if you like—I can take abuse," he said. "But leave my family alone."

Clamor   5. It seems that every courtroom drama includes a scene in which a(n) ___ erupts, with the judge pounding the gavel and shouting "Order in the court!"

equivocal   6. When Ben asked Jenna if she loved him, her ___ response—"Oh, Ben, I love everybody"—left him more confused than ever.

rescind   7. Angry over a council member's racist statements, a citizens' group decided to ___ its invitation to have him speak at its annual fundraising dinner.

duplicity   8. City supervisors said the repairs to our street would take a month, but they took almost a year. We don't know if this was ___ on the city's part, or an honest miscalculation.

Stagnant   9. Sales had been ___ for months, so the company began an aggressive new ad campaign in the hope that merchandise would begin moving again.

Uniform   10. "No longer will each department handle billing its own way," the boss announced. "From now on, we will all use identical forms and a(n) ___ set of procedures."

NOTE: Now check your answers to these items by turning to page 175. Going over the answers carefully will help you prepare for the next two practices, for which answers are not given.

Sentence Check 2

Using the answer lines provided, complete each item below with **two** words from the box. Use each word once.

irresolute
Untenable   1–2. Eddie paused, ___, outside the professor's office. He wanted to argue about his poor grade, but he hesitated because he was afraid she would consider his reasons ___.

Vilify
Stagnant   3–4. "Don't expect me to ___ the mayor," said the opposing candidate. "He's a decent, honest man. But our city has grown sluggish and ___ during his administration. It's time to break out of our torpor° and move forward again!"

Contract
equivocal

5–6. Asked whether the college should expand or ___, the president gave a(n) ___ answer: "Growth is positive, but we may need to draw inward and sharpen our focus."

Uniform
Clamor

7–8. People used to describe the United States as a "melting pot," taking in immigrants and blending them so they would coalesce° into a(n) ___ mixture. However, those wishing to keep their ethnic heritage objected to this description, often with a(n) ___ of protest.

Rescind
duplicty

9–10. The new office manager promised to ___ some pointless rules about using the copier, but he seems to be guilty of ___. The silly rules are still in place.

Final Check: *Memory Aids*

Here is a final opportunity for you to strengthen your knowledge of the ten words. First read the following selection carefully. Then fill in each blank with a word from the box at the top of the previous page. (Context clues will help you figure out which word goes in which blank.) Use each word once.

How can you remember the word (1) "_Vilify_"? Think of saying something *vile*, and there you are: "to speak *evil* of." For (2) "_stagnant_," you could think of *st-* as in standing *still*—not moving. And (3) "_Clamour_" is easier to remember if you think of a *claim*, which is also a demand, though not necessarily a loud one. If you've ever used a copying machine—a scanner or photocopier—to make duplicates, exact doubles of an original document, you'll have no trouble remembering that (4) "_duplicity_" means "double-dealing," or "dishonesty." To remember the adjective (5) "_Uniform_," just think of what people in the Air Force or the Navy wear so that they all look the same.

A prefix—a word part at the beginning of a longer word—can also be a memory aid. Remember that the prefix *ir-* means "not" and *resolve* means "make up your mind," and you won't forget that (6) "_irresolute_" means "not having made up your mind." To remember (7) "_Untenable_," think of holding something with your *ten* fingers. Add the prefix *un*, which also means "not," and you have it: "not holdable." The prefix *con-*, meaning "together," will help you recall what (8) "_Contract_" means: think of making something smaller by pulling or pushing its parts closer *together*. And one meaning of the prefix *re-* is "back" or "backward," which can remind (which means "take your mind *back* to") you of the fact that (9) "_rescind_" means "take back" or "repeal."

Sometimes the best way to learn a word is to cut it in half, scrutinize° both halves, and see what they say. Think of *equal* and *voice* to remember that (10) "_equivocal_" describes something which can be understood in more than one way—as if *equal voices* were speaking.

Try making up your own memory aids. Even if they sound frivolous° or ludicrous°, you'll find that they're a powerful tool and an exemplary° learning method.

Scores	Sentence Check 2 ___%	Final Check ___%

Enter your scores above and in the **Vocabulary Performance Chart** on the inside back cover of the book.

d Not on the exam nor final

affable	loquacious
apocryphal	obtuse
desultory	opaque
garbled	paucity
irascible	recapitulate

Ten Words in Context

In the space provided, write the letter of the meaning closest to that of each **boldfaced** word. Use the context of the sentences to help you figure out each word's meaning.

1 affable
(ăf'ə-bəl)
- *adjective*

● Dobermans and pit bulls are often thought of as unfriendly dogs, while golden retrievers and Labradors are seen as **affable**.

● "I wish my new boss were more **affable**," Jothi said. "She seems so stern that I'm afraid to ask her a question when I don't understand something."

__ *Affable* means A. bad-tempered. B. good-natured. C. intelligent.

2 apocryphal
(ə-pŏk'rə-fəl)
- *adjective*

● A hero of American folklore is the giant lumberjack Paul Bunyan, whose footprints supposedly formed the Great Lakes. Clearly, this story is **apocryphal**.

● There is a story in our family that my great-great-grandfather was a train robber, but I think the story is **apocryphal**. I've never seen any proof.

__ *Apocryphal* means A. fictitious. B. difficult to understand. C. true.

3 desultory
(dĕs'əl-tôr'ē)
- *adjective*

● When the shoe repair shop lost my boots, the clerk's search was so **desultory** and disorganized that I had to go through the shelves and find them myself.

● Darrin went to the emergency room with a severe stomachache, but the doctor on duty gave him only a quick, **desultory** examination and sent him home.

__ *Desultory* means A. fake. B. random. C. intensive.

4 garbled
(gär'bəld)
- *adjective*

● When Tim printed his essay, a computer error made it come out **garbled**. Only meaningless symbols and numbers appeared on the page.

● The children played a game in which each one whispered a message to the next child in line. The first child whispered, "My favorite color is purple," but the message the last child heard was **garbled**: "You shouldn't holler at your uncle."

__ *Garbled* means A. lengthy. B. shortened. C. distorted.

5 irascible
(ĭ-răs'ə-bəl)
- *adjective*

● "The holidays are supposed to be a happy time," sighed Martina. "But with all the extra work and guests, I find myself becoming **irascible**—I'm a real grouch."

● "I know my patients are improving when they become grumpy," said Dr. Imiri. "An **irascible** patient is on the road to recovery."

__ *Irascible* means A. bad-tempered. B. nervous. C. depressed.

6 loquacious
(lō-kwā'shəs)
- *adjective*

● Kyle, who prefers to sleep or read on a long plane trip, says it never fails: he always ends up with a **loquacious** seat companion who wants to chat nonstop.

● The British have an amusing way of describing **loquacious** people: they say that such a person can "talk the hind leg off a donkey."

__ *Loquacious* means A. talking too much. B. aggressive. C. irritable.

7 obtuse
(ŏb-toos′)
- *adjective*

- Children can be remarkably **obtuse** about understanding school subjects like math, but their wits sharpen amazingly when they're learning a new video game.
- Today, in front of Gillian, Harvey mentioned the surprise party we're planning for her. I kicked him under the table, hoping to shut him up, but he's so **obtuse** he just said, "Ow! Why did you kick me?"

__ *Obtuse* means   A. angry.   (B.) stupid.   C. thoughtful.

8 opaque
(ō-pāk′)
- *adjective*

- We attempted to follow the movie's complex plot, but the characters' motives and reactions remained **opaque**. We finally gave up trying to understand it.
- Articles on Einstein's theory of relativity usually start reassuringly, noting that there is no reason why this theory should be **opaque** to the ordinary reader. Then they proceed to make it even more confusing.

__ *Opaque* means   A. fascinating.   (B.) difficult to understand.   C. improbable.

9 paucity
(pô′sĭ-tē)
- *noun*

- The speaker's elegant language could not conceal his **paucity** of ideas. He had nothing meaningful to say.
- Serena wanted to get away from her small town because of its **paucity** of intellectual life. It didn't even have a library or a bookstore.

__ *Paucity* means   A. repetition.   B. conflict.   (C.) lack.

10 recapitulate
(rē′kə-pĭch′ə-lāt′)
- *verb*

- "To **recapitulate** what we told you on the phone," said Ms. Brown to the baby sitter, "we'll be home at eleven o'clock, and you can reach us at the Athens Café."
- Before an exam, Ms. Chiu always has a review session in which she **recapitulates** some of the most important material the class has studied.

__ *Recapitulate* means   (A.) to sum up.   B. to ignore.   C. to contradict.

Matching Words with Definitions

Following are definitions of the ten words. Clearly write or print each word next to its definition. The sentences above and on the previous page will help you decide on the meaning of each word.

1. _apocryphal_   Of doubtful authenticity; not genuine
2. _desultory_   Moving from one thing to another in an unplanned way
3. _loquacious_   Very talkative
4. _affable_   Friendly; easy to get along with
5. _irascible_   Easily angered; irritable
6. _opaque_   Difficult to understand or explain; obscure; incomprehensible
7. _Recapitulate_   To summarize or repeat briefly
8. _Obtuse_   Slow to understand; dull
9. _Paucity_   A scarcity; an insufficiency
10. _garbled_   Mixed up to such an extent as to be misleading or incomprehensible

CAUTION: Do not go any further until you are sure the above answers are correct. Then you can use the definitions to help you in the following practices. Your goal is eventually to know the words well enough so that you don't need to check the definitions at all.

Sentence Check 1

Using the answer line provided, complete each item below with the correct word from the box. Use each word once.

A. **affable**	B. **apocryphal**	C. **desultory**	D. **garbled**	E. **irascible**
F. **loquacious**	G. **obtuse**	H. **opaque**	I. **paucity**	J. **recapitulate**

apocryphal   1. Many Spanish explorers in the 1700s lost their lives searching for the ___ "fountain of youth."

garbled   2. After a stroke, some people partially lose their ability to speak. Until they recover, their words come out ___ and unclear.

loquacious   3. People often become ___ when they're nervous. Unfortunately, not only do they talk too much, but what they say isn't very interesting.

opaque   4. The words of the poem sounded lovely, but their meaning was ___. Even the teacher found it difficult to explain.

affable   5. Although Ms. Henderson is a(n) ___ instructor, don't let her good nature make you think that she's a pushover. She's nice and friendly, but she's also a demanding teacher.

irascible   6. Deepak always seems to have a chip on his shoulder, and he gets angry over the slightest thing. I don't know what makes him so ___.

desultory   7. Jon's paper was a(n) ___ effort. He started late and then just threw some disconnected notes together. No wonder he got a D.

paucity   8. "We seem to have a(n) ___ of singers this year," said the chorus director. Only three students had shown up for the auditions, possibly indicating a dearth° of interest in joining the group.

recapitulate   9. Before I left the office, my doctor ___(e)d her advice to me: "Get extra rest, drink plenty of fluids, and don't worry."

obtuse   10. "I've been hinting that my birthday would be a good time for Jeff to give me an engagement ring," Jan said, "but he seems completely ___. I don't think he gets the point."

NOTE: Now check your answers to these items by turning to page 175. Going over the answers carefully will help you prepare for the next two practices, for which answers are not given.

Sentence Check 2

Using the answer lines provided, complete each item below with **two** words from the box. Use each word once.

irascible / *affable*   1–2. Lara had heard that the famous pianist was ___ and brusque°, but when she asked him for his autograph, he was very ___. He signed her program and gave her a charming smile.

desultory / *recapitulate*   3–4. The lecture was ___, with the speaker hopping confusingly from one topic to another. At the end, when he said, "To ___," it was hard to imagine which of his unrelated, rambling points he might choose to repeat.

_____apocryphal_____
_____opaque_____

5–6. Many widespread e-mails are ___—that is, they report information that is exaggerated, misleading, or just plain not true. The reasons people would originally write such e-mails are ___. Do they do it for attention? Or do they actually believe what they are writing is factual?

_____loquacious_____
_____obtuse_____

7–8. When Anya's ___ husband talks too much, she tries to remind him of the need for brevity° by raising her eyebrows and clearing her throat, but he's often too ___ to take the hint.

_____garbled_____
_____paucity_____

9–10. The weather report on the radio was ___ by static. Was the announcer predicting a(n) "___" of rain, meaning none, or a "possibility" of rain, meaning we might get drenched?

Final Check: *A Formula for Teaching*

Here is a final opportunity for you to strengthen your knowledge of the ten words. First read the following selection carefully. Then fill in each blank with a word from the box at the top of the previous page. (Context clues will help you figure out which word goes in which blank.) Use each word once.

There is a famous formula for communicating ideas to people: *Step 1*—Tell them what you're going to tell them. *Step 2*—Tell them. *Step 3*—Tell them what you've told them. The formula is said to have been invented long ago by the Army. That story may be (1)__apocryphal__, but it is probably authentic. The Army had to teach many things quickly to all kinds of fledgling° recruits, and often it had a(n) (2)__paucity__ of good instructors: too few teachers, with too little training. Moreover, there were all kinds of instructors. Some were tough and (3)__irascible__, with a quick temper and no patience for a learner who seemed slow, irresolute°, or (4)__obtuse__. Others were (5)__affable__ and (6)__loquacious__, and although these good-natured, talkative men might teach well, they could also waste time on incidental° matters or give confusing, (7)__garble__ instructions. The three-step formula would keep all teaching focused.

The formula is simple to use, and it is effective in writing as well as teaching. In step 1, you announce what you intend to say: how to disassemble and reassemble a rifle, how to apply for a job—whatever it is you want to communicate. In step 2, you say it. In step 3, you say it (briefly) again: you (8)__Recapitulate__ it as a summary and a reminder.

No formula is foolproof, but being cognizant° of this one will definitely help you avoid planless, (9)__desultory__ writing and writing that is unclear, equivocal°, vague, or (10)__opaque__. What worked for the Army can work for you.

| Scores | Sentence Check 2 _____% | Final Check _____% |

accolade	edifice
assuage	gravity
cacophony	infraction
censure	profane
diatribe	somber

Ten Words in Context

In the space provided, write the letter of the meaning closest to that of each **boldfaced** word. Use the context of the sentences to help you figure out each word's meaning.

1 accolade
(ăk′ə-lād′)
- *noun*

- Many people rushed out to try the new Thai restaurant on Wayne Avenue after it received an **accolade** in a newspaper review.
- Although it was filmed in 1941, *Citizen Kane* continues to earn **accolades** as one of the best movies ever made.

___ *Accolade* means   A. an expression of approval.   B. an apology.   C. a greeting.

2 assuage
(ə-swāj′)
- *verb*

- My brother's apology helped to **assuage** my anger at him.
- The grief one feels over the loss of a loved one never fully goes away, but time does **assuage** the pain.

___ *Assuage* means   A. to increase.   B. to explain.   C. to make less severe.

3 cacophony
(kə-kŏf′ə-nē)
- *noun*

- "I bought my daughter an iPod," Gordon confessed, "so I wouldn't have to listen to the **cacophony** that she calls music."
- When we listen to the **cacophony** of orchestra members tuning their instruments, it is hard to believe that they will soon produce a beautiful symphony.

___ *Cacophony* means   A. harmony.   B. unpleasant noise.   C. silence.

4 censure
(sĕn′shər)
- *noun*

- After Aaron got his ear pierced, he had to deal not only with his father's **censure**, but also with his grandfather's sarcastic remarks and icy stares.
- Jodi's parents were strongly opposed to her engagement. Unable to stand up to their **censure**, she broke up with her boyfriend.

___ *Censure* means   A. disapproval.   B. tolerance.   C. neglect.

5 diatribe
(dī′ə-trīb′)
- *noun*

- A reporter covering a preacher's sermon sat through an hour-long **diatribe** about wickedness. He later wrote, "Mr. Blank spoke on sin. He was against it."
- The art teacher, normally soft-spoken, subjected the class to a loud **diatribe** when he discovered that someone had spilled Coca-Cola on his computer.

___ *Diatribe* means   A. a calm discussion.   B. a physical attack.   C. a verbal attack.

6 edifice
(ĕd′ə-fĭs)
- *noun*

- On the college's hundredth anniversary, a plaque was put up in honor of the architect who had designed its first **edifice**, now the administration building.
- The company president decided to continue to rent office space, rather than buy a building. "It would be nice to move into a fine new **edifice**," she said, "but I'd rather spend the money on higher salaries and a better product."

___ *Edifice* means   A. a structure.   B. an expense.   C. a design.

7 gravity
(grăv′ĭ-tē)
- *noun*

- "I'm not sure you understand the **gravity** of the crimes you are accused of," the lawyer told his client. "Do you realize you could go to prison for a very long time?"
- The anxious parents waited in the emergency room to learn the **gravity** of their son's condition.

___ *Gravity* means   A. grief.   B. seriousness.   C. usefulness.

8 infraction
(ĭn-frăk′shən)
- *noun*

- "In my class, there will be no texting or other cell-phone use," said the instructor. "Any **infraction** of this rule will lead to a lower grade."
- Mrs. Hoeffel charges her kids for household **infractions**. For instance, there is a five-cent fine for leaving towels on the bathroom floor and a twenty-five-cent fine for failing to turn off the living-room lights at bedtime.

___ *Infraction* means   A. an exception.   B. an explanation.   C. a violation.

9 profane
(prō-fān′)
- *adjective*

- Karen refuses to use **profane** language. She says "Oh my gosh" instead of "Oh my God."
- Movies may get an "R" rating because of violence, sexual scenes, or **profane** dialog.

___ *Profane* means   A. lacking reverence.   B. ungrammatical.   C. hard to understand.

10 somber
(sŏm′bər)
- *adjective*

- When I saw the doctor's **somber** expression, I was afraid she had bad news for me.
- The dark colors and heavy furniture in the house give it a **somber** look—I think it would be hard to laugh or even smile there.

___ *Somber* means   A. very serious.   B. cheerful.   C. restful.

Matching Words with Definitions

Following are definitions of the ten words. Clearly write or print each word next to its definition. The sentences above and on the previous page will help you decide on the meaning of each word.

1. _____ Praise

2. _____ A building, especially of large, imposing size

3. _____ A breaking of a law or rule

4. _____ A bitter, abusively critical speech or piece of writing; denunciation

5. _____ To relieve; lessen

6. _____ Solemn; sad and depressing; melancholy

7. _____ Blame; a rebuke

8. _____ Severity; weighty importance

9. _____ Showing disrespect or contempt for sacred things; irreverent

10. _____ Harsh, discordant sounds

CAUTION: Do not go any further until you are sure the above answers are correct. Then you can use the definitions to help you in the following practices. Your goal is eventually to know the words well enough so that you don't need to check the definitions at all.

Sentence Check 1

Using the answer line provided, complete each item below with the correct word from the box. Use each word once.

| A. accolade | B. assuage | C. cacophony | D. censure | E. diatribe |
| F. edifice | G. gravity | H. infraction | I. profane | J. somber |

_____ 1. If parents use ___ language around children, the children will most likely repeat it—not only at home but also in public, and at the most embarrassing moments possible.

_____ 2. Many birds sing sweetly, but crows don't—instead, they produce a harsh ___ of cawing.

_____ 3. Judging from the ___s the new movie has been receiving, it's sure to be nominated for several Academy Awards.

_____ 4. The Little League team lost the championship game, but the coach ___(e)d the kids' disappointment by taking them out for banana splits.

_____ 5. "Because of the ___ of the international situation," announced the newscaster, "we will stay on the air with constant news updates throughout the evening."

_____ 6. The doctor received a letter of ___ from the local medical association for his negligent° treatment of a sick homeless man.

_____ 7. Jessie's apartment house is an ornate ___ dating from the nineteenth century.

_____ 8. Students are sent to detention for a variety of ___s, such as fighting, talking in class, or being disrespectful to a teacher.

_____ 9. On the day of the queen's funeral, the national radio station played only ___ music, as if to commiserate° with a country in mourning.

_____ 10. The nutritionist lectured passionately on the folly of eating red meat. Then, tired and hungry after her ___, she went out to dinner at Steak 'n' Ribs.

NOTE: Now check your answers to these items by turning to page 176. Going over the answers carefully will help you prepare for the next two practices, for which answers are not given.

Sentence Check 2

Using the answer lines provided, complete each item below with **two** words from the box. Use each word once.

_____
_____ 1–2. The old mansion is a(n) ___-looking ___, dark and dismal. It would be a perfect setting for a horror movie.

_____
_____ 3–4. Not so long ago, using ___ language "in the presence of ladies" was an offense of considerable ___. In some places, swearing in public was even punishable by arrest.

_____
_____ 5–6. True, chewing gum is a(n) ___ of school rules, but these days, hardly anybody thinks such a minor offense is worthy of ___.

_____   7–8. The rock concert was so heavily miked that the ___ gave Jade a pounding
_____   headache. When she got home, she put an ice pack on her forehead to ___ the
                             throbbing pain.

_____   9–10. The senator's hackneyed° speech was one he had given a hundred times.
_____   After a(n) ___ against graft, corruption, and decadence°, he ended with ___s
                             to motherhood, the flag, and apple pie.

Final Check: *The One-Room Schoolhouse*

Here is a final opportunity for you to strengthen your knowledge of the ten words. First read the following
selection carefully. Then fill in each blank with a word from the box at the top of the previous page.
(Context clues will help you figure out which word goes in which blank.) Use each word once.

For many years, the one-room rural schoolhouse was part of the American scene. This tiny
(1)_____ did have only one room, where all the pupils, ranging in age from five
or six to their teens, sat together with one teacher—a young man or woman looking at them with a(n)
(2)_____ expression. The teacher might have just graduated from a "normal school"
(a teacher-training institute) but would be trying to seem as serious and dignified as possible. School was
held mostly in winter, because the pupils were farm children who had to work from spring planting until
the harvest was in.

If you could go back in time and enter such a schoolhouse, you would hear a clamor°—a(n)
(3)_____ of voices as many of the pupils, grouped by grades, "said" their
lessons all at once. The smallest children would be memorizing the alphabet; the oldest might be
reciting some famous speech from the past, perhaps an eloquent° (4)_____
delivered in the Roman senate, where speakers used powerful, passionate language to vilify°
their opponents. All of the students would be wearing long woolen underwear and writhing° and
scratching to (5)_____ the itching. A wood-burning stove heated
the room, more or less. The "big boys" would keep the woodbox filled, or a pupil might have to
fetch wood as a punishment for some (6)_____ of a rule, such as
(7)_____ language, although misbehavior of such (8)_____
was rare.

These one-room schools held a special place in the hearts of Americans. In fact, at one time in American
history, any political speech was sure to draw (9)_____ if it did not include a(n)
(10)_____ in praise of the "little red schoolhouse."

Scores   Sentence Check 2 _____%   Final Check _____%

Enter your scores above and in the **Vocabulary Performance Chart** on the inside back cover of the book.

blasphemy	incite
enmity	languish
erroneous	peruse
garner	recluse
heretic	renounce

Ten Words in Context

In the space provided, write the letter of the meaning closest to that of each **boldfaced** word. Use the context of the sentences to help you figure out each word's meaning.

1 blasphemy
(blăs′fə-mē)
- *noun*

- Some of the world's greatest thinkers, such as Copernicus, have been accused of **blasphemy** because their ideas challenged the teachings of the Church.
- The Smiths have lived so long in Boston and think it is such a wonderful city that they feel it's almost **blasphemy** to consider living anywhere else.

__ *Blasphemy* means   A. physical violence.   B. an insult to something holy.   C. daydreaming.

2 enmity
(ĕn′mĭ-tē)
- *noun*

- After their divorce, Han tried not to feel **enmity** toward his ex-wife. He knew that anger and bitterness would be bad for their children.
- Lila seems to feel real **enmity** toward her boss; she criticizes everything he says or does.

__ *Enmity* means   A. admiration.   B. affection.   C. hostility.

3 erroneous
(ĭ-rō′nē-əs)
- *adjective*

- Many first-graders have the **erroneous** idea that their teacher lives at the school.
- Because the newspaper had printed an **erroneous** date and time for the community meeting, few people showed up when it actually took place.

__ *Erroneous* means   A. error-free.   B. wrong.   C. original.

4 garner
(gär′nər)
- *verb*

- Once a year, the company president sends around a questionnaire to **garner** ideas from the employees about how to improve workplace conditions.
- Although *Avatar* did not win any major Academy Awards in 2010, it **garnered** praise from environmentalists everywhere for its themes of a world in balance and the connections among all living things.

__ *Garner* means   A. to gather.   B. to distribute.   C. to reject.

5 heretic
(hĕr′ĭ-tĭk)
- *noun*

- Martin Luther was originally a Catholic priest, but when he began to disagree with the Church's teachings, he was labeled a **heretic** and left the priesthood.
- People who believed that the world was round, not flat, were once considered lunatics or **heretics**.

__ *Heretic* means   A. a conservative.   B. a rebel.   C. a genius.

6 incite
(ĭn-sīt′)
- *verb*

- The smell of blood in the water can **incite** sharks to attack.
- No one knows what **incited** the usually gentle dog to bite the mail carrier.

__ *Incite* means   A. to prevent.   B. to urge on.   C. to forbid.

7 languish
(lăng′gwĭsh)
- *verb*

- Children who **languish** in institutions, such as orphanages, often improve dramatically when they are adopted into loving homes.
- Some people **languish** in the summer heat, but others love the hot weather and feel full of energy and strength.

__ *Languish* means   A. to thrive.   B. to misunderstand.   C. to do poorly.

8 peruse
(pə-rōōz′)
- *verb*

- When the list of people killed in the plane crash was posted, the passengers' anxious relatives **perused** it fearfully.
- To **peruse** a train timetable, with its tiny type and tinier footnotes, you need good eyesight and plenty of patience.

__ *Peruse* means   A. to inspect.   B. to glance at.   C. to explain.

9 recluse
(rĕk′lōōs′)
- *noun*

- Local old-timers tell stories about Wild Man Bill, a **recluse** who lived in a cave and came into town only once a year to buy supplies.
- While she was suffering from depression, Linda became a **recluse**, rarely leaving her home and not wanting to see even her closest friends.

__ *Recluse* means   A. a hermit.   B. a popular person.   C. a busy person.

10 renounce
(rĭ-nouns′)
- *verb*

- Great-Uncle Abe was a member of the Communist Party when he was a young man, but he soon decided to **renounce** communism and become a Republican.
- Edward VIII was briefly king of England, but he **renounced** his throne in 1936 in order to marry Wallis Simpson, a divorced commoner.

__ *Renounce* means   A. to announce.   B. to remember.   C. to give up.

Matching Words with Definitions

Following are definitions of the ten words. Clearly write or print each word next to its definition. The sentences above and on the previous page will help you decide on the meaning of each word.

1. _____ Hatred

2. _____ To examine; read with great care

3. _____ Mistaken; in error

4. _____ A person who leads a solitary life; someone who withdraws from others

5. _____ Disrespect toward something sacred or important; irreverence

6. _____ To reject; cast off; disown

7. _____ To lose strength; fail in health; be weak

8. _____ To stir up

9. _____ A person who holds unpopular or unaccepted beliefs; dissenter; nonconformist

10. _____ To collect

CAUTION: Do not go any further until you are sure the above answers are correct. Then you can use the definitions to help you in the following practices. Your goal is eventually to know the words well enough so that you don't need to check the definitions at all.

Sentence Check 1

Using the answer line provided, complete each item below with the correct word from the box. Use each word once.

A. **blasphemy**	B. **enmity**	C. **erroneous**	D. **garner**	E. **heretic**
F. **incite**	G. **languish**	H. **peruse**	I. **recluse**	J. **renounce**

_____ 1. The poet Elizabeth Barrett ___(e)d on her couch for years, a semi-invalid, until she fell in love with Robert Browning and found the strength to elope with him.

_____ 2. My grandmother is horrified that my brother wears jeans to church. She thinks doing so is close to ___, but he says, "I'm not being disrespectful; I just like to be comfortable!"

_____ 3. "I am dropping out of the race," the candidate stated after losing badly in the primary election. "I have ___(e)d all hope of becoming President."

_____ 4. My girlfriend and I decided to go our separate ways without ___. We both agreed that we didn't want to spend our lives together, but we intended to remain friends.

_____ 5. Obviously, Jamie has a(n) ___ idea of where babies come from. She announced that her father and mother had bought her in a toy store.

_____ 6. Since I ___ so many compliments every time I wear this sweater, I must conclude that it is a very good color and style for me.

_____ 7. Some people have no respect for anyone else's religious beliefs. According to them, if you don't believe as they do, you are a(n) ___.

_____ 8. The appearance of a hawk in the sky ___(e)d the other birds to attack, fearing that it intended to kill and eat their progeny°.

_____ 9. Mrs. Sheridan rarely leaves her house. She is simply a harmless old ___, but the neighborhood kids think she must be a witch or a criminal.

_____ 10. Irina ___(e)d the contract slowly, reading every bit of the fine print and asking what the legal jargon° meant. She didn't want to sign anything that she might regret later.

NOTE: Now check your answers to these items by turning to page 176. Going over the answers carefully will help you prepare for the next two practices, for which answers are not given.

Sentence Check 2

Using the answer lines provided, complete each item below with **two** words from the box. Use each word once.

_____
_____ 1–2. Many people think that referring to Christmas as "Xmas" is ___, but this idea is ___. In fact, the X is the Greek symbol for Christ.

_____
_____ 3–4. By "skim reading," you can ___ a lot of information, even though you do not ___ every word of a book or article. Instead, you run your eye quickly over the page to find what you need.

_____   5–6. It's hard to see how anyone can manage to ___ the world and become a(n) ___. How do hermits earn a living, for instance? And what happens when they get called for jury duty?

_____   7–8. A(n) ___ is likely to earn the ___ of people who hold more conventional beliefs and do not like to have their ideas challenged.

_____   9–10. The young revolutionary was sent to prison for trying to ___ a riot, but he didn't ___ there. Instead, he became a voracious° reader; kept a passionate, eloquent° diary; and emerged ready to rebel again.

Final Check: *Galileo*

Here is a final opportunity for you to strengthen your knowledge of the ten words. First read the following selection carefully. Then fill in each blank with a word from the box at the top of the previous page. (Context clues will help you figure out which word goes in which blank.) Use each word once.

The great scientist Galileo Galilei, usually known simply as "Galileo," was a brilliant man who was far ahead of his time. But instead of earning accolades°, his discoveries earned him the (1)_____ of the powerful Catholic Church, which tried for years to silence him. Born in 1564 in Pisa, Italy, Galileo became a student of mathematics. He invented a device for making mathematical measurements and found the first dependable way of keeping time. But his true passion was kindled° when he learned of the first telescope, which had been invented in Holland. He (2)_____(e)d every piece of writing he could find about the new invention, then built much stronger telescopes and began to study the sky. The information he (3)_____(e)d led to some startling realizations. He found out that several ideas taught as facts by the universities and the Church were (4)_____. For instance, the Church insisted that the moon was a perfectly smooth ball. Galileo, however, could see that the moon's surface was not uniform°, but was dotted with mountains and valleys. More important, the Church insisted that the Earth was the center of the universe. Galileo's studies showed that the Earth and other planets rotated around the sun. To the Church, this idea was (5)_____: an infraction° of its own teachings. Church officials called the scientist a(n) (6)_____ for saying that the universe did not rotate around the Earth. They feared that Galileo's findings would (7)_____ people to question the Church in other ways. Therefore, they demanded that Galileo (8)_____ his own findings. But he ignored their reproach° and continued to write about what he knew to be true. For the last eight years of his life, Galileo (9)_____(e)d under "house arrest," forbidden to leave his own home. Even while he was forced to live as a(n) (10)_____, he continued to study and to write about his discoveries. More than three hundred years after his death, Galileo was pardoned by the Church, which finally admitted that he had been right all along.

Scores	Sentence Check 2 _____%	Final Check _____%

Enter your scores above and in the **Vocabulary Performance Chart** on the inside back cover of the book.

The box at the right lists twenty-five words from Unit Two. Using the clues at the bottom of the page, fill in these words to complete the puzzle that follows.

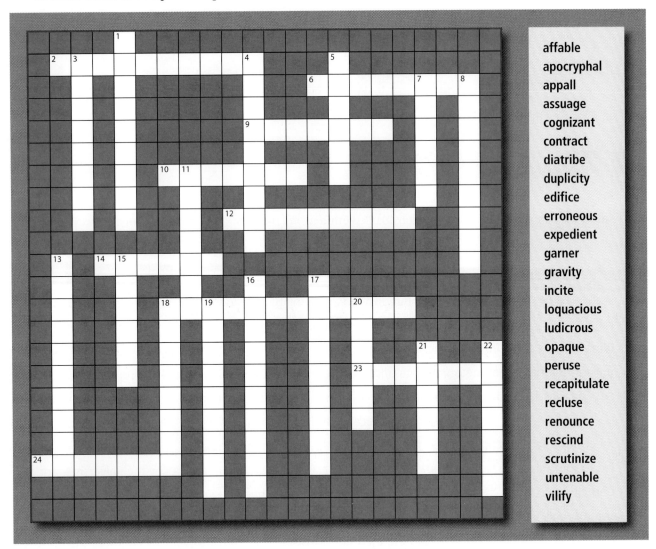

affable
apocryphal
appall
assuage
cognizant
contract
diatribe
duplicity
edifice
erroneous
expedient
garner
gravity
incite
loquacious
ludicrous
opaque
peruse
recapitulate
recluse
renounce
rescind
scrutinize
untenable
vilify

ACROSS

2. To examine carefully
6. A bitter, abusively critical speech or piece of writing
9. A large building
10. Severity; weighty importance
12. Unable to be held or defended
14. Difficult to understand or explain
18. To summarize or repeat briefly
23. Friendly
24. To relieve or lessen

DOWN

1. Laughable
3. To reduce in size
4. Self-serving; convenient
5. To make abusive statements about
7. To stir up
8. Mistaken
11. A person who leads a solitary life
13. Very talkative
15. To examine; read with great care

16. Not genuine
17. Deliberate deceit
18. To reject or cast off
19. Aware
20. To horrify
21. To collect
22. To take back

PART A

Choose the word that best completes each item and write it in the space provided.

_____ 1. The man next door is a(n) ___. He never emerges from his house, and no one has seen him for years.

    A. recluse   B. heretic   C. edifice   D. hindrance

_____ 2. Our family decided to ___ television for one month. We wanted to see if we could survive without watching TV.

    A. recapitulate   B. garner   C. incite   D. renounce

_____ 3. The famous story of George Washington and the cherry tree is ___. There is no evidence that it ever happened at all.

    A. somber   B. affable   C. lavish   D. apocryphal

_____ 4. Instead of addressing the issues, many politicians just badmouth and ___ their opponents.

    A. recapitulate   B. rescind   C. vilify   D. assuage

_____ 5. Having a pet is a(n) ___ of the rules in his apartment, so Curtis keeps his turtle hidden in a box under his bed.

    A. accolade   B. clamor   C. infraction   D. cacophony

_____ 6. In earlier times, many books used asterisks instead of actually printing ___ words. For instance, a character might say: "D*** you!" or "Oh, my G**!"

    A. erroneous   B. profane   C. ludicrous   D. affable

_____ 7. When children ask a parent for something, they hate to get the ___ answer, "We'll see."

    A. equivocal   B. loquacious   C. lavish   D. garbled

_____ 8. The ___ expression on the surgeon's face made it plain that the operation had gone badly.

    A. ludicrous   B. stagnant   C. affable   D. somber

_____ 9. Derek knew that his great-grandmother's grave was somewhere in the old cemetery, but to find it, he had to ___ the inscriptions on more than a hundred headstones.

    A. kindle   B. peruse   C. vilify   D. rescind

_____ 10. Todd listened in frustration to his voice mail. Something had gone wrong with his recording machine, and all the messages were hopelessly ___.

    A. irascible   B. garbled   C. cognizant   D. lavish

(Continues on next page)

_____ 11. It is a crime to ___ others to riot.

      A. assuage   B. scrutinize   C. incite   D. recapitulate

_____ 12. There is an old saying, "He travels fastest who travels alone." It implies that a traveling companion can be a(n) ___.

      A. hindrance   B. edifice   C. heretic   D. diatribe

_____ 13. The new movie was expected to ___ praise from the reviewers. But they hated it, and it was a flop.

      A. rescind   B. renounce   C. scrutinize   D. garner

PART B

Write **C** if the italicized word is used **correctly**. Write **I** if the word is used **incorrectly**.

____ 14. Teenagers often peer into a mirror and *scrutinize* their reflections closely. It's as if they are trying to figure out who they are.

____ 15. The college admissions office says that there is a *paucity* of applicants this year. More than 6,000 people have applied for the 120 places in the freshman class.

____ 16. For kids, a birthday is a celebration. But when middle-aged people have a birthday, their friends don't know whether to congratulate them or *commiserate* with them.

____ 17. The boss was in a bad mood today. He was so *affable* and grouchy that no one wanted to cross his path.

____ 18. Francie's husband is so *loquacious* that she says she can hardly get two words out of him. They often sit through an entire meal in complete silence.

____ 19. For Valentine's Day, Wendell sent his girlfriend a box of matches, with a note: "I hope these will *kindle* a flame of love in your heart."

____ 20. "What a miserable performance!" said Holly as she left the theater. "I've never seen such terrible acting! The entire cast deserves an *accolade*."

____ 21. According to the Bible, "A soft answer turneth away wrath," meaning that a gentle reply will *assuage* someone's anger.

____ 22. Two TV sets, three CD players, and a radio were all blaring away at once. The *cacophony* was unbearable.

____ 23. The candidate found it *expedient* to get votes by promising a tax cut. As soon as he took office, though, he raised taxes.

____ 24. The city will *contract* significantly in the coming decade. The population is expected to double, and many new developments are being built on the outskirts.

____ 25. The notice posted on the door of the bank seemed to suggest *duplicity* on the part of the management. It read, "To serve you better, we are closing this branch."

Score   (Number correct) _____ x 4 = _____%

Enter your score above and in the **Vocabulary Performance Chart** on the inside back cover of the book.

PART A

On the answer line, write the word from the box that completes each item below. Use each word once.

A. appall	B. blasphemy	C. censure	D. cognizant	E. desultory
F. edifice	G. enmity	H. erroneous	I. gravity	J. heretic
K. irascible	L. languish	M. lavish		

_____ 1. Dorrie and Ed celebrated their first anniversary with a(n) ___ dinner at the best restaurant in town.

_____ 2. The teenagers who were caught trying to sneak into the movie without buying tickets treated their arrest as a joke. They didn't seem to realize the ___ of the situation.

_____ 3. The Greek poet Homer observed that "praise from a friend or ___ from a foe" doesn't carry much weight. But people pay attention when our own friends criticize us or our enemies praise us!

_____ 4. In the Middle Ages, when the Catholic Church was all-powerful, a(n) ___ was likely to be burnt at the stake.

_____ 5. City Hall was once the tallest ___ in town, but now it is dwarfed by the huge new skyscrapers all around it.

_____ 6. The ___ between the two nations has existed for centuries. They have gone to war against each other so often that everyone has lost count.

_____ 7. Conditions in the hospital ___ the staff, the patients, and visitors. The hospital building is old-fashioned, overcrowded, run-down, and dirty.

_____ 8. Elise is getting very deaf, but she doesn't seem to be ___ of her impairment. She says, "I would hear perfectly well if people spoke up instead of always mumbling!"

_____ 9. Many people think that if you toss a coin and get ten heads in a row, the next toss is sure to be tails, but this idea is ___. On any toss, heads and tails are equally likely.

_____ 10. Dad is a(n) ___ man. He continually loses his temper.

_____ 11. Flat-faced dogs tend to ___ in very hot weather. They suffer so much because they do not have a long enough nose to cool the air they inhale.

_____ 12. When LaTanya lost her wristwatch, she made only a(n) ___ effort to find it, because she had never really liked it much.

_____ 13. Some mild expressions, such as "gosh-darn it," "golly," and "gee," developed as a substitute for stronger words that would be considered ___.

(Continues on next page)

PART B

Write **C** if the italicized word is used **correctly**. Write **I** if the word is used **incorrectly**.

_____ 14. When it comes to mathematics, Mei Ling is really *obtuse*. She can do complicated calculations in her head, and she can always solve the toughest problems.

_____ 15. In a textbook, the purpose of chapter summaries is to *recapitulate* the main points and the most important concepts.

_____ 16. When Lani asked her father for a car, his response was a *diatribe*. He said, "Okay."

_____ 17. Beata's wedding gown was the most beautiful I've ever seen. She looked *ludicrous*.

_____ 18. The classroom was completely silent as Harold walked forward to give his speech. The *clamor* made him feel even more nervous.

_____ 19. Swollen by melting snow and spring rains, the *stagnant* brook tumbled and rushed along.

_____ 20. To give its series of texts a *uniform* appearance, the publisher designed matching covers for all the books.

_____ 21. Pam has a *negligent* attitude toward her job. She arrives late and leaves early, her desk is a mess, and she is always behind in her work.

_____ 22. The employees asked the company to *rescind* its tradition of giving a year-end bonus. They wanted to make sure the bonuses would continue in the future.

_____ 23. Alex sent me a letter in code. It was completely *opaque* to me.

_____ 24. Jonas is *irresolute* about whether to major in English or history. He just can't make up his mind.

_____ 25. The candidate said she favored "clean government, better schools, and good community relations." No one could disagree with any of that, so she was in an *untenable* position.

Score   (Number correct) _____ x 4 = _____ %

PART A: Synonyms

In the space provided, write the letter of the choice that is most nearly the **same** in meaning as the **boldfaced** word.

_____ 1. **accolade**   A. condemnation   B. commendation   C. conspiracy   D. commitment

_____ 2. **apocryphal**   A. fictitious   B. proven   C. uninteresting   D. applicable

_____ 3. **appall**   A. to horrify   B. to please   C. to appeal to   D. to defend

_____ 4. **blasphemy**   A. silence   B. curiosity   C. piousness   D. contempt

_____ 5. **commiserate**   A. to sympathize   B. to confer   C. to exaggerate   D. to observe

_____ 6. **diatribe**   A. a denunciation B. a diary   C. a diagram   D. harmony

_____ 7. **duplicity**   A. honesty   B. hardship   C. friendship   D. trickery

_____ 8. **edifice**   A. something educational B. something constructed C. an expense D. a gift

_____ 9. **equivocal**   A. noncommittal   B. nonsensical   C. nongrammatical   D. nonverbal

_____ 10. **garbled**   A. boring   B. fascinating   C. distorted   D. essential

_____ 11. **gravity**   A. vagueness   B. deceptiveness   C. seriousness   D. duration

_____ 12. **heretic**   A. a herald   B. a nonconformist C. an heir   D. a nominee

_____ 13. **incite**   A. to arouse   B. to understand   C. to misunderstand D. to injure

_____ 14. **infraction**   A. an offense   B. an insight   C. a rule   D. an illness

_____ 15. **irascible**   A. irrelevant   B. warm-hearted   C. hot-tempered   D. stingy

_____ 16. **kindle**   A. to discourage   B. to forbid   C. to ignore   D. to ignite

_____ 17. **ludicrous**   A. unnoticeable   B. heartbreaking   C. absurd   D. terrifying

_____ 18. **peruse**   A. to read   B. to write   C. to say   D. to hear

_____ 19. **recapitulate**   A. to introduce   B. to state again C. to hint   D. to conceal

_____ 20. **recluse**   A. a lawbreaker   B. a loner   C. a leader   D. a learner

_____ 21. **renounce**   A. to search for   B. to desire   C. to possess   D. to give up

_____ 22. **rescind**   A. to repeat   B. to recognize   C. to reveal   D. to cancel

_____ 23. **scrutinize**   A. to prevent   B. to forget   C. to close one's eyes to D. to look at closely

_____ 24. **untenable**   A. unforgettable   B. insupportable   C. unforeseeable   D. undeniable

_____ 25. **vilify**   A. to admire   B. to malign   C. to trust   D. to help

(Continues on next page)

PART B: Antonyms

In the space provided, write the letter of the choice that is most nearly **opposite** in meaning to the **boldfaced** word.

_____	26. **affable**	A. affordable	B. rich	C. unfriendly	D. unqualified
_____	27. **assuage**	A. to assign	B. to assert	C. to make worse	D. to make fun of
_____	28. **cacophony**	A. harmony	B. conflict	C. noise	D. confusion
_____	29. **censure**	A. praise	B. ridicule	C. disgust	D. anger
_____	30. **clamor**	A. intensity	B. stress	C. conflict	D. silence
_____	31. **cognizant**	A. intelligent	B. ignorant	C. informed	D. insightful
_____	32. **contract**	A. to expand	B. to reduce	C. to watch	D. to wait for
_____	33. **desultory**	A. unfortunate	B. fortunate	C. purposeful	D. random
_____	34. **enmity**	A. hope	B. mistrust	C. friendship	D. strife
_____	35. **erroneous**	A. interesting	B. correct	C. incomplete	D. deceptive
_____	36. **expedient**	A. selfish	B. unselfish	C. planned	D. accidental
_____	37. **garner**	A. to precede	B. to follow	C. to lose	D. to gain
_____	38. **hindrance**	A. a burden	B. a help	C. a nuisance	D. a mystery
_____	39. **irresolute**	A. puzzled	B. hopeful	C. certain	D. fearful
_____	40. **languish**	A. to search	B. to find	C. to thrive	D. to die
_____	41. **lavish**	A. generous	B. expensive	C. permanent	D. stingy
_____	42. **loquacious**	A. enthusiastic	B. silent	C. insane	D. sane
_____	43. **negligent**	A. conscientious	B. sloppy	C. forgetful	D. successful
_____	44. **obtuse**	A. clever	B. thickheaded	C. obese	D. obedient
_____	45. **opaque**	A. opposite	B. similar	C. clear	D. murky
_____	46. **paucity**	A. health	B. absence	C. abundance	D. shortage
_____	47. **profane**	A. probable	B. improbable	C. reverent	D. outraged
_____	48. **somber**	A. cheerful	B. cheerless	C. solemn	D. sudden
_____	49. **stagnant**	A. in memory	B. in motion	C. in view	D. invisible
_____	50. **uniform**	A. similar	B. varying	C. unchanging	D. wordy

Score   (Number correct) _____ x 2 = _____%

Enter your score above and in the **Vocabulary Performance Chart** on the inside back cover of the book.

Unit Three

Chapter 11

aesthetic	peerless
catalyst	propriety
disparage	virtuoso
ingratiate	vitriolic
insipid	whimsical

Chapter 12

amicable	immutable
devious	ponderous
dissonance	predecessor
efface	rebuff
garrulous	static

Chapter 13

acquiesce	delineate
articulate	diffident
belittle	laconic
bombastic	scanty
conciliatory	subjugate

Chapter 14

anarchy	quixotic
authoritarian	salutary
depravity	suppress
meager	temerity
predilection	turbulence

Chapter 15

callous	paragon
desecrate	provincial
evanescent	steadfast
heed	supercilious
indigent	usurp

aesthetic	peerless
catalyst	propriety
disparage	virtuoso
ingratiate	vitriolic
insipid	whimsical

Ten Words in Context

In the space provided, write the letter of the meaning closest to that of each **boldfaced** word. Use the context of the sentences to help you figure out each word's meaning.

1 aesthetic
(ĕs-thĕt′ĭk)
- *adjective*

● A vegetable garden not only is practical but has **aesthetic** value, too; the shining green peppers, red tomatoes, and purple eggplants are a beautiful sight.
● Your green plaid pants and orange flowered shirt do not make a very **aesthetic** combination.

___ *Aesthetic* means   A. pleasing to the senses.   B. moral.   C. financial.

2 catalyst
(kăt′l-ĭst)
- *noun*

● World War II was a **catalyst** for social change. When women took factory jobs, filling in for men who were away fighting, the concept of "women's work" was permanently expanded.
● Seeing a friend die of an overdose was a **catalyst** for Herbert's decision to stop abusing drugs.

___ *Catalyst* means   A. something that causes or speeds up a process.   B. something that prevents a process.   C. something that is harmful.

3 disparage
(dĭ-spăr′ĭj)
- *verb*

● An ironclad rule of politics used to be "Never **disparage** anyone in your party." For the sake of unity, party members weren't supposed to criticize each other.
● "I've lost respect for Cheryl," Shawna said. "She'll pretend to be your friend, but then she'll **disparage** you behind your back."

___ *Disparage* means   A. to discourage.   B. to say bad things about.   C. to ignore.

4 ingratiate
(ĭn-grā′shē-āt′)
- *verb*

● When he was stopped for speeding, Luke tried hard to **ingratiate** himself with the officer by complimenting the police department, but he got a ticket anyway.
● It's sickening the way Howie **ingratiates** himself with his boss by agreeing with her about every little thing and telling her how wonderful she is.

___ *Ingratiate* means   A. to argue with someone.   B. to flatter someone.   C. to make demands.

5 insipid
(ĭn-sĭp′ĭd)
- *adjective*

● A French novelist once said, "A story without love is like beef without mustard—an **insipid** dish."
● The cast tried hard to put some sparkle and zest into the play, but the script was so pointless and **insipid** that their efforts fell flat.

___ *Insipid* means   A. disgusting.   B. inspiring.   C. boring.

6 peerless
(pîr′lĭs)
- *adjective*

● "She's **peerless**," the singer's fans insisted. "No one can compete with her."
● When their beloved teacher retired, her students presented her with a plaque: "To a **peerless** educator and a matchless friend."

___ *Peerless* means   A. without an equal.   B. critical.   C. perceptive.

7 propriety
(prə-prī′ĭ-tē)
- *noun*

● Helen, a newspaper reporter, is concerned about the **propriety** of her writing stories about the town council when her husband is a member of the council.

● People questioned the **propriety** of the woman's beginning to date only two weeks after her husband had been killed.

__ *Propriety* means   A. opportunity.   B. correctness.   C. cost.

8 virtuoso
(vûr′chōō-ō′sō)
- *noun*

● Woody Allen has a funny line about a woman who gave up her lifetime ambition of becoming a violin **virtuoso** when she realized she would have to study the violin.

● The pianist was disappointed by the review of his performance: "He is competent, but no **virtuoso**—that spark of genius is missing."

__ *Virtuoso* means   A. a moral person.   B. a repairperson.   C. a master performer.

9 vitriolic
(vĭt′rē-ŏl′ĭk)
- *adjective*

● Some people who call in to radio talk shows make shockingly **vitriolic** remarks; they seem to be using the show as an outlet for their most bitter, vicious thoughts.

● A famous piece of advice: When you are furious at someone, write him or her a **vitriolic** letter, using the ugliest, most cutting words you can find. Read it a few times to make sure it's as hateful as possible. Then tear it up and throw it away.

__ *Vitriolic* means   A. debatable.   B. sharp and bitter.   C. insane.

10 whimsical
(wĭm′zĭ-kəl *or*
hwĭm′zĭ-kəl)
- *adjective*

● Toni and Ed's decision to marry seemed **whimsical**. They had known each other for only three days.

● Some of the policies at our school seem pointless and **whimsical**. For example, students are allowed to audit courses in science but not in math, the library is closed every other Tuesday, and coffee is not served in the dining hall.

__ *Whimsical* means   A. impulsive.   B. appropriate.   C. frightening.

Matching Words with Definitions

Following are definitions of the ten words. Clearly write or print each word next to its definition. The sentences above and on the previous page will help you decide on the meaning of each word.

1. _____ Having a sense of beauty; giving an impression of beauty; artistic

2. _____ To charm; win favor; make oneself agreeable

3. _____ Sharply critical; harsh; biting

4. _____ An expert, particularly in the arts

5. _____ A person or thing that brings about change

6. _____ Appropriateness

7. _____ To speak ill of; criticize; put down

8. _____ Dull; tasteless; unexciting

9. _____ So superior as to be without equal; incomparable; unsurpassed

10. _____ Determined by impulse; odd; arbitrary

CAUTION: Do not go any further until you are sure the above answers are correct. Then you can use the definitions to help you in the following practices. Your goal is eventually to know the words well enough so that you don't need to check the definitions at all.

Sentence Check 1

Using the answer line provided, complete each item below with the correct word from the box. Use each word once.

A. aesthetic	B. catalyst	C. disparage	D. ingratiate	E. insipid
F. peerless	G. propriety	H. virtuoso	I. vitriolic	J. whimsical

_____ 1. Mozart was considered a(n) ___ at an early age: he was performing before royalty by age six.

_____ 2. Mr. Lattimore is an unpopular teacher because his criticism is so ___. He is not only harsh about students' work but is also highly critical of students personally.

_____ 3. Though I like tea, I find it ___ without lemon to liven it up.

_____ 4. At first, Dad said we couldn't keep the little dog, but then Muffin ___(ed) herself by sitting down in front of him and politely offering her paw.

_____ 5. "Don't ___ the instructor for failing you," my advisor said. "Instead, I'd suggest you stop bad-mouthing her and work harder." It was good advice.

_____ 6. "Well, I see that our ___ ball club has been beaten again," Matt said sarcastically, as the baseball team lost its ninth game in a row.

_____ 7. I thought my grandmother's sense of ___ would be offended by my sister's plan to be married barefoot in a meadow, but Grandma loved the idea.

_____ 8. The ___ that started World War I was the assassination of an Austrian archduke—after that, fighting broke out among many factions.

_____ 9. "I've asked Sylvia to help me redecorate my apartment," Lee said, "because she has the best ___ know-how of all my friends."

_____ 10. Getting a pet should not be a(n) ___, spur-of-the-moment decision. Owning a dog or cat is a long-term commitment that requires thought and planning.

NOTE: Now check your answers to these items by turning to page 176. Going over the answers carefully will help you prepare for the next two practices, for which answers are not given.

Sentence Check 2

Using the answer lines provided, complete each item below with **two** words from the box. Use each word once.

_____
_____ 1–2. "It pains me to ___ the new library," wrote the architecture critic, "but the building is needlessly ugly. All ___ considerations have been completely ignored."

_____
_____ 3–4. The composer Franz Liszt was also a piano ___, a master performer who was considered ___: no other musician in his time had such amazing technique.

_____
_____ 5–6. "Our school has too many odd, ___ rules," Reba said. "Elect me student body president, and I promise to be a(n) ___ for change. I'll work hard to rescind° these quirky regulations."

_____   7–8. At work, Edgar tries to ___ himself with his supervisors by behaving with
_____   the utmost ___. He intends to win their approval by the correctness of his
                                   appearance and manners.

_____   9–10. The review of the new restaurant was ___. "Most of the food is ___, and
_____   what isn't tasteless is disgusting," it read. "The waiters belong in a zoo. The
                                   decor is ludicrous°—it looks like something left over from a horror movie."

Final Check: *Isadora Duncan*

Here is a final opportunity for you to strengthen your knowledge of the ten words. First read the following
selection carefully. Then fill in each blank with a word from the box at the top of the previous page.
(Context clues will help you figure out which word goes in which blank.) Use each word once.

Isadora Duncan was a famous dancer born in 1877. She was known for her dramatic personality
as well as her revolutionary way of dancing. She rejected the traditional style of ballet, considering it
boring and (1)_____. She had an affinity° for dance that was naturally
(2)_____, capturing the beauty of the wind, flowers, and stars. To express
that idea, she danced barefoot, wearing voluminous° fluttering silk scarves. Her dancing was
(3)_____, based on the inspiration of the moment, and was never quite the same
twice. In her private life, too, Duncan cared little for most people's ideas of (4)_____;
she had two children before marrying. When she did marry, she chose a Russian poet seventeen years
younger than she.

At first, audiences did not know what to make of Duncan's unusual dance style. The critics' reviews
were (5)_____. They (6)_____(e)d and vilified°
Duncan, calling her a joke and a fake. But her talent and charm enabled Duncan to overcome such
censure° and (7)_____ herself with the public. She was eventually seen as a(n)
(8)_____ of her own free-spirited style.

In 1927, when Duncan was living in France, she admired a sports car driven by a guest. He offered to
take her for a drive. She agreed. Wrapping one of her trademark long silk scarves around her neck, she
called to the others, "Goodbye, my friends, I am off to glory!" The car started off. The end of Duncan's scarf
became tangled in one of its wheels, and Duncan was strangled.

In her lifetime, Duncan was regarded as a(n) (9)_____ dancer with an
unusual style. Today she is remembered as a(n) (10)_____ for many of the
new developments in modern dance.

Scores	Sentence Check 2 _____ %	Final Check _____ %

Enter your scores above and in the **Vocabulary Performance Chart** on the inside back cover of the book.

amicable	immutable
devious	ponderous
dissonance	predecessor
efface	rebuff
garrulous	static

Ten Words in Context

In the space provided, write the letter of the meaning closest to that of each **boldfaced** word. Use the context of the sentences to help you figure out each word's meaning.

1 amicable
(ăm′ĭ-kə-bəl)
- *adjective*

● Who says that cats and dogs are enemies? Our dog and two cats live together in the most **amicable** way.

● Because the two countries had always maintained **amicable** relations, they were able to settle their border dispute through friendly talks.

___ *Amicable* means   A. hostile.   B. peaceable.   C. cute.

2 devious
(dē′vē-əs)
- *adjective*

● Beware of **devious** advertising. For example, a sign may say in huge letters "PRICES SLASHED 75 PERCENT" and then in tiny type "on selected items only."

● Aimee's mother didn't want to ask her directly if she and her boyfriend were going to get married, so she used more **devious** wording: "Do you and Dave have any plans for the future?"

___ *Devious* means   A. obvious.   B. rude.   C. sneaky.

3 dissonance
(dĭs′ə-nəns)
- *noun*

● Over time, people's ideas of **dissonance** in music change. Chords that sounded harsh and grating to previous generations now seem pleasant to us.

● Kids like to create **dissonance** on a piano by using both arms to slam down all the keys at once.

___ *Dissonance* means   A. an unpleasant sound.   B. a rare sound.   C. an everyday sound.

4 efface
(ĭ-fās′)
- *verb*

● When Joanie and Gary broke up, she said, "I've thrown away all his letters and photographs. Now I wish I could **efface** my memories."

● Last Thanksgiving, the turkey slid off its platter onto the dining-room rug. We scrubbed and rubbed, but we weren't able to **efface** the stain completely.

___ *Efface* means   A. to face up to.   B. to remove all traces of.   C. to try to preserve.

5 garrulous
(găr′ə-ləs)
- *adjective*

● Our waiter at dinner last night was extremely **garrulous**. He hung around our table telling us long stories when all we wanted was to eat in peace.

● Because Arnie is so **garrulous**, I always need an excuse to escape. Today I broke into his non-stop talk with, "I'd love to hear more, but I have a class now."

___ *Garrulous* means   A. long-winded.   B. short-tempered.   C. open-minded.

6 immutable
(ĭ-myōō′tə-bəl)
- *adjective*

● Does Mr. Madison ever smile? The frown on his face seems **immutable**.

● For years, my aunt has followed an **immutable** schedule: she always gets up at 6:30 a.m., works out for a half hour, and then has a soft-boiled egg and toast.

___ *Immutable* means   A. changeless.   B. flawless.   C. fearless.

7 ponderous
(pŏn'dər-əs)
- *adjective*

● Ads for the circus always used to describe the elephants as "**ponderous** pachyderms."

● There used to be a theory that dinosaurs became extinct because they grew too large for their own good. They were so huge and **ponderous** that they could hardly move.

__ *Ponderous* means   A. living in ponds.   B. delicate.   C. weighty.

8 predecessor
(prĕd'ĭ-sĕs'ər)
- *noun*

● It won't be easy to get used to the new boss. She seems quiet, formal, and serious, whereas her **predecessor** was easygoing and loved to laugh.

● When they moved into their new apartment, the Martins had to get rid of a lot of junk that their **predecessors** had left behind.

__ *Predecessor* means   A. someone earlier.   B. someone later.   C. someone who predicts.

9 rebuff
(rĭ-bŭf')
- *verb*

● Here's a good way to **rebuff** a telephone pollster who's trying to find out which candidate you're supporting. Just say, "I'm sorry, but I never discuss politics with strangers."

● The new puppy bounded joyfully up to the resident housecat. But the cat **rebuffed** his advances with a loud hiss and a scratch to his nose.

__ *Rebuff* means   A. to treat coldly.   B. to welcome warmly.   C. to reward.

10 static
(stăt'ĭk)
- *adjective*

● "This scene is too **static**," the director said to the actors. "It's dead. We've got to get some action into it."

● A still life, as the name suggests, is a **static** painting: it might show, for example, a bowl of apples. By contrast, an action painting shows a dramatic scene full of movement.

__ *Static* means   A. silent.   B. inactive.   C. stressful.

Matching Words with Definitions

Following are definitions of the ten words. Clearly write or print each word next to its definition. The sentences above and on the previous page will help you decide on the meaning of each word.

1. _____ To reject bluntly; snub

2. _____ Not straightforward; tricky; shifty

3. _____ Never changing or varying

4. _____ Heavy, labored; massive; lacking grace

5. _____ A person who comes before another in time

6. _____ Friendly; showing goodwill

7. _____ Not moving or progressing; still

8. _____ To wipe out; erase; remove completely

9. _____ A harsh, disagreeable combination of sounds

10. _____ Talkative to an annoying degree

CAUTION: Do not go any further until you are sure the above answers are correct. Then you can use the definitions to help you in the following practices. Your goal is eventually to know the words well enough so that you don't need to check the definitions at all.

Sentence Check 1

Using the answer line provided, complete each item below with the correct word from the box. Use each word once.

A. **amicable**	B. **devious**	C. **dissonance**	D. **efface**	E. **garrulous**
F. **immutable**	G. **ponderous**	H. **predecessor**	I. **rebuff**	J. **static**

_____ 1. Zach quickly ___s anyone who calls to try to sell him something or raise funds. "I'm not interested," he says, and hangs up.

_____ 2. Do you think surprise quizzes are a useful teaching tool? Or do you consider them ___ and unfair?

_____ 3. The hardest of all stains to ___ is blueberry. If you drop blueberry pie on a white shirt, you'll have to throw the shirt away or dye it blue.

_____ 4. Whenever I visit my ___ Uncle Hal, I tell him I have another appointment in an hour. Otherwise, I would be forced to sit and listen to him all day.

_____ 5. Everyone dreads the principal's speeches. Her slow, labored way of talking and long pauses make even a short talk ___.

_____ 6. As I walked through the hall of the music school, I could hear three instrumental classes in three rooms playing three different pieces all at once. This ___ made my ears ache, so I fled into the street.

_____ 7. Wanting to be on ___ terms with her new neighbors, Meg brought them a homemade pie to welcome them to the neighborhood.

_____ 8. Did you ever wonder why people in old photographs look frozen in stiff, ___ poses? It's because they could not move while the film was being exposed—a process that took a long time.

_____ 9. Although the car Jasmin just bought is four years old, it looks like new. Whoever was her ___ in owning it took very good care of it.

_____ 10. The stars may look unchanging, but in fact they are not ___. Stars are born, and eventually die, over billions of years.

NOTE: Now check your answers to these items by turning to page 176. Going over the answers carefully will help you prepare for the next two practices, for which answers are not given.

Sentence Check 2

Using the answer lines provided, complete each item below with **two** words from the box. Use each word once.

_____
_____ 1–2. Marcy and Jack worked out a(n) ___ divorce. But the goodwill they put into the final settlement could not ___ the memory of the months of anger that came before it.

_____
_____ 3–4. It's strange but true: one ___, constant law of nature is that nothing is ever constant or ___—everything changes all the time.

_____
_____ 5–6. When she started her new job, Robin tried in ___ ways to find out why her ___ had left. She didn't want to ask directly whether he had quit or been fired.

_____   7–8. Flora and Bruno couldn't agree on what kind of art to put in their living
_____   room. She rejected a large piece of sculpture he had chosen, saying it was too
                                     ___, and he ___(e)d her when she suggested an abstract painting.

_____   9–10. The concert was awful. The band was too loud and badly out of tune—
_____   creating cacophony°, not music. In addition, a(n) ___ person beside me kept
                                     up an incessant° stream of conversation, adding to the general ___.

Final Check: *Miles Standish*

Here is a final opportunity for you to strengthen your knowledge of the ten words. First read the following selection carefully. Then fill in each blank with a word from the box at the top of the previous page. (Context clues will help you figure out which word goes in which blank.) Use each word once.

"If you want something done right, do it yourself." Such is the message of "The Courtship of Miles Standish," a poem by one of America's most famous poets, Henry Wadsworth Longfellow.

Now, the first thing you need to know about "Miles Standish" is that the story is apocryphal°. Miles Standish was a real person, and so were John Alden and Priscilla Mullins, the other two principal characters in the poem. And John and Priscilla got married, as the poem says, and had fifteen children, which it doesn't say. But as far as we know, Miles's "courtship" was the product of Longfellow's imagination. Nevertheless, the poem tells a good story. This is how it goes:

Miles Standish, a scarred veteran of many battles, was the leader of the Puritan colony in Plymouth, Massachusetts. As the poem opens, Miles shares a secret with his young friend John Alden. Miles is in love with Priscilla. Priscilla's (1)_____ in Miles's heart was his wife, Rose, who died soon after the Pilgrims landed in the New World. Since Rose's death, Miles says, his life has been dull and (2)_____. He asks John to do him a favor. "Go to the damsel Priscilla, the loveliest maiden of Plymouth, / Say that a blunt old Captain, a man not of words but of actions, / Offers his hand and his heart, the hand and heart of a soldier."

The problem is that unbeknownst to Miles Standish, John is also in love with Priscilla. Horrified, he tries to get out of the errand, suggesting that Miles speak to Priscilla himself. But Miles's determination is (3)_____. Also, he says he is a(n) (4)_____ speaker, not graceful and eloquent° like John. He fears he would either say too little or be too (5)_____ to win her favor. And while he is brave in battle, he says, he fears Priscilla will (6)_____ his offer.

Unable to refuse his friend, John goes to Priscilla and blurts out Miles Standish's offer of marriage. Priscilla is first amazed, then indignant. "If the great Captain of Plymouth is so very eager to wed me, / Why does he not come himself, and take the trouble to woo me?" John tries to explain that the Captain is a very busy man, but Priscilla's irritation is not assuaged°. A man who was *really* in love, she tells John, would find time to win her heart. John stumbles on, describing all the Captain's good qualities: his courage, his skill, his honor. As he talks, he seems to (7)_____ his own feelings and think only of his friend. To Priscilla, who has been hoping to hear John's own declaration of love, his words are (8)_____, not sweet music. Finally she boldly interrupts, "Why don't you speak for yourself, John?"

The rest of the poem describes how John returns to Miles and tells him the truth. Initially Standish is furious, believing that John has been (9)_____, going behind his back to win the girl. But he overcomes his feelings of enmity° and maintains his (10)_____ relationship with John and Priscilla. He comes to their wedding and gives them his blessing. And perhaps he has learned that when it comes to romancing a woman, it's best to do the job yourself!

Scores   Sentence Check 2 _____%   Final Check _____%

Enter your scores above and in the **Vocabulary Performance Chart** on the inside back cover of the book.

acquiesce	delineate
articulate	diffident
belittle	laconic
bombastic	scanty
conciliatory	subjugate

Ten Words in Context

In the space provided, write the letter of the meaning closest to that of each **boldfaced** word. Use the context of the sentences to help you figure out each word's meaning.

1 acquiesce
(ăk′wē-ĕs′)
- *verb*

- When the reporter was ordered to reveal who had given her information about a gambling ring, she had to decide whether to **acquiesce** or go to jail.
- The students asked if they could use their notes during the test. They were pleased when the teacher **acquiesced**.

___ *Acquiesce* means   A. to consent.   B. to conquer.   C. to refuse.

2 articulate
(är-tĭk′yə-lĭt)
- *adjective*

- John Kennedy was known as one of our most **articulate** presidents. He expressed himself beautifully, whether he was giving a speech or just joking with reporters.
- Molly is unusually **articulate** for a three-year-old. She always speaks in complete sentences and uses a quite grown-up vocabulary.

___ *Articulate* means   A. artificial.   B. using words effectively.   C. quiet.

3 belittle
(bĭ-lĭt′l)
- *verb*

- One unpleasant little girl at the daycare center constantly **belittles** the other children, saying things like, "Can't your parents buy you nicer clothes than that?"
- It is rude to accept an invitation to dinner and then **belittle** your host's cooking.

___ *Belittle* means   A. to praise.   B. to emphasize.   C. to put down.

4 bombastic
(bŏm-băs′tĭk)
- *adjective*

- I don't like to invite Jerry to dinner because he is so **bombastic**. He bores everyone with his endless pretentious talk.
- "At this point in time there is little reason to think that the suspected perpetrator will soon be apprehended" is a **bombastic** way of saying, "The crook got away."

___ *Bombastic* means   A. wordy and pretentious.   B. down-to-earth.   C. fascinating.

5 conciliatory
(kən-sĭl′ē-ə-tôr′ē)
- *adjective*

- Our new toaster broke down after one use, but when we returned it, the clerk was not **conciliatory**. He said, "You must have done something wrong to it."
- When a small child throws a temper tantrum, should a parent be **conciliatory** and try to comfort the child? Or is it better to use firm discipline?

___ *Conciliatory* means   A. soothing.   B. persistent.   C. proud.

6 delineate
(dĭ-lĭn′ē-āt′)
- *verb*

- The history teacher carefully **delineated** the scene of the battle: where the opposing troops were, how the supply lines were set up, and where the nearby towns and roads were located.
- "One picture is worth a thousand words" suggests that to **delineate** something, a drawing is often more useful than phrases and sentences.

___ *Delineate* means   A. to change.   B. to recall.   C. to describe.

7 diffident
(dĭf′ĭ-dənt)
- *adjective*

- Although Jay is outgoing with other men, he is shy and **diffident** with women and therefore finds it hard to get a date.

- Choosing a puppy out of the litter, Jeanine was drawn to a **diffident** little one who hung back timidly while the others played roughly.

___ *Diffident* means   A. different.   B. angry.   C. hesitant.

8 laconic
(lə-kŏn′ĭk)
- *adjective*

- Frieda is a woman of very few words. When she received an impassioned twenty-page letter from her boyfriend imploring her to marry him, she sent this **laconic** reply: "Sure."

- During World War II, General McAuliffe of the 101st Airborne Division gained fame for his **laconic** reply to a German commander who was demanding that he surrender: "Nuts."

___ *Laconic* means   A. sweet.   B. brief.   C. secretive.

9 scanty
(skăn′tē)
- *adjective*

- Office supplies are so **scanty** this year that most people have to buy their own pens and notepads.

- The poor little maple tree is not doing well. Its leaves are **scanty**, and it is barely growing.

___ *Scanty* means   A. insufficient.   B. plentiful.   C. permanent.

10 subjugate
(sŭb′jə-gāt′)
- *verb*

- Judges are expected to **subjugate** their feelings during a trial. But keeping their emotions under tight control is not always easy.

- Many developing nations were **subjugated** by colonial powers in years past. In some cases, the wounds of their earlier defeat remain painful.

___ *Subjugate* means   A. to explore.   B. to dominate.   C. to study.

Matching Words with Definitions

Following are definitions of the ten words. Clearly write or print each word next to its definition. The sentences above and on the previous page will help you decide on the meaning of each word.

1. _____ Using high-sounding language without much meaning; overblown

2. _____ To consent without protest; comply; assent

3. _____ To make something seem less worthy or less important; disparage°

4. _____ Lacking self-confidence; timid

5. _____ Using as few words as possible; concise; to the point

6. _____ Barely sufficient; barely adequate

7. _____ Well-spoken

8. _____ To bring under control; enslave; conquer

9. _____ To represent in words or pictures; describe; portray

10. _____ Tending to win over or to calm by agreeing to demands; soothing

CAUTION: Do not go any further until you are sure the above answers are correct. Then you can use the definitions to help you in the following practices. Your goal is eventually to know the words well enough so that you don't need to check the definitions at all.

Sentence Check 1

Using the answer line provided, complete each item below with the correct word from the box. Use each word once.

A. **acquiesce**	B. **articulate**	C. **belittle**	D. **bombastic**	E. **conciliatory**
F. **delineate**	G. **diffident**	H. **laconic**	I. **scanty**	J. **subjugate**

_____ 1. Knowing a lot does not necessarily make people effective communicators. They need to be ___ in order to reach others with their words.

_____ 2. M. Harrison is an unpopular teacher because of the way he ___s his students, ; disparaging° remarks like, "I've given up expecting good work from

_____ 3. A ___ person is not likely to do well in a sales job, where confidence and ease . talking to strangers are important qualities.

_____ 4. My neighbor is so ___ that it's difficult to hold a conversation with him. He usually confines his remarks to "Hmm," "Oh," and "I see."

_____ 5. When we asked the movie star for her autograph, she ___(e)d pleasantly, saying, "I'll be happy to."

_____ 6. Prehistoric cave paintings in France and Spain ___ not just animals but the act of hunting—to show hunters what they were about to experience.

_____ 7. It's obvious that the Hallers have not lived in their apartment very long. The furnishings are ___ — just a couch, a bed, and a kitchen table.

_____ 8. The famous novel *1984* concerns a government that ___s its people by constantly spying on them and punishing them for any independent thought.

_____ 9. When we had to work over a weekend taking inventory, our boss was ___: she told us we could dress casually, and she kept sending out for food, coffee, and sodas.

_____ 10. I've read this ___ editorial in the newspaper three times, and I'm still not sure what is being said. It's a lot of fancy words, but what does it mean?

NOTE: Now check your answers to these items by turning to page 176. Going over the answers carefully will help you prepare for the next two practices, for which answers are not given.

Sentence Check 2

Using the answer lines provided, complete each item below with **two** words from the box. Use each word once.

_____
_____ 1–2. "Don't put yourself down," the self-help book urged. "If you constantly ___ yourself, you will become too timid and ___ to tackle anything important."

_____
_____ 3–4. When people are ___, it is sometimes because they feel they are not ___ enough. Believing that they can't express themselves well, they decide to say very little.

_____   5–6. When Jake tried to ___ the plan for his term paper to Tricia, he realized that

_____   his ideas were too ___— he needed to do further research.

_____   7–8. The invaders did not find it easy to ___ the town. Refusing to ___, the

_____   townspeople kept on fighting, building by building, street by street, for many
weeks.

_____   9–10. At the dinner party, Hana was seated next to a(n) ___ man who kept spouting

_____   all his overblown opinions in a loud voice. She is the ___ type, though, so
she pretended to be interested in his diatribe°.

Final Check: *Men, Women, and Talk*

Here is a final opportunity for you to strengthen your knowledge of the ten words. First read the following selection carefully. Then fill in each blank with a word from the box at the top of the previous page. (Context clues will help you figure out which word goes in which blank.) Use each word once.

Feminists, sociologists, and psychologists have been taking a long, hard look at—or listening in on—how men and women talk to each other. Their idea is that just as men (1)_____ women economically and politically—earning far more than women and enjoying greater power—men also (2)_____ women in conversation. That is an interesting theory, but unfortunately, when these observers (3)_____ their findings, their results are contradictory.

Some researchers say that men, garrulous° and long-winded, dominate conversations. They find that men are (4)_____, liking to announce their opinions in lofty language and lay down the law. Men are also loquacious°—never allowing women to get a word in edgewise, except to (5)_____ with a brief murmur of agreement or to be (6)_____ if a disagreement seems to be arising. According to this theory, most women are too (7)_____ to speak out; but if a woman does try, the man will ignore or rebuff° her, and if this snub doesn't shut her up, he'll interrupt her. In extreme cases, he may have to resort to a vitriolic° remark or profane° language to shock her into silence.

Other researchers find just the opposite. They say that men are (8)_____, making a(n) (9)_____ contribution, or none, to a conversation. The poor woman tries desperately to keep the talk going, while the man, parsimonious° with words, just grunts "Hmm" or "Um." Women are generally said to be more verbal and (10)_____ than men, so when a man clams up, he's exploiting this trait to control the situation.

It's hard to know what to make of this equivocal° research, but the men seem to be in a no-win situation. Whether they talk or don't talk, they're accused of being domineering and a hindrance° to conversation. It would be fascinating to hear the researchers debate this—especially if half of them were men and half were women!

| Scores | Sentence Check 2 _____% | Final Check _____% |

Enter your scores above and in the **Vocabulary Performance Chart** on the inside back cover of the book.

anarchy	quixotic
authoritarian	salutary
depravity	suppress
meager	temerity
predilection	turbulence

Ten Words in Context

In the space provided, write the letter of the meaning closest to that of each **boldfaced** word. Use the context of the sentences to help you figure out each word's meaning.

1 anarchy
(ăn′ər-kē)
- *noun*

- The day after the earthquake, the city was in a state of **anarchy**, with people looting stores, stealing cars, and destroying property.
- Following the revolution, there was a period of **anarchy**, with several different groups claiming to govern the country and no one really in control.

___ *Anarchy* means   A. poverty.   B. disorder.   C. sorrow.

2 authoritarian
(ə-thôr′ĭ-târ′ē-ən)
- *adjective*

- Ms. Pettigrew is easygoing outside the classroom, but when class is in session, she is a tough, **authoritarian** teacher.
- Some parents let their children argue over every decision, while others are **authoritarian** and expect to be obeyed immediately.

___ *Authoritarian* means   A. favoring freedom.   B. favoring firm discipline.   C. uncertain.

3 depravity
(dĭ-prăv′ĭ-tē)
- *noun*

- Do you think the death penalty is justified for crimes of shocking **depravity**?
- In the horror movie, the **depravity** of the villain was rendered in gory detail. I still have nightmares about it.

___ *Depravity* means   A. passion.   B. anger.   C. wickedness.

4 meager
(mē′gər)
- *adjective*

- The furniture in the apartment was **meager**, consisting of just a cot, one chair, and a small desk.
- Holly triple-spaced her paper and left very wide margins, but it still fell far short of the five pages that had been assigned. Her instructor wrote on it, "This is a **meager** effort."

___ *Meager* means   A. inaccurate.   B. inadequate.   C. inspired.

5 predilection
(prĕd′l-ĕk′shən)
- *noun*

- Maddie always had a **predilection** for vegetarianism. She stopped eating meat when she was only five.
- Like most Labrador retrievers, Beau has a **predilection** for water—he will jump into any pool, pond, or river he sees.

___ *Predilection* means   A. a liking.   B. an avoidance.   C. a fear.

6 quixotic
(kwĭk-sŏt′ĭk)
- *adjective*

- Angel quit his job to protest his company's hiring policies, without considering the consequences of this **quixotic** gesture. Now he cannot support his family.
- Jim Smith's candidacy in the race for governor seems **quixotic**. He has some grand, lofty ideas, but he's an unknown with no sources of funding.

___ *Quixotic* means   A. noble but unwise.   B. sensible but unfair.   C. sneaky.

7 salutary
(săl′yə-tĕr′ē)
- *adjective*

- Studies have shown that garlic has several **salutary** effects, including boosting the body's ability to fight off illness.
- The doctor recommended that Mrs. Thornton take extra calcium, which has the **salutary** effect of strengthening the bones.

___ *Salutary* means   A. wholesome.   B. unknown.   C. dangerous.

8 suppress
(sə-prĕs′)
- *verb*

- Bonnie couldn't **suppress** a giggle in church when the minister, calling for prayer, said, "With eyes bowed and heads closed . . ."
- "I am opposed to censorship in any form," said the lecturer. "When free speech is **suppressed**, all other freedoms are soon crushed as well."

___ *Suppress* means   A. to arouse.   B. to reveal.   C. to keep down.

9 temerity
(tə-mĕr′ĭ-tē)
-*noun*

- People who rush into marriage often regret their **temerity** later. There's an old saying: "Marry in haste; repent at leisure."
- Flagged down for a minor traffic violation, the driver had the **temerity** to try to outrace the police car. This foolhardy attempt landed him in jail.

___ *Temerity* means   A. fear.   B. regret.   C. recklessness.

10 turbulence
(tûr′byə-ləns)
- *noun*

- "We may experience some **turbulence**," the pilot announced. A moment later, the plane was shaking so violently that some passengers began to scream.
- The kindergarten room was a scene of **turbulence**, with the kids racing around, throwing things, and yelling at the top of their lungs.

___ *Turbulence* means   A. wild disorder.   B. a turning point.   C. a repeat performance.

Matching Words with Definitions

Following are definitions of the ten words. Clearly write or print each word next to its definition. The sentences above and on the previous page will help you decide on the meaning of each word.

1. _____ Violent irregularity, disturbance, or agitation, as of motion, air, or water

2. _____ Lacking in quality or quantity; insufficient

3. _____ Idealistic but impractical

4. _____ To put down by force; control

5. _____ Lawlessness; lack of government; absence of authority or rules

6. _____ Rash boldness; audacity; nerve

7. _____ Promoting good health; beneficial

8. _____ Evil; moral corruption

9. _____ Demanding or expecting total obedience

10. _____ A natural preference; tendency to like something

CAUTION: Do not go any further until you are sure the above answers are correct. Then you can use the definitions to help you in the following practices. Your goal is eventually to know the words well enough so that you don't need to check the definitions at all.

Sentence Check 1

Using the answer line provided, complete each item below with the correct word from the box. Use each word once.

A. anarchy	B. authoritarian	C. depravity	D. meager	E. predilection
F. quixotic	G. salutary	H. suppress	I. temerity	J. turbulence

_____ 1. After being served only ___ refreshments at the meeting, Julio stopped at a fast-food restaurant on the way home for a cheeseburger.

_____ 2. Mom was a great believer in the ___ effects of fresh air and sunshine, so she encouraged us children to play outside as much as possible.

_____ 3. The famous novel *Lord of the Flies* describes young boys living alone on an island with no adult supervision, no rules, and no laws, and what happens during that period of ___.

_____ 4. People who regularly ___ anger can develop physical ailments. Rage that must stay hidden can show up as a rash, a headache, or an upset stomach—and can even be a catalyst° for a heart attack or stroke.

_____ 5. Though it took place more than sixty years ago, the ___ of the Nazis continues to shock and disturb us.

_____ 6. It's easy to see that Amanda is the oldest child in her family. Her ___ manner shows that she's accustomed to being in charge.

_____ 7. Chaos theory seeks to describe ___ in natural systems such as whirlpools and tornadoes, in which motion is wild and unpredictable.

_____ 8. Few children have a(n) ___ for liver, broccoli, and spinach. People develop a liking for such foods later in life, if at all.

_____ 9. The foolish young man decided to try to jump across the railroad track before the train passed by. His ___ resulted in his losing a leg and nearly cost him his life.

_____ 10. Aunt Julie e-mails her Congressional representative regularly on issues she cares about. She says, "Maybe it's ___—maybe nobody ever reads what I write—but at least I feel like I'm trying to make a difference."

NOTE: Now check your answers to these items by turning to page 176. Going over the answers carefully will help you prepare for the next two practices, for which answers are not given.

Sentence Check 2

Using the answer lines provided, complete each item below with **two** words from the box. Use each word once.

_____
_____ 1–2. The students were so afraid of their strict, ___ principal that if they met him in the hallway, few of them even had the ___ to say "good morning."

_____
_____ 3–4. The adjective "___" comes from a famous tale of a romantic, befuddled Spanish knight who had a(n) ___ for setting forth on impossible and sometimes ludicrous° quests.

_____   5–6. Water turns white with ___ when a swift current crashes against rocks.
_____   White-water canoeing is a challenge because a lightweight, frail canoe gives
                                 only ___ protection.

_____   7–8. Cutting down on fats is ___, but if your diet is usually healthful, having an
_____   occasional hamburger or milkshake is not a sign of ___—you needn't feel
                                 guilty.

_____   9–10. Obedience training will not ___ your dog's natural spirit. A wolf pack does
_____   not live in a state of ___, but establishes rules of order; and dogs, like their
                                  wolf relatives, also need to learn rules of propriety°.

Final Check: *Is Human Nature Good or Evil?*

Here is a final opportunity for you to strengthen your knowledge of the ten words. First read the following
selection carefully. Then fill in each blank with a word from the box at the top of the previous page.
(Context clues will help you figure out which word goes in which blank.) Use each word once.

Whether human beings are naturally good or naturally evil is an age-old debate, and how people
answer this question has influenced their ideas about government. Those who believe that a(n)
(1)_____ toward evil is inborn and immutable° tend to think that a government
must be (2)_____: strong, with laws that are strict and strictly enforced. They
are not misanthropes,° they insist—simply realists who know that people are basically devious° and corrupt
and cannot change. Under a weak government, they argue, (3)_____ will result:
humanity will, on the whole, behave viciously and brutally.

In contrast are those who believe that human beings are born good and would remain good if
powerful governments did not (4)_____ their freedom. They argue that when
a government crushes freedom, it also subjugates° basic human decency, and therefore all governments
should contract° and become weak, with scanty° laws—just a bare minimum of rules to keep things
running smoothly. One extreme view actually favors (5)_____: no government
and no laws. Anarchists are often accused of recommending chaotic (6)_____,
or at best of being (7)_____ idealists. They respond, though, that the effect
would be (8)_____, a healthy society.

The debate remains unsettled. Not surprisingly, evidence favoring total absence of government is
(9)_____, since societies see it as risky; and few of them, if any, have had the
(10)_____ to try it. But the human experience with all-powerful governments—
from the tyrants of centuries past to the dictatorships of our own time—has not been encouraging. As in so
many disputes, we may feel that the most sagacious° decision is to take a middle ground.

Scores   Sentence Check 2 _____%   Final Check _____%

callous	paragon
desecrate	provincial
evanescent	steadfast
heed	supercilious
indigent	usurp

Ten Words in Context

In the space provided, write the letter of the meaning closest to that of each **boldfaced** word. Use the context of the sentences to help you figure out each word's meaning.

1 callous
(kăl′əs)
- *adjective*

- Only the most **callous** person is not touched by pictures of starving children in refugee camps.
- Doctors and nurses in emergency rooms may seem **callous**, but if they let themselves become upset by the suffering they see, they could not do their jobs.

___ *Callous* means
   A. unfamiliar. –   B. unfeeling.   C. unqualified.

2 desecrate
(dĕs′ĭ-krāt′)
- *verb*

- Food vendors, postcard stands, and the like are not allowed at the war memorial. Such commercial ventures would **desecrate** this shrine to the war dead.
- New Englanders feel that clam chowder is **desecrated** by the addition of tomatoes. There's not a speck of tomato in pure New England chowder.

___ *Desecrate* means
   A. to adorn.   B. to dishonor.   C. to finish.

3 evanescent
(ĕv′ə-nĕs′ənt)
- *adjective*

- My grandmother seemed to have an **evanescent** scent of vanilla about her. When I hugged her, I would sometimes catch a sweet whiff of it.
- It is a wonderful, rare thing to get a glimpse of the northern lights, which appear as **evanescent** flickers of color on the horizon.

___ *Evanescent* means
   A. briefly present.   B. long-lasting.   C. imaginary.

4 heed
(hēd)
- *verb*

- Parents often wish that children were more willing to **heed** their advice.
- The senator was voted out of office after just one term because he refused to **heed** the voters' wishes.

___ *Heed* means
   A. to listen to.   B. to misunderstand.   C. to ignore.

5 indigent
(ĭn′dĭ-jənt)
- *adjective*

- The nun Mother Teresa was famous for her work among the **indigent** people of India, the people she called "the poorest of the poor."
- A soup kitchen and free clothing outlet has opened on West Avenue to help the city's **indigent** population.

___ *Indigent* means
   A. important.   B. well-behaved.   C. needy.

6 paragon
(păr′ə-gŏn′)
- *noun*

- The Acme Company presented itself as a **paragon** of business ethics. Therefore, the public was surprised at reports that Acme was dumping toxic wastes into streams and that its executives had fled the country with the stockholders' money.
- The New England town meeting is frequently described as a **paragon** of democracy. All citizens can participate and make their voices heard.

___ *Paragon* means
   A. an ancestor.   B. an imitation.   C. an ideal example.

7 provincial
(prə-vĭn′shəl)
- *adjective*

- Just because Ivan lives in the country, do not think he is **provincial**. On the contrary, he is a well-educated man who reads a great deal and keeps up with what's going on in the world.

- The local paper is too **provincial** for me. Its stories are written from a very limited point of view that doesn't consider other ways of looking at questions.

__ *Provincial* means   A. narrow-minded.   B. broad-minded.   C. calm.

8 steadfast
(stĕd′făst′)
- *adjective*

- For the last 11 years, my grandmother has been a **steadfast** volunteer for the Meals on Wheels program. Every Tuesday and Thursday evening, no matter what the weather, she delivers meals to neighbors who cannot leave their homes.

- On their golden anniversary, Dad made a touching toast to Mom, saying that she had been his "**steadfast** companion for half a century."

__ *Steadfast* means   A. forgetful.   B. faithful.   C. grateful.

9 supercilious
(sōō′pər-sĭl′ē-əs)
- *adjective*

- After a conference with her son's teacher, Jane was fuming because of the teacher's **supercilious** attitude. "She treated me like dirt under her feet," Jane said bitterly.

- The **supercilious** hotel clerk lost his job when he asked a plainly-dressed foreign-looking woman in the lobby to leave. She was the hotel owner's mother.

__ *Supercilious* means   A. snobbish.   B. sensitive.   C. supportive.

10 usurp
(yōō-sûrp′)
- *verb*

- In the novel, the evil prince arranged to have the elderly king kidnapped. He then **usurped** the throne, declaring himself king and threatening to hang as a traitor anyone who objected.

- If you get a puppy, it is important to reassure your old dog that the newcomer won't **usurp** his place in your affections. Give the old dog plenty of extra love to show him he still comes first—the puppy won't mind.

__ *Usurp* means   A. to share.   B. to take over.   C. to support.

Matching Words with Definitions

Following are definitions of the ten words. Clearly write or print each word next to its definition. The sentences above and on the previous page will help you decide on the meaning of each word.

1. _____   To treat with extreme disrespect; to violate the sacredness (of something highly valued)

2. _____   Gradually disappearing; fading away like a vapor

3. _____   A model of excellence or perfection

4. _____   Limited and narrow in outlook; unsophisticated

5. _____   To seize power or position by force or without right

6. _____   Proud; scornful; looking down on others

7. _____   Not having enough to live on; very poor; impoverished

8. _____   Firmly and consistently loyal

9. _____   Hardened in mind or feelings

10. _____   To pay attention to

CAUTION: Do not go any further until you are sure the above answers are correct. Then you can use the definitions to help you in the following practices. Your goal is eventually to know the words well enough so that you don't need to check the definitions at all.

Sentence Check 1

Using the answer line provided, complete each item below with the correct word from the box. Use each word once.

A. **callous**	B. **desecrate**	C. **evanescent**	D. **heed**	E. **indigent**
F. **paragon**	G. **provincial**	H. **steadfast**	I. **supercilious**	J. **usurp**

_____ 1. Tyrell is the most ___ player on his soccer team. He's totally committed, and he never misses a game or a practice session.

_____ 2. My mother and her sister Belle have not been on speaking terms for years. "I wouldn't let Belle come in our door," Mother says. "Her presence would ___ our home!"

_____ 3. The farm geese moved restlessly as the wild geese flew overhead. They were unsure whether they should stay around their little pond or ___ the call of their wild cousins and fly south.

_____ 4. In the small town where I grew up, there was a simple-minded, ___ man everyone knew as Tom. The local restaurants gave him meals, and members of several churches provided him with clothes.

_____ 5. When I woke up, I could remember few details of my dream. Like many dreams, it was ___, quickly slipping away from my memory.

_____ 6. Some parents fear that letting their children watch violent TV shows will make the children ___, uncaring about the suffering of others.

_____ 7. With most people having easy access to the Internet and 24-hour news channels, it is growing more difficult to be truly ___. It's almost impossible to completely ignore the world outside your own little community.

_____ 8. Not realizing that Dad is the only one who ever sits in the brown recliner, my date innocently sat there. "Who is this person who has the temerity° to ___ my throne?" Dad roared at the poor boy.

_____ 9. The elegant boutique in town must go out of its way to find ___ clerks. The last time I walked in, the woman there glanced at my shabby raincoat and said haughtily, "I doubt that we have anything in your price range."

_____ 10. Reading about our town's Woman of the Year made me so depressed that I wanted to go back to bed. This ___ not only runs her own successful business, has a happy marriage, and raises apparently peerless° children, but she also makes all her own clothes from cotton she spins herself.

NOTE: Now check your answers to these items by turning to page 176. Going over the answers carefully will help you prepare for the next two practices, for which answers are not given.

Sentence Check 2

Using the answer lines provided, complete each item below with **two** words from the box. Use each word once.

_____ 1–2. When I took my old wind-up watch in for cleaning, the ___ clerk belittled°
_____ it, sneering, "No one wears those anymore." I didn't ___ him, but simply said, "Please have it ready by tomorrow."

_____   3–4. Father used to say, "Don't harden your heart against the poor." Having been
_____   ___ once himself, he felt strongly about teaching his progeny° never to
                            become ___.

_____   5–6. It's common for older children to fear that a baby will ___ their place in the
_____   family. Hostility toward the newcomer is usually ___, though, if the older
                            children are made to feel loved and wanted.

_____   7–8. The dog is often said to be a(n) ___ of ___ friendship. In fact, a traditional
_____   name for a dog, "Fido," is Latin for "I am faithful."

_____   9–10. Bettina was opposed to the exhibition of pop art, arguing that it would ___
_____   the halls of the traditional old museum. "Don't be so ___!" her boyfriend
                            said. "Broaden your aesthetic° horizons."

Final Check: *The Strange Case of X*

Here is a final opportunity for you to strengthen your knowledge of the ten words. First read the following selection carefully. Then fill in each blank with a word from the box at the top of the previous page. (Context clues will help you figure out which word goes in which blank.) Use each word once.

　　　X is a writer, and his case is a strange one: He still uses a typewriter—a manual typewriter. No, X is not (1)_____. He doesn't live in a primitive village where computers are unheard of; he lives in a modern city. No, X is not (2)_____ either. He is not a starving artist suffering from a paucity° of funds; he's a successful professional who could well afford a computer. When asked about his refusal to (3)_____ the call of the computer, X gives an eloquent° reply:

　　　"My typewriter has been my loyal, (4)_____ companion for years. How could I be so heartless, so (5)_____, as to toss it aside and let a computer (6)_____ its place? Also, computers cost much more than typewriters; why be prodigal° and spend a lot of money on something I don't need? And best of all, the manual typewriter is a(n) (7)_____ of all that is best in technology. It burns no fossil fuels. It does not pollute the atmosphere. It does not deplete the ozone layer. Why should I (8)_____ the purity of my office with a computer?"

　　　Also, for a long time, X predicted that computers would prove to be (9)_____. He reasoned: Why rush out to buy something that will be just a passing fad? But he seems to have been wrong about that, and now some of his (10)_____ friends (he calls them "computer snobs") look down on him and say he is being quixotic°.

　　　I often think about X's case. In fact, I thought of him just yesterday when my computer told me it had a "disk read error" and I would have to restart. I thought of him again this afternoon when it had a "system failure" that managed to efface° all the files on its hard drive. I wonder if X and his indefatigable° typewriter might have the last laugh.

| Scores | Sentence Check 2 _____% | Final Check _____% |

The box at the right lists twenty-five words from Unit Three. Using the clues at the bottom of the page, fill in these words to complete the puzzle that follows.

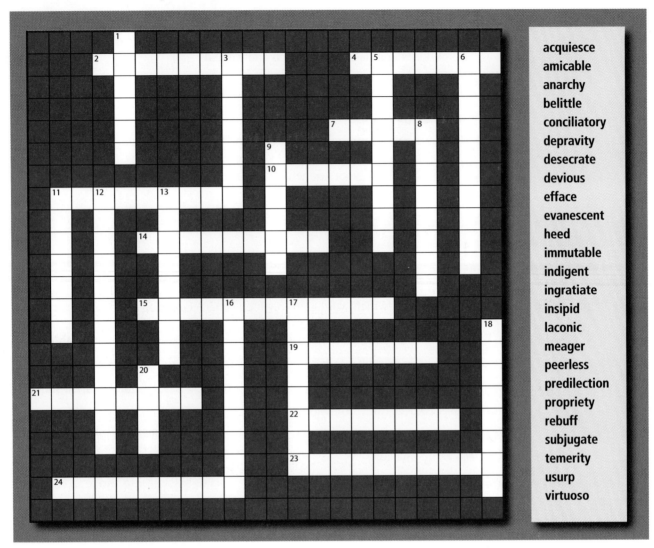

acquiesce
amicable
anarchy
belittle
conciliatory
depravity
desecrate
devious
efface
evanescent
heed
immutable
indigent
ingratiate
insipid
laconic
meager
peerless
predilection
propriety
rebuff
subjugate
temerity
usurp
virtuoso

ACROSS

2. To treat with extreme disrespect
4. Using as few words as possible
7. To seize power or position by force or without right
10. To wipe out
11. Evil
14. Appropriateness
15. Tending to win over or to calm by agreeing to demands
19. Dull; tasteless; unexciting
21. Very poor
22. To make something seem less worthy or less important
23. Gradually disappearing
24. To bring under control; enslave

DOWN

1. To reject bluntly; snub
3. Lawlessness
5. To consent without protest
6. To charm; win favor
8. Incomparable
9. Lacking in quality or quantity
11. Not straightforward; tricky
12. A natural preference
13. An expert, particularly in the arts
16. Never changing
17. Friendly; showing goodwill
18. Rash boldness; audacity; nerve
20. To pay attention to

PART A

Choose the word that best completes each item and write it in the space provided.

_____ 1. Little Tomas was very upset when his baby sister was born. He was obviously afraid that she would ___ his place in the family.

    A. ingratiate   B. acquiesce   C. delineate   D. usurp

_____ 2. When Meg started her new job, she wasn't quite sure what "dress-down Friday" meant there. She wondered about the ___ of wearing sneakers and blue jeans.

    A. predecessor   B. depravity   C. propriety   D. turbulence

_____ 3. In writing a math problem on the board, the professor made an elementary mistake in multiplication, but no one in the class had the ___ to tell her.

    A. temerity   B. dissonance   C. catalyst   D. anarchy

_____ 4. A(n) ___ law of nature is Murphy's Law: "If something can go wrong, it will."

    A. conciliatory   B. insipid   C. bombastic   D. immutable

_____ 5. Sam tried to comb his ___ hair over his bald spot, but there wasn't enough to cover it.

    A. provincial   B. ponderous   C. immutable   D. scanty

_____ 6. Luz felt ___ about taking a course in public speaking. She didn't think she would be brave enough to stand up and address a roomful of people.

    A. peerless   B. evanescent   C. diffident   D. amicable

_____ 7. Serena didn't really want to go out with Ernie, but she was too kindhearted to ___ him.

    A. delineate   B. rebuff   C. ingratiate   D. desecrate

_____ 8. "Our rule against eating at your desk isn't just ___," the boss explained. "Crumbs and leftover food attract mice and roaches."

    A. whimsical   B. peerless   C. steadfast   D. insipid

_____ 9. Among land animals, the cheetah is the fastest runner. This ___ sprinter can reach speeds of up to 75 miles per hour.

    A. peerless   B. bombastic   C. meager   D. whimsical

_____ 10. When the Acme Company downsized, it showed a(n) ___ disregard for the employees' feelings. The termination notices were issued on Christmas Eve.

    A. articulate   B. callous   C. static   D. conciliatory

(Continues on next page)

_____ 11. Isaac is majoring in math. This is not surprising, since he has always had a(n) ___ for mathematics.

     A. predecessor   B. depravity   C. predilection   D. anarchy

_____ 12. Many people think of dogs as loyal companions, but a cat can be just as faithful and ___.

     A. steadfast   B. articulate   C. provincial   D. vitriolic

_____ 13. ___ parents lay down the law and expect their children to obey immediately, with no questions or comments.

     A. Conciliatory   B. Evanescent   C. Authoritarian   D. Indigent

PART B

Write **C** if the italicized word is used **correctly**. Write **I** if the word is used **incorrectly**.

_____ 14. Some teachers believe they must be very strict and set many rules in order to prevent *anarchy* in the classroom.

_____ 15. When people disagree with you, don't automatically *disparage* them and their ideas. Instead of sneering, try keeping an open mind—you may learn something.

_____ 16. Carina and Scott constantly boast and brag about how marvelous, talented, and bright their children are. Everyone is tired of hearing them *belittle* their kids.

_____ 17. The Nazis proclaimed that their state would be *evanescent*. They predicted that it would last a thousand years.

_____ 18. I chose my winter coat only because it looked great, then found that it didn't keep me warm. I wish I had focused on practical rather than *aesthetic* qualities.

_____ 19. Arthur Bryant's is a restaurant in Kansas City famous for its spicy, *insipid* barbecued spareribs.

_____ 20. The "one-liner," as its name implies, is a *laconic* type of joke.

_____ 21. Mozart is considered a *paragon* among composers. Many people think his music is the finest ever written.

_____ 22. Labor-management relations at the Acme Company are very *amicable*. In the past five years, there have been several walkouts, one lockout, and two long, bitter strikes.

_____ 23. Eating a steady diet of fast food and soda is one of the most *salutary* habits anyone can develop.

_____ 24. The boys' choir is famous for its sweet, harmonious sound. This *dissonance* has made it a worldwide favorite.

_____ 25. Monica wants to have the apartment all to herself on Friday night so she can invite her boyfriend over for a romantic dinner. She hopes her roommate will *acquiesce* and go out for the evening.

Score   (Number correct) _____   x 4 = _____%

PART A

On the answer line, write the word from the box that completes each item below. Use each word once.

A. **catalyst**	B. **conciliatory**	C. **delineate**	D. **depravity**	E. **garrulous**
F. **heed**	G. **indigent**	H. **quixotic**	I. **provincial**	J. **subjugate**
K. **supercilious**	L. **turbulence**	M. **virtuoso**		

_____ 1. Sometimes a kid just seems to be a(n) ___ for trouble. Minutes after he walks into a room, sparks begin to fly and fights break out.

_____ 2. The New York Philharmonic orchestra boasts that every one of its hundred musicians is a(n) ___ .

_____ 3. "Don't go out in this freezing cold without a coat," said Dick's mom; "you'll catch pneumonia!" He did not ___ her warning. He went out coatless and caught pneumonia.

_____ 4. "The human race is sunk in ___!" thundered the street preacher. "Repent before it is too late!"

_____ 5. The boss was ashamed that he had lost his temper and yelled at his secretary. As a(n) ___ gesture, he sent her a beautiful box of candy.

_____ 6. The clothing exchange at the church was meant to benefit ___ people, but it soon became popular with bargain hunters who were far from poor.

_____ 7. The ___ waiter in the fancy restaurant looked down his nose at us because we didn't know how to pronounce the names of the wines.

_____ 8. The opening chapters of the novel ___ daily life in a small Southern town.

_____ 9. After a siege lasting a month, the attackers were easily able to ___ the city. The inhabitants were too weak and tired to fight the conquerors off.

_____ 10. A rich woman in a short story, bored with life, finds a beggar sleeping on her doorstep. In a sudden ___ gesture, she gives him all her money and the key to her house.

_____ 11. A tornado is a condition of extreme ___: strong, violently whirling winds.

_____ 12. Aline has a(n) ___ outlook on life. She has little interest in anything beyond her own narrow neighborhood—the rest of the world doesn't exist for her.

_____ 13. When my ___ cousin gets started talking on the phone, he can't seem to stop. A call from him may last an hour or two.

(Continues on next page)

PART B

Write **C** if the italicized word is used **correctly**. Write **I** if the word is used **incorrectly**.

_____ 14. When DeShawn got an A on his paper, he was unable to *suppress* his feelings. He let out a whoop of joy right in the middle of class.

_____ 15. At Easter, several members of the congregation worked together to decorate the church with spring flowers and *desecrate* the altar with lilies.

_____ 16. "This fine novel is beautifully written and a joy to read," the reviewer wrote. That *vitriolic* comment made the author glow with pride.

_____ 17. Judy's severe stutter makes her especially *articulate*.

_____ 18. Trying to *ingratiate* himself with his instructor, Lorin told her, "You are the most inspiring teacher this college has ever had."

_____ 19. Kwan has trouble making ends meet on his *meager* salary. He has to watch every penny and stick to a strict budget.

_____ 20. Everyone enjoyed the lecture because it was so *bombastic*. The speaker was down-to-earth, relaxed, casual, and plainspoken, and he used simple, everyday examples.

_____ 21. Op art—or optical art—looks *static*. Sharply slanting or curving lines and intensely bright colors are used to give these paintings a sense of pulsing, shimmering movement.

_____ 22. The outgoing mayor was gracious as he left office. Referring to the new mayor, he said, "I wish my *predecessor* well as she takes up the leadership of our city."

_____ 23. Sherri's father would love to know how much money she earns, but he doesn't want to ask her, so he tries to find out in *devious* ways.

_____ 24. Greek music is so lively and *ponderous* that diners in Greek restaurants just can't keep their feet from tapping. Often, they suddenly start dancing in the aisles between the tables.

_____ 25. To *efface* the memory of her grandparents, April had their wedding picture enlarged and framed and hung it in her living room.

Score   (Number correct) _____ x 4 = _____ %

PART A: Synonyms

In the space provided, write the letter of the choice that is most nearly the **same** in meaning as the **boldfaced** word.

_____ 1. **acquiesce**　　A. to acquire　　B. to agree　　C. to become acquainted　　D. to disagree

_____ 2. **aesthetic**　　A. referring to beauty　　B. referring to science　　C. strenuous　　D. influential

_____ 3. **articulate**　　A. well-spoken　　B. well-paid　　C. well-meant　　D. well-off

_____ 4. **bombastic**　　A. bitter　　B. modest　　C. explosive　　D. wordy

_____ 5. **catalyst**　　A. a disaster　　B. a catalogue　　C. an agent of change　　D. an analyst

_____ 6. **delineate**　　A. to detest　　B. to defeat　　C. to describe　　D. to disgust

_____ 7. **depravity**　　A. immorality　　B. immediacy　　C. humor　　D. charity

_____ 8. **desecrate**　　A. to disguise　　B. to discourage　　C. to dishonor　　D. to discover

_____ 9. **efface**　　A. to preserve　　B. to repair　　C. to blot out　　D. to use up

_____ 10. **ingratiate**　　A. to gain favor　　B. to fall out of favor　　C. to initiate　　D. to integrate

_____ 11. **paragon**　　A. a part of a whole　　B. a geometric shape　　C. a straight line　　D. a model

_____ 12. **peerless**　　A. unavoidable　　B. unnoticed　　C. unequaled　　D. uncertain

_____ 13. **predilection**　　A. a fear　　B. a liking　　C. a mistake　　D. a loss

_____ 14. **propriety**　　A. outrage　　B. appropriateness　　C. scarcity　　D. panic

_____ 15. **provincial**　　A. profitable　　B. urban　　C. relaxed　　D. narrow

_____ 16. **quixotic**　　A. having your ear to the ground　　B. having your head in the clouds　　C. having your tongue in your cheek　　D. having one foot in the grave

_____ 17. **rebuff**　　A. to retire　　B. to retain　　C. to reject　　D. to require

_____ 18. **subjugate**　　A. to overcome　　B. to subsidize　　C. to exaggerate　　D. to surrender

_____ 19. **supercilious**　　A. snobby　　B. sleepy　　C. silly　　D. sorry

_____ 20. **suppress**　　A. to supply　　B. to defeat　　C. to desire　　D. to rescue

_____ 21. **temerity**　　A. a sense of humor　　B. a sense of responsibility　　C. caution　　D. boldness

_____ 22. **usurp**　　A. to give up　　B. to seize　　C. to study　　D. to avoid

_____ 23. **virtuoso**　　A. an expert　　B. a learner　　C. a villain　　D. a saint

_____ 24. **vitriolic**　　A. sweet like sugar　　B. stinging like acid　　C. smooth like cream　　D. wholesome like bread

_____ 25. **whimsical**　　A. without goodness　　B. without reason　　C. funny　　D. serious

(Continues on next page)

PART B: Antonyms

In the space provided, write the letter of the choice that is most nearly **opposite** in meaning to the **boldfaced** word.

_____ 26. **amicable**   A. loving   B. hostile   C. gentle   D. old

_____ 27. **anarchy**   A. odds and ends   B. pros and cons   C. wear and tear
                            D. law and order

_____ 28. **authoritarian** A. strict   B. democratic   C. fictional   D. factual

_____ 29. **belittle**   A. to watch   B. to remember   C. to seek   D. to praise

_____ 30. **callous**   A. lightheaded   B. sure-footed   C. softhearted   D. sharp-eyed

_____ 31. **conciliatory**   A. argumentative   B. peaceable   C. timid   D. cooperative

_____ 32. **devious**   A. sly   B. honest   C. wily   D. sad

_____ 33. **diffident**   A. different   B. similar   C. fearful   D. assertive

_____ 34. **disparage**   A. to attack   B. to praise   C. to greet   D. to listen to

_____ 35. **dissonance**   A. harmony   B. strife   C. noise   D. stress

_____ 36. **evanescent**   A. eventful   B. uneventful   C. brief   D. permanent

_____ 37. **garrulous**   A. underhanded   B. evenhanded   C. short-spoken   D. long-winded

_____ 38. **heed**   A. to hear   B. to focus on   C. to ignore   D. to study

_____ 39. **immutable**   A. constant   B. changeable   C. visible   D. universal

_____ 40. **indigent**   A. angry   B. faraway   C. nearby   D. rich

_____ 41. **insipid**   A. bland   B. zesty   C. flavorless   D. dreary

_____ 42. **laconic**   A. terse   B. wordy   C. traditional   D. new

_____ 43. **meager**   A. ample   B. measurable   C. deficient   D. empty

_____ 44. **ponderous**   A. predictable   B. random   C. light   D. weighty

_____ 45. **predecessor**   A. a predicament   B. a successor   C. an ancestor   D. an enemy

_____ 46. **salutary**   A. useful   B. unhealthy   C. unusual   D. noticeable

_____ 47. **scanty**   A. insufficient   B. incredible   C. logical   D. plentiful

_____ 48. **static**   A. moving   B. quiet   C. difficult   D. easy

_____ 49. **steadfast**   A. steady   B. true-blue   C. treacherous   D. trustworthy

_____ 50. **turbulence**   A. uproar   B. poverty   C. conflict   D. calm

Score   (Number correct) _____ x 2 = _____%

Enter your score above and in the **Vocabulary Performance Chart** on the inside back cover of the book.

Unit Four

buoyant	marred
enervate	parochial
incorrigible	partisan
inexorable	pique
irrefutable	satirical

Ten Words in Context

In the space provided, write the letter of the meaning closest to that of each **boldfaced** word. Use the context of the sentences to help you figure out each word's meaning.

1 buoyant
(boi′ənt)
- *adjective*

- Helium balloons are **buoyant** because the helium gas in them is lighter than air.
- To help her daughter float in the pool, Barbara bought her a swimsuit that has a **buoyant** tube around the waist.

___ *Buoyant* means   A. capable of floating.   B. tending to sink.   C. invisible.

2 enervate
(ĕn′ər-vāt′)
- *verb*

- The doctor warned me that my husband's medication might **enervate** him. "While he's taking it," she said, "just let him rest as much as he needs to."
- The heat wave completely **enervated** Janine. By the sixth day of 90-degree temperatures, she could barely drag herself out of bed.

___ *Enervate* means   A. to frighten.   B. to exhaust.   C. to awaken.

3 incorrigible
(ĭn-kôr′ĭ-jə-bəl)
- *adjective*

- The dog trainer shook her head in frustration. "I'll give you your money back," she told Prince's owners. "This dog is **incorrigible**. I can't teach him a thing."
- Jake has lost many friends because he is such an **incorrigible** practical joker. He hides frogs in people's beds, puts tacks on their chairs, and sprinkles "sneezing powder" on their food.

___ *Incorrigible* means   A. incurable.   B. intelligent.   C. influential.

4 inexorable
(ĭn-ĕk′sər-ə-bəl)
- *adjective*

- Although my grandmother is still in pretty good health, old age is taking its slow, **inexorable** toll on her.
- The Martins have an **inexorable** rule against smoking in their home—no one is allowed to do it, ever.

___ *Inexorable* means   A. lenient.   B. unyielding.   C. not exact.

5 irrefutable
(ĭ-rĕf′yə-tə-bəl *or* ĭr′ĭ-fyoo′tə-bəl)
- *adjective*

- "It's **irrefutable**!" Mike said. "I saw it with my own eyes in a magazine at the supermarket! Humans are definitely being kidnapped by aliens from Saturn!"
- Although many people claim to have seen the Loch Ness monster, no one has ever come up with **irrefutable** proof that any such creature exists.

___ *Irrefutable* means   A. easy to understand.   B. unprejudiced.   C. indisputable.

6 marred
(mărd)
- *verb*

- The shore, once so peaceful and lovely, is now **marred** by a row of fast-food stands.
- The automobile company's reputation was **marred** when it was learned that executives had ignored a dangerous problem with the cars' brakes.

___ *Marred* means   A. improved.   B. disguised.   C. damaged.

7 parochial
(pə-rō′kē-əl)
- *adjective*

● Many young people arrive at college with little knowledge of the world, but meeting students and instructors from other places and other cultures helps them overcome their **parochial** outlook.

● Aunt Violet is interested only in her small circle of family and friends. When we tell her she has a **parochial** attitude, she says, "I don't know about other people, and I don't care."

__ *Parochial* means   A. timid.   B. limited.   C. lacking enthusiasm.

8 partisan
(pär′tĭ-zən)
- *adjective*

● The League of Women Voters is not **partisan**. In every election, it remains neutral and provides information about all the candidates.

● Rachel's highly **partisan** comments sometimes annoy her friends, but her strong views might make her a real asset to a debating team.

__ *Partisan* means   A. uncaring.   B. objective.   C. one-sided.

9 pique
(pēk)
- *noun*

● When her husband told her that she talked too much, a Frenchwoman retorted, "Very well; I'll never talk again." Her **pique** lasted the rest of her life; despite the pleas of her family, she went to her grave still silent.

● Macy's art project got more attention than Laila's. Out of **pique**, Laila told people that Macy had stolen the idea for the project from someone else.

__ *Pique* means   A. a sense of injury.   B. a sense of duty.   C. a sense of humor.

10 satirical
(sə-tĭr′ĭ-kəl)
- *adjective*

● The TV shows *The Colbert Report* and *The Daily Show with Jon Stewart* take a **satirical** look at current events, mixing political criticism with humor.

● The governor was angry about a **satirical** article in the newspaper that amused readers by making fun of his many broken promises.

__ *Satirical* means   A. admiring.   B. criticizing through ridicule.   C. boring.

Matching Words with Definitions

Following are definitions of the ten words. Clearly write or print each word next to its definition. The sentences above and on the previous page will help you decide on the meaning of each word.

1. _____ Not capable of being influenced or prevented; relentless; unstoppable

2. _____ Restricted to a narrow scope or outlook; narrow-minded

3. _____ Attacking human vice or foolishness through irony or wit

4. _____ To weaken; rob of strength or energy

5. _____ Impossible to disprove

6. _____ A feeling of resentment or anger because of wounded pride

7. _____ Able to float or rise

8. _____ Strongly supporting a specific party, cause, or person

9. _____ Made less perfect through injury or damage

10. _____ Uncontrollable; unmanageable; not capable of being corrected or reformed

CAUTION: Do not go any further until you are sure the above answers are correct. Then you can use the definitions to help you in the following practices. Your goal is eventually to know the words well enough so that you don't need to check the definitions at all.

Sentence Check 1

Using the answer line provided, complete each item below with the correct word from the box. Use each word once.

A. **buoyant**	B. **enervate**	C. **incorrigible**	D. **inexorable**	E. **irrefutable**
F. **marred**	G. **parochial**	H. **partisan**	I. **pique**	J. **satirical**

_____ 1. Buoys are markers that float in the water to warn of dangerous spots. Their name is related to the word "___," which means "able to float."

_____ 2. Our mayor is a paragon° among politicians. Her spotless record has never been ___ by even a hint of wrongdoing.

_____ 3. Shows like *Saturday Night Live* take a(n) ___ attitude toward the famous and powerful, making fun of celebrities and government officials alike.

_____ 4. When his opponent won the tennis match with a lucky shot, Nicky refused to shake hands. His ___ seemed childish to the spectators.

_____ 5. Lem's instructor was impressed with his paper, which was a powerful combination of facts and ___ logic.

_____ 6. The farmland in this area is slowly being swallowed up by the ___ spread of housing developments.

_____ 7. The automobile accident ___(e)d Carlos for weeks, causing him to languish° at home, even though he had not been badly injured. His doctors said this was normal and that his energy would soon return.

_____ 8. "You'll have to leave now," the shop owner said to the parents and their badly behaved children. "How dare you let your ___ kids run unsupervised through the store, crashing into customers and breaking merchandise?"

_____ 9. Oliver takes a(n) ___ approach to life. He is intensely committed and sees everything as a struggle between opponents.

_____ 10. Although Uncle Don has spent his whole life in a small country town, he has never been ___: everything in the wide world interests him.

NOTE: Now check your answers to these items by turning to page 176. Going over the answers carefully will help you prepare for the next two practices, for which answers are not given.

Sentence Check 2

Using the answer lines provided, complete each item below with **two** words from the box. Use each word once.

_____
_____ 1–2. When the ___ march of time brings wrinkles, a woman may feel that her face is hopelessly ___—but a man thinks he now looks "distinguished."

_____
_____ 3–4. Margo is very ___, and her narrow-mindedness seems to be ___: no one has ever persuaded her to broaden her provincial° outlook on life.

_____
_____ 5–6. When summer's heat and humidity threaten to ___ me, I like to float in a pool on a(n) ___ cushion, preferably one that also holds a frosty drink.

_____   7–8. The students who put on the ___ show decided not to be ___ when they
_____   lampooned° their victims. They made fun of everyone, regardless of race,
                                   creed, ethnic origin, or political affiliation.

_____   9–10. Instead of being a good sport and admitting that his opponent's articulate°,
_____   carefully worked-out argument was ___, Perry quit the debating team in a fit
                                   of ___.

Final Check: *The Salem Witches*

Here is a final opportunity for you to strengthen your knowledge of the ten words. First read the following
selection carefully. Then fill in each blank with a word from the box at the top of the previous page.
(Context clues will help you figure out which word goes in which blank.) Use each word once.

A tragic chapter in American history began with almost unbelievably trivial occurrences. The witch
trials held in Salem, Massachusetts, in 1692 resulted in the execution of nineteen accused witches and the
imprisonment of many others. At the height of the witchcraft frenzy, incidents between neighbors that
would ordinarily cause only (1)_____ resulted in accusations of involvement with the devil.
A frivolous° or (2)_____ remark might be taken as serious, leading to the unfortunate
speaker's trial and even death.

The witchcraft trials, which have (3)_____ the reputation of Salem for more than
three centuries, began when several young girls accused a slave woman named Tituba of casting spells
on them. They claimed that she could read their minds and that she tormented them, causing them to fall
into fits, writhe°, make animal noises, and scream at invisible enemies. Why did the girls make such claims?
A possible explanation is that one girl, Abigail Williams, was angry at Tituba. Abigail was a badly behaved
child whom Tituba had sometimes punished for her (4)_____ conduct. The girls may
also have wanted to get out of work by claiming that the "spells" (5)_____(e)d them,
leaving them too tired to do their chores.

Although the girls' stories seemed untenable°, even ludicrous°, they were believed. Many people in
1692 were uneducated, (6)_____, and thus intensely fearful of the unknown. Tituba
was a good target for their fears: she was foreign, black, and known to be highly capable. Why did her
garden yield more vegetables than other women's? Why were the animals she raised so fat and healthy?
The successes she had garnered° seemed to her neighbors (7)_____ proof that Tituba
was in league with the devil.

Once Tituba had been accused of witchcraft, a(n) (8)_____ tide of suspicion
seemed to sweep over the village. The townspeople turned on one another like savage animals,
accusing friends and relatives of being witches. The trials were a mockery of justice. The judges were
entirely (9)_____, convinced from the beginning that the "witches" were guilty.
The accused were subject to ridiculous tests, such as having to recite the Lord's Prayer backwards.
Some were thrown into water, on the theory that an innocent person would sink, while a witch was
(10)_____ and would escape unscathed° from drowning.

After nineteen people had been executed for witchcraft, eighteen by hanging and one by being
crushed with stones, the governor of Massachusetts stopped the trials. Over a hundred people were in
prison awaiting trial at the time. They were released. (Tituba was among them.) Later, some of the girls who
had brought the original accusations admitted that they had been pretending.

Scores	Sentence Check 2 _____ %	Final Check _____ %

Enter your scores above and in the **Vocabulary Performance Chart** on the inside back cover of the book.

cajole	reverent
capitulate	stupor
egregious	sycophant
premonition	urbane
prestigious	zany

Ten Words in Context

In the space provided, write the letter of the meaning closest to that of each **boldfaced** word. Use the context of the sentences to help you figure out each word's meaning.

1 cajole
(kə-jōl′)
- *verb*

- No matter how I **cajoled** him, the police officer continued to write me a ticket for speeding.
- Once my mother told us children "Absolutely not," we knew better than to try to **cajole** her into changing her mind. Begging only made her angry.

___ *Cajole* means   A. to plead with.   B. to laugh at.   C. to hate.

2 capitulate
(kə-pĭch′ə-lāt′)
- *verb*

- Although Stacy has said she will never speak to Karen again, I expect her to **capitulate** shortly—I think she will soon miss her old friend.
- Mr. Henderson resisted the idea of his daughter going on dates, but he **capitulated** when she became a high-school senior.

___ *Capitulate* means   A. to be capable.   B. to repeat.   C. to yield.

3 egregious
(ĭ-grē′jəs)
- *adjective*

- "You certainly made an **egregious** fool of yourself," George's wife said after the party. "Did you have to sing and dance with a lampshade on your head?"
- "It was an **egregious** mistake to paint our office hot pink," admitted the president of the accounting firm. "No one seems to take us seriously anymore."

___ *Egregious* means   A. obviously bad.   B. minor.   C. easily overlooked.

4 premonition
(prĕ′mə-nĭsh′ən)
- *noun*

- Although I'd had a **premonition** that I shouldn't get on the airplane, nothing bad happened. It was a perfectly ordinary flight.
- "Wait!" called out the fortuneteller as Malik walked past. "I have a **premonition** about you! For only five dollars, I'll tell you your future."

___ *Premonition* means   A. a memory.   B. a warning in advance.   C. a plan.

5 prestigious
(prĕ-stē′jəs)
- *adjective*

- Are those name-brand jeans really better than less expensive ones, or are you just paying more for the **prestigious** label?
- A Rolls-Royce car, Dom Perignon champagne, a Harvard education, a Tiffany diamond—all these are regarded as the most **prestigious** items of their kinds.

___ *Prestigious* means   A. common.   B. highly valued.   C. beautiful.

6 reverent
(rĕv′ər-ənt)
- *adjective*

- A huge, awesome natural wonder, such as the Grand Canyon or Niagara Falls, makes most visitors feel **reverent**.
- As we walked through the art museum, our teacher spoke in hushed, **reverent** tones about the masterpieces we were seeing.

___ *Reverent* means   A. scornful.   B. amused.   C. worshipful.

7 stupor
(stoo′pər)
- *noun*

- At one time, patients who had surgery requiring general anesthesia would remain in a **stupor** for many hours afterward. But with today's improved anesthetics, they often regain full consciousness within minutes.
- A recent study reported that many truck drivers get too little sleep on long trips and often drive in a **stupor**, not aware that their senses are dulled.

__ *Stupor* means   A. a state of anxiety.   B. a state of grief.   C. a drowsy state.

8 sycophant
(sĭk′ə-fənt)
- *noun*

- "I don't expect a class full of **sycophants**," the teacher told her argumentative students, "but couldn't you agree with me about something just once?"
- The manager of the restaurant where Ted works had a truly crazy idea about how to reorganize the kitchen. Ted, always the **sycophant**, told him the plan was brilliant.

__ *Sycophant* means   A. a chatterbox.   B. a flatterer.   C. a traitor.

9 urbane
(ûr-bān′)
- *adjective*

- The new student dressed all in black and spoke perfect French, making her seem more **urbane** and sophisticated than her classmates.
- The critics loved the new movie by a director whose trademark was worldly-wise, **urbane** comedy. "As witty, clever, and artful as ever!" they wrote.

__ *Urbane* means   A. impulsive.   B. refined.   C. careful.

10 zany
(zā′nē)
- *adjective*

- The audience at the circus roared with delight at the clowns' **zany** tricks.
- As kids, my brother and I couldn't get enough of *Mad*, a **zany** magazine whose motto was "Humor in a jugular vein."

__ *Zany* means   A. absurdly funny.   B. understated.   C. scary.

Matching Words with Definitions

Following are definitions of the ten words. Clearly write or print each word next to its definition. The sentences above and on the previous page will help you decide on the meaning of each word.

1. _____ To give in

2. _____ Feeling or expressing respect or awe

3. _____ Having an honored name or reputation; having prestige

4. _____ A state of mental numbness; a daze

5. _____ A person who tries to win favor through flattery

6. _____ Wildly silly or comical

7. _____ Smooth in manner; elegant; polished; suave

8. _____ A feeling that something bad is going to happen

9. _____ Highly noticeable in a negative way; conspicuously bad

10. _____ To persuade with flattery; to sweet-talk

CAUTION: Do not go any further until you are sure the above answers are correct. Then you can use the definitions to help you in the following practices. Your goal is eventually to know the words well enough so that you don't need to check the definitions at all.

Sentence Check 1

Using the answer line provided, complete each item below with the correct word from the box. Use each word once.

A. cajole	B. capitulate	C. egregious	D. premonition	E. prestigious
F. reverent	G. stupor	H. sycophant	I. urbane	J. zany

_____ 1. Mom resisted getting a cell phone for a long time, but she finally ___(e)d after getting a flat tire and having no way to call a tow truck.

_____ 2. Mack comes up with one ___ get-rich-quick scheme after another. He says we may find them silly now, but he'll have the last laugh: one of them will win him fame and fortune.

_____ 3. "When my uncle is being annoying at family dinners, I wish you wouldn't be so nice to him," Amy told her husband. "He doesn't need a(n) ___ to make him think he's clever and amusing."

_____ 4. I had a(n) ___ that Lisa and Todd would not hit it off, and I was right. They were in a heated argument within five minutes of being introduced.

_____ 5. To give himself a better chance of getting the job, the applicant faked letters of recommendation from people with ___ positions in the community.

_____ 6. The owner of the restaurant is a gracious, ___ woman, always poised and at ease greeting celebrities. And she is just as courteous and amicable° to all her customers.

_____ 7. ___ is one symptom of hypothermia—very low body temperature—in the elderly. Their memory loss and dazed condition may be curable simply by turning up the heat.

_____ 8. The children managed to ___ their parents into letting them stay up long past their usual bedtime.

_____ 9. "Don't wear those torn jeans to the funeral," Maude told her son. "Put on a suit and tie so you'll seem properly ___."

_____ 10. Renata's first public performance as a pianist was a(n) ___ disaster. The piano bench collapsed under her, much to the amusement of the audience.

NOTE: Now check your answers to these items by turning to page 176. Going over the answers carefully will help you prepare for the next two practices, for which answers are not given.

Sentence Check 2

Using the answer lines provided, complete each item below with **two** words from the box. Use each word once.

_____
_____ 1–2. "What ___ idiot erased all our computer files?" the boss yelled. Monica had a(n) ___ of disaster: she had just used the computer.

_____
_____ 3–4. Are you more in the mood for a(n) ___, sophisticated comedy—maybe something starring George Clooney—or something goofy and ___, such as an Adam Sandler or Will Ferrell film?

_____   5–6. When he was told he had won a(n) ___ scholarship, Ramon was so
_____   overwhelmed with the honor that he walked around in a dreamy ___ for the
                                  rest of the day.

_____   7–8. If children want an expensive toy, they will usually try to ___ a parent into
_____   buying it for them—whichever parent they think is more likely to ___.

_____   9–10. ___s are respectful, even ___, because it is expedient°. Their goal is to
_____   ingratiate° themselves—usually by "buttering up" the instructor or boss—for
                                   some personal advantage.

Final Check: _Fashion Show_

Here is a final opportunity for you to strengthen your knowledge of the ten words. First read the following selection carefully. Then fill in each blank with a word from the box at the top of the previous page. (Context clues will help you figure out which word goes in which blank.) Use each word once.

Never again will I let anyone talk me into attending a fashion show. My sister, who lives in New York, loves to go to these shows. The last time I visited her, she (1)_____(e)d me into going with her. "Julie, I have _no_ interest in doing this," I protested. But she kept pleading, promising me, "You'll love it. You're lucky I could even get tickets for it—Dominic is one of the most (2)_____ designers in the world." I hated to rebuff° her, so finally I (3)_____(e)d, and off we went.

When we arrived at Dominic's showroom, I saw dozens of weirdly-dressed men and women flowing in. "I have a(n) (4)_____ that this is going to be even more awful than I feared," I said to Julie. "Suppose I go to a movie and meet you later?" But she dragged me in.

When Dominic, handsome in a dark suit, came onstage to introduce the show, I thought maybe it would be OK after all. I liked his elegant European accent and (5)_____ manner as he told us that we were about to see the most creative, exciting clothes he had ever designed.

Colored lights flashed and loud music boomed as the models began walking down the runway. I stared in amazement. What they were wearing was as (6)_____ as any Halloween costume. One dress was made of tinfoil. Another was made of soup cans that had been flattened and fastened together with tiny chains. A third dress was printed with targets that had holes in the center. I stared at Dominic, who was standing next to the stage. He was surrounded by (7)_____s praising the "beauty" and "originality" of the absurd clothes. I whispered to my sister, "This is a joke, right?" She dug her elbow into my side, saying "Hush!" I looked around at the other people in the audience. They maintained a(n) (8)_____ silence, as if they were in church—except for one woman who glared at me, as if accusing me of blasphemy°.

It didn't get better. I sat in a(n) (9)_____ of disbelief, my mouth hanging open. As the lights came up, Julie sighed happily, "Wasn't it _wonderful?_" "Julie," I replied, "I have never in my life seen such a(n) (10)_____ display of wasted talent and bad taste." "You're obtuse°— you just don't get it—you lack the aesthetic° sense to appreciate Dominic's work," Julie replied. Her final reproach° was, "You're simply too provincial°."

Maybe she's right. Maybe I'm not sophisticated. But at least I know what I _don't_ like.

Scores   Sentence Check 2 _____%   Final Check _____%

aberration	formidable
composure	inscrutable
congenital	precocious
elusive	trepidation
extol	virulent

Ten Words in Context

In the space provided, write the letter of the meaning closest to that of each **boldfaced** word. Use the context of the sentences to help you figure out each word's meaning.

1 aberration
(ăb′ə-rā′shən)
- *noun*

- Yes, we had a poor meal at Antonio's Restaurant, but that was an **aberration**. Generally the food there is excellent.
- We have seen many **aberrations** in the weather this year. For instance, it snowed in June, and it reached 70 degrees on Christmas Day.

___ *Aberration* means   A. something abnormal.   B. something typical.   C. something impossible.

2 composure
(kəm-pō′zhər)
- *noun*

- When Kaylin served as a juror, she was impressed by the foreman's **composure** as he announced the jury's verdict. Afterward, though, he said to her, "I may have looked calm, but I was shaking inside."
- Grandma's **composure** was legendary. When her house was flooded, the Red Cross arrived to find her perched in an upstairs window, calmly knitting. "Why fuss?" she said. "I knew you'd get here sooner or later."

___ *Composure* means   A. understanding.   B. cool-headedness.   C. selfishness.

3 congenital
(kən-jĕn′ĭ-tl)
- *adjective*

- Before the Jacksons' baby son was born, doctors knew he had a **congenital** heart defect. He had surgery to correct it when he was only two months old.
- Both of Ravi's parents are deaf. His father's deafness is **congenital**, but his mother's was caused by an ear infection when she was very young.

___ *Congenital* means   A. unusual.   B. existing from birth.   C. insufficient.

4 elusive
(ĭ-lōō′sĭv)
- *adjective*

- Marta tried to follow the lecture, but the ideas seemed **elusive**. "The point escaped me," she admitted later.
- There was a faint, **elusive** scent in the air. Was it flowers, or was it someone's perfume? We couldn't be sure.

___ *Elusive* means   A. difficult to capture.   B. horrible.   C. common.

5 extol
(ĭk-stōl′)
- *verb*

- Advertisements all **extol** whatever product they are selling, saying that it is the best of its type.
- The review of this movie **extols** it as one of the best films of the year.

___ *Extol* means   A. to glorify.   B. to combine.   C. to complete.

6 formidable
(fôr′mĭ-də-bəl)
- *adjective*

- The movers stood on the sidewalk, considering the **formidable** task of getting a grand piano up a long, narrow flight of stairs.
- When Joe and Mia learned they were going to have triplets, they wondered how they could handle such a **formidable** responsibility.

___ *Formidable* means   A. formless.   B. previous.   C. difficult.

7 inscrutable
(ĭn-skrōō′tə-bəl)
- *adjective*

- "How can I write a paper on the meaning of this poem when I don't understand it myself?" Kiri moaned. "It's completely **inscrutable** to me."
- When the artist Vincent van Gogh cut off his ear, his motive seemed completely **inscrutable**. One possible solution to the mystery is that he may have been poisoned by the lead in his paints, leading to brain damage.

__ *Inscrutable* means   A. looked at closely.   B. mysterious.   C. clear.

8 precocious
(prĭ-kō′shəs)
- *adjective*

- *Matilda* is an amusing book by Roald Dahl about a **precocious** little girl who reads an entire library of books before she begins first grade.
- Ms. Wolf is quite excited about one of her piano students, a **precocious** boy who not only plays very well but is already composing his own music.

__ *Precocious* means   A. prejudiced.   B. advanced for one's age.   C. tending to misbehave.

9 trepidation
(trĕp′ĭ-dā′shən)
- *noun*

- "It is with some **trepidation** that I put my plan before you," the consultant told the board of directors nervously, "since it involves moving the company to Siberia."
- "Yes," Grandpa remembered, "I experienced some **trepidation** on my wedding day. In fact, you could say I was scared to death."

__ *Trepidation* means   A. enthusiasm.   B. boredom.   C. anxiety.

10 virulent
(vîr′yə-lənt)
- *adjective*

- The mayor bitterly protested the newspaper's **virulent** attacks on her administration: "I demand an end to these attempts to poison the public's mind against me."
- Lung cancer is one of the most **virulent** forms of cancer, but though it is deadly, it is also highly preventable. Quitting smoking reduces the risk dramatically.

__ *Virulent* means   A. constant.   B. inconsistent.   C. destructive.

Matching Words with Definitions

Following are definitions of the ten words. Clearly write or print each word next to its definition. The sentences above and on the previous page will help you decide on the meaning of each word.

1. _____ Calmness of mind or manner; self-possession

2. _____ Very challenging; demanding

3. _____ An oddity; something different from what is normal or expected

4. _____ To praise highly; exalt

5. _____ Tending to escape; hard to catch hold of or identify

6. _____ Alarm or dread

7. _____ Very injurious; lethal; deadly

8. _____ Showing unusually early development or maturity, especially in mental ability

9. _____ Difficult to interpret or understand; puzzling

10. _____ Referring to a condition present at birth; inborn

CAUTION: Do not go any further until you are sure the above answers are correct. Then you can use the definitions to help you in the following practices. Your goal is eventually to know the words well enough so that you don't need to check the definitions at all.

Sentence Check 1

Using the answer line provided, complete each item below with the correct word from the box. Use each word once.

A. aberration	B. composure	C. congenital	D. elusive	E. extol
F. formidable	G. inscrutable	H. precocious	I. trepidation	J. virulent

_____ 1. That little boy's good nature is ___; he's been smiling since the day he was born.

_____ 2. Heidi adores her new job. She ___s everything about it, from her affable° coworkers to the great coffee in the lunchroom.

_____ 3. Wendy's friends vowed to maintain their ___ at her funeral, no matter how much they might break down and cry later in private.

_____ 4. As the great detective peered through his magnifying glass at the fingerprint, his expression was ___. No one could tell what he might be thinking.

_____ 5. Jian had a terrifying experience during the blackout—he was stuck in an elevator for seven hours. Now he never enters an elevator without ___.

_____ 6. One of Mrs. Thompson's first-graders is so ___ that she is reading at a high-school level and actually helps teach the other children.

_____ 7. After an hour of angry, ___ criticism from the audience, the company president stalked out of the stockholders' meeting. "I quit," he said. "Let someone else take all this abuse."

_____ 8. Jermain was trying to write a song, but the melody remained ___. Bits of it drifted into his mind but proved to be evanescent°, fading away before he could write them down.

_____ 9. Keeping up with housework, raising children, holding a job, and maintaining friendships is a(n) ___ task, yet many people somehow manage to do it all with only brief respites° from all their responsibilities.

_____ 10. Chicken eggs with two yolks are a(n) ___, but although they are unusual, you do find one from time to time.

NOTE: Now check your answers to these items by turning to page 176. Going over the answers carefully will help you prepare for the next two practices, for which answers are not given.

Sentence Check 2

Using the answer lines provided, complete each item below with **two** words from the box. Use each word once.

_____
_____ 1–2. People who ___ the wonders of modern medicine are sure to mention the victory over smallpox. This ___, deadly disease has been completely wiped out.

_____
_____ 3–4. Walking to the front of the class to give her speech, Cyndi felt such ___ that she could hardly keep her ___. She wanted to scream and run out of the room.

_____   5–6. Glenn has only one arm, and people assume that he must have lost the other
_____   in an accident. But in fact, this ___ is ___: he was born that way.

_____   7–8. Parents are not always cognizant° of the fact that having a very bright child
_____   can be a(n) ___ challenge. ___ kids need special nurturing to develop their
                               talents.

_____   9–10. In a well-written murder mystery, the solution to the crime should be ___,
_____   not easy to pinpoint. At the same time, the characters mustn't be completely
                               ___—the author should give some hints about their inner secrets and possible
                               motives.

Final Check: *Math Anxiety*

Here is a final opportunity for you to strengthen your knowledge of the ten words. First read the following selection carefully. Then fill in each blank with a word from the box at the top of the previous page. (Context clues will help you figure out which word goes in which blank.) Use each word once.

No one ever talks about "history anxiety" or even "chemistry anxiety," but "math anxiety" is common and widespread. It's amazing how many otherwise intelligent, capable people will tell you that they approach mathematics with fear and trembling. As a mathematician, I'm puzzled by their (1)_____. But I don't think math anxiety is (2)_____— people aren't born with a fear of math. I think it gets passed on like a(n) (3)_____ disease: one person catches it from another.

Picture a typical scene. A kid says to Dad or Mom, "Could you help me with my homework?" Dad (Mom) says "Sure" but then sees that the homework is a math problem, turns pale with terror, and loses his (her) (4)_____. "Math? Don't ask me to help with that. I can't do math. I always hated math." The kid gets the message: Mom (Dad) "can't do math," so it must be fearsome stuff. In fact, it must be a totally opaque°, (5)_____ mystery. If a child happens to have a predilection° for math and isn't terrified by it, that's considered a(n) (6)_____, almost freakish. What is this kid, a(n) (7)_____ genius or something?

In fact, though, math is not all that (8)_____; it's no harder to handle than other subjects, and it's less challenging than some. Allow me to (9)_____ the virtues of a math course. One, no labs. Two, no 500-word papers on the worst teacher you ever had. Three, no dreary hours in the library taking voluminous° notes on the Corn Laws. Four, in math—unlike history or sociology—the answers to questions are usually quite straightforward, even if they seem (10)_____ at first. They tend to be either right or wrong. True, a math course requires brainwork, but I hope you don't consider that a hindrance°. Muster your courage and give it a try. You too can overcome math anxiety!

Scores   Sentence Check 2 _____%   Final Check _____%

Enter your scores above and in the **Vocabulary Performance Chart** on the inside back cover of the book.

accommodate	officious
clairvoyant	preclude
contiguous	spurn
debilitate	stealthy
obliterate	taciturn

Ten Words in Context

In the space provided, write the letter of the meaning closest to that of each **boldfaced** word. Use the context of the sentences to help you figure out each word's meaning.

1 accommodate
(ə-kŏm′ə-dāt′)
- *verb*

- Most minivans can **accommodate** seven passengers.
- The hotel **accommodated** the extra children by putting cots in their parents' room.

___ *Accommodate* means   A. to accompany.   B. to eliminate.   C. to hold.

2 clairvoyant
(klâr-voi′ənt)
- *adjective*

- The back pages of many magazines are filled with ads for fortunetellers, palm-readers, psychics, and other supposedly **clairvoyant** people.
- The famous magician Harry Houdini exposed many people who falsely claimed to be **clairvoyant**. Being trained in stage magic, Houdini recognized the tricks used by those who pretended to see the future or talk with the dead.

___ *Clairvoyant* means   A. seeing beyond the senses.   B. well educated.   C. well traveled.

3 contiguous
(kən-tĭg′yoo-əs)
-*adjective*

- Portugal is unusual in that it is **contiguous** to just one other country. It shares a border only with Spain.
- The shopping center in Rodrigo's town has two **contiguous** supermarkets. No one can figure out why they were built side by side.

___ *Contiguous* means   A. contrasting.   B. alternating.   C. adjoining.

4 debilitate
(dĭ-bĭl′ĭ-tāt′)
- *verb*

- Influenza can seriously **debilitate** elderly patients, so older people should be sure to get a flu shot each year.
- Six of our star basketball players are graduating this year. That is likely to **debilitate** the team next season.

___ *Debilitate* means   A. to improve slightly.   B. to weaken.   C. to encourage.

5 obliterate
(ə-blĭt′ə-rāt′)
- *verb*

- At the ancient battlefield, the years had **obliterated** all traces of the bloody conflict. Nothing could be seen but grass and wildflowers.
- The commencement speaker said, "This is a proud day in your lives. I hope that time will never **obliterate** your memories of it."

___ *Obliterate* means   A. to preserve.   B. to add to.   C. to wipe out.

6 officious
(ə-fĭsh′əs)
- *adjective*

- Every college dorm seems to have one **officious** person who takes it upon himself or herself to monitor the noise level, reorganize the laundry room, and generally make everyone toe the line.
- Jayson's marriage is under a severe strain because his in-laws are too **officious**. They constantly intrude on him and his wife with suggestions, plans, and unasked-for help.

___ *Officious* means   A. interfering.   B. easily offended.   C. boring.

7 preclude
(prĭ-klōod′)
- *verb*

● When Sean asked if I liked the short story he'd written, my natural politeness **precluded** me from answering honestly.

● The president of the Acme Company told the employees, "Declining sales and a costly lawsuit **preclude** any pay raises this year."

___ *Preclude* means   A. to rule out.   B. to include.   C. to predict.

8 spurn
(spûrn)
- *verb*

● After he was **spurned** by the first girl he invited to the prom, Taylor felt too scared to ask anyone else.

● The employees **spurned** the contract their company offered them and went on strike instead.

___ *Spurn* means   A. to accept.   B. to reject.   C. to meet.

9 stealthy
(stĕl′thē)
- *adjective*

● The cat crept up on the bird in a slow, **stealthy** manner, keeping low to the ground and making no sound.

● All the preparations for Raymond's surprise party had to be **stealthy**. We didn't want him to know what was going on, so we kept our activities hidden.

___ *Stealthy* means   A. secretive.   B. stupid.   C. unsteady.

10 taciturn
(tăs′ĭ-tûrn′)
- *adjective*

● Uncle Maury is a **taciturn** man. At dinner this Thanksgiving, he made only one remark: "Please pass the gravy."

● Joelle listens very sympathetically to other people's troubles, but she's **taciturn** about her own. If she has a problem, you're unlikely to hear about it from her.

___ *Taciturn* means   A. opinionated.   B. uninformed.   C. reluctant to talk.

Matching Words with Definitions

Following are definitions of the ten words. Clearly write or print each word next to its definition. The sentences above and on the previous page will help you decide on the meaning of each word.

1. _____ To deprive of strength or energy

2. _____ Having the supposed power to see things not perceived by the normal senses

3. _____ Offering unwanted advice or services; meddlesome

4. _____ To make impossible in advance; prevent

5. _____ Sharing an edge or a boundary

6. _____ To destroy or erase completely

7. _____ To reject or refuse with scorn

8. _____ Habitually nontalkative; uncommunicative

9. _____ Moving or acting in a cautious, deceptive way; sneaky

10. _____ To provide with something needed; make or have room for

CAUTION: Do not go any further until you are sure the above answers are correct. Then you can use the definitions to help you in the following practices. Your goal is eventually to know the words well enough so that you don't need to check the definitions at all.

Sentence Check 1

Using the answer line provided, complete each item below with the correct word from the box. Use each word once.

A. accommodate	B. clairvoyant	C. contiguous	D. debilitate	E. obliterate
F. officious	G. preclude	H. spurn	I. stealthy	J. taciturn

_____ 1. The children sitting on the beach burst into tears when the tide came in and a wave ___(e)d their elaborate sand drawing.

_____ 2. If you are naturally ___, don't become a TV sportscaster. Sports announcers have to be garrulous°—they're expected to talk nonstop.

_____ 3. Moving with slow, ___ steps, the hungry leopard approached the unsuspecting antelope.

_____ 4. My brother ran for city council, but his campaign was ___(e)d by lack of funds. In the end, he had to drop out of the race.

_____ 5. The army base where Dad was stationed was ___ to the grounds of a mental hospital. The soldiers made a lot of jokes about who belonged where.

_____ 6. "Don't ask me to order your meal," Liz pleaded with her mother at the restaurant. "I'm not ___; I don't know what you'll like or not like."

_____ 7. In the fairy tale "King Thrushbeard," a proud princess ___s a good king's offer of marriage but later learns to love and admire him.

_____ 8. Ron's house is specially built to ___ his wheelchair. It has ramps instead of stairs, and extra-wide doors.

_____ 9. Reiko decided to get married in the winter, even though the cold weather would ___ an outdoor reception.

_____ 10. Grandfather's home health aide is too ___. Not content with just doing her job, she bustles in each day full of self-importance and tries to run his life.

NOTE: Now check your answers to these items by turning to page 176. Going over the answers carefully will help you prepare for the next two practices, for which answers are not given.

Sentence Check 2

Using the answer lines provided, complete each item below with **two** words from the box. Use each word once.

_____
_____ 1–2. My roommate, claiming to be ___, offered to reveal my future by reading my palm. I didn't want to rebuff° or ___ her, so I agreed, but I thought it was all nonsense.

_____
_____ 3–4. The largest edifice° in Deepvale, the high school, was too small to ___ all the flood victims, so some of them were taken to a(n) ___ town for shelter.

_____
_____ 5–6. A migraine headache can completely ___ the victim. It may cause nausea and can be severe enough to ___ all activity: the sufferer cannot even sit up or keep his or her eyes open.

_____   7–8. The student in charge of planning a surprise baby shower for our librarian
_____   promised to make all the arrangements in a(n) ___ way. But since she is not
                                 at all ___, we were afraid she would blurt out the secret.

_____   9–10. Some ___ soul went around the dorm putting signs in the kitchens and
_____   bathrooms: "Do not make a mess." We were annoyed, but instead of taking
                                  them down, we decided simply to ___ the word "not."

Final Check: *The Roma*

Here is a final opportunity for you to strengthen your knowledge of the ten words. First read the following selection carefully. Then fill in each blank with a word from the box at the top of the previous page. (Context clues will help you figure out which word goes in which blank.) Use each word once.

Few groups in the world today are so little understood as the people called "Gypsies." It is significant that even the word *Gypsy* is based on a misunderstanding. *Gypsy* comes from *Egyptian*; Gypsies were once thought to have originated in Egypt. In fact, though, this idea was erroneous°: the Gypsy people originated in northwest India. It is more proper to call them the Roma; the language they speak is known as Romany.

Centuries ago, the Roma began wandering westward out of India. They became established in Hungary and in (1)_____ countries, such as Romania, Austria, and Czechoslovakia. Traditionally the Roma (2)_____(e)d the notion of settling permanently in one place. Traveling in groups by horse-drawn wagons, they meandered° all across Europe. The men were known as skillful horse-trainers, blacksmiths, musicians, and carvers. Many of the women claimed to be (3)_____ and would tell fortunes for a fee. Then as now, the Roma inspired strong feelings in others. Their affinity° for free-spirited wandering, their colorful dress, their music and dance, and their unusual language all fascinated outsiders. But other characteristics made non-Roma suspicious of them. The Roma kept to themselves; with outsiders, they were generally (4)_____. Moving constantly, they did not consider themselves citizens of any particular country, but were loyal only to themselves. Rumors followed the Roma; people claimed that they were (5)_____ bandits who stole livestock and sometimes children. They were even suspected of witchcraft. In 1721, the German emperor wanted the Roma suppressed° and their culture (6)_____(e)d. Many Roma in Germany were tracked down and killed.

In modern times, the Roma have not fared much better. Many countries have been unwilling to (7)_____ them or even tolerate them. It is estimated that half a million Roma were killed during the Nazi Holocaust. In parts of Europe, Roma children are often taken away for adoption or put in institutions by (8)_____ government agents who disapprove of the Roma culture. Skinheads and neo-Nazis have made the Roma a target of hate crimes. All these losses have (9)_____(e)d the Roma community.

There are probably eight to ten million Roma in the world today, with perhaps one million in the United States. Most Roma no longer travel but live in settled communities. Their steadfast° family ties and their long history of persecution (10)_____ any real trust of outsiders. Thus even today, they tend to be a people apart.

Scores	Sentence Check 2 _____%	Final Check _____%

Enter your scores above and in the **Vocabulary Performance Chart** on the inside back cover of the book.

cordial	indoctrinate
defame	submissive
discordant	sullen
grueling	thwart
indict	wanton

Ten Words in Context

In the space provided, write the letter of the meaning closest to that of each **boldfaced** word. Use the context of the sentences to help you figure out each word's meaning.

1 cordial
(kôr′jəl)
- *adjective*

● Moving into their new apartment, Lee and Ron received a **cordial** welcome from their next-door neighbors, who brought them flowers and a chocolate cake.

● "I hate having to act sweet and **cordial** to my in-laws," Rosa complained, "when I really don't like them very much."

___ *Cordial* means   A. grumpy.   B. gracious.   C. sophisticated.

2 defame
(dĭ-fām′)
- *verb*

● Li thought he knew who had stolen his iPod, but he wasn't sure, and he didn't want to **defame** the person by making a false accusation. He didn't know what to do.

● After the test, the instructor quietly drew Annie aside. "I don't want to **defame** you," she said, "but I think you were cheating. Can you explain why you kept looking at your cell phone during the test?"

___ *Defame* means   A. to dispute.   B. to misunderstand.   C. to slander.

3 discordant
(dĭ-skôr′dnt)
- *adjective*

● The colors in the living room are **discordant**. We should have realized that orange, purple, and lime green would clash.

● The performance of the marching band has improved amazingly. At the beginning of the school year it was **discordant**, but now it's in perfect tune.

___ *Discordant* means   A. not visible.   B. not intended.   C. not in harmony.

4 grueling
(grōō′ə-lĭng)
- *adjective*

● Before running the marathon, Dolores worked hard—training, eating carefully, and preparing her mind and body for the **grueling** race.

● In Japan, high-school seniors spend weeks cramming for the **grueling** exam that will determine whether or not they go to college.

___ *Grueling* means   A. stressful.   B. relaxing.   C. amusing.

5 indict
(ĭn-dīt′)
- *verb*

● You can't really **indict** a cat for killing birds; the cat is only doing what is natural.

● In many divorces, each person **indicts** the other as being more to blame for the marriage's breakdown.

___ *Indict* means   A. to advise.   B. to accuse.   C. to inform.

6 indoctrinate
(ĭn-dŏk′trə-nāt′)
- *verb*

● Nazi leaders **indoctrinated** their followers with the idea that there was a "master race" which deserved to rule over the rest of humanity.

● Elsie criticized her brother for teaching his children that his religious beliefs were the only acceptable ones. But he responded, "It's not wrong to **indoctrinate** your children with the truth."

___ *Indoctrinate* means   A. to instruct.   B. to tease.   C. to blame.

7 submissive
(səb-mĭs′ĭv)
- *adjective*

● Some dogs are dominant, seeking to establish power over other dogs. Other dogs are **submissive**, immediately showing that they will offer no resistance.

● Strict parents expect their children to be **submissive**. By contrast, easygoing parents focus less on being obeyed and more on developing a child's independence.

___ *Submissive* means   A. unresisting.   B. depressed.   C. affectionate.

8 sullen
(sŭl′ən)
- *adjective*

● "Leave the table and go to your room!" said little Ann's father when she wouldn't stop kicking her brother. "And wipe that **sullen** look off your face, or no TV for a week."

● Cary's girlfriend has been **sullen** and silent for days. "What's wrong, sweetie?" he asks. "Nothing!" she snaps.

___ *Sullen* means   A. frightened.   B. disagreeable.   C. overexcited.

9 thwart
(thwôrt)
- *verb*

● The burglars' attempt to break into our house was **thwarted** by our dog, who barked loudly and frightened them off.

● "Lack of education will **thwart** all your ambitions," warned the guidance counselor, "so stay in school."

___ *Thwart* means   A. to block.   B. to hide.   C. to assist.

10 wanton
(wŏn′tən)
- *adjective*

● As Vernon worked at his term paper at his desk near an open window, a sudden, **wanton** gust of wind scattered the pages and his notes in all directions.

● **Wanton** violence is terrifying because we can see no sense in it and therefore cannot think how to prevent or avoid it.

___ *Wanton* means   A. disguised.   B. obvious.   C. mindless.

Matching Words with Definitions

Following are definitions of the ten words. Clearly write or print each word next to its definition. The sentences above and on the previous page will help you decide on the meaning of each word.

1. _____   To damage the good name or reputation of

2. _____   Physically or mentally exhausting

3. _____   To teach a specific body of doctrine or point of view, excluding other opinions; to impose a partisan° or one-sided way of thinking

4. _____   Giving in to the authority of others; obedient

5. _____   Quietly resentful; bitter; irritable

6. _____   To oppose and defeat; obstruct, frustrate

7. _____   Lacking agreement; lacking harmony

8. _____   To charge with an offense; blame

9. _____   Warm and friendly

10. _____   Senseless

CAUTION: Do not go any further until you are sure the above answers are correct. Then you can use the definitions to help you in the following practices. Your goal is eventually to know the words well enough so that you don't need to check the definitions at all.

Sentence Check 1

Using the answer line provided, complete each item below with the correct word from the box. Use each word once.

A. **cordial**	B. **defame**	C. **discordant**	D. **grueling**	E. **indict**
F. **indoctrinate**	G. **submissive**	H. **sullen**	I. **thwart**	J. **wanton**

_____ 1. The meal took a lot of work, but the results were ___. Pork and sauerkraut do not go very well with ice cream and cake for dessert.

_____ 2. A grand jury hears evidence and then decides whether the evidence is sufficient to ___ someone for a crime.

_____ 3. The prisoner's wife said he had been ___(e)d, but she would clear his name.

_____ 4. The employees seemed ___ about having to work late. Hoping to improve their mood, the boss sent out for coffee and sandwiches.

_____ 5. "The movie is excellent, but watching it is a(n) ___ experience," Rafael warned his friends. "The story is so tragic that it drains you emotionally."

_____ 6. Don't let "test anxiety" ___ your efforts to earn good grades. Learn how to avoid it by being well prepared and developing a positive attitude.

_____ 7. Members of racist hate groups, such as the Ku Klux Klan, ___ their children with the belief that one racial group is better than another.

_____ 8. "As flies to ___ boys, are we to the gods; they kill us for their sport." These words from Shakespeare's *King Lear* mean that fate can injure us senselessly.

_____ 9. In public, my grandmother was ___ to my grandfather, agreeing with whatever he said. In private, however, she bossed him around a good deal.

_____ 10. Even after their divorce, Max and Amy remained ___ to each other. "We were always good friends," Max tells people, "and we still are."

NOTE: Now check your answers to these items by turning to page 176. Going over the answers carefully will help you prepare for the next two practices, for which answers are not given.

Sentence Check 2

Using the answer lines provided, complete each item below with **two** words from the box. Use each word once.

_____
_____ 1–2. A false friend is one who is ___ to you to your face but then tries to disparage° and ___ you behind your back.

_____
_____ 3–4. To ___ political prisoners with government propaganda that would obliterate° their previous beliefs, the secret police subjected them to a(n) ___ "reeducation" program and even to torture.

_____
_____ 5–6. The grand jury refused to ___ the murder suspect, because the meager° evidence against him did not hold together—there was too much contradictory, ___ testimony.

_____
_____ 7–8. When small children try to do something dangerous, it is necessary to ___ them, even if being stopped makes them angry, querulous°, and ___.

_____ 9–10. A child who is "different" will often be the object of teasing and even ___ cruelty from other children, whether the child is ___ or fights back.

_____

Final Check: *The Jonestown Tragedy*

Here is a final opportunity for you to strengthen your knowledge of the ten words. First read the following selection carefully. Then fill in each blank with a word from the box at the top of the previous page. (Context clues will help you figure out which word goes in which blank.) Use each word once.

Cults are religious communities that isolate their members from mainstream society. They demand steadfast° devotion from their members, who in turn depend on the cult for their own sense of self-worth. This isolation and loyalty can produce bizarre results. One of the most bizarre, and tragic, cult-related stories occurred in 1978 in Jonestown, a settlement in the South American country of Guyana. It involved a man named Jim Jones and an organization called the People's Temple.

By most accounts, Jones was a sincere and helpful young pastor when he founded the People's Temple in Indiana in the 1950s. He preached about racial harmony and social justice. His congregation was a mixture of black and white, mostly low-income people. In 1965, Jones and about one hundred of his followers moved to San Francisco. Here, Jones became increasingly authoritarian°. He insisted that members of the temple call him "Father." In his sermons, he continued to (1)_____ American society as racist and unjust. But he also began attacking many individuals he claimed were enemies of the Temple. He predicted a nuclear war that would destroy the world, but promised that Temple members would survive if they were (2)_____ to his will. Increasingly Jones (3)_____(e)d the members with the idea that he alone deserved their loyalty.

By 1977, things were not going well for the Temple. Some members—a(n) (4)_____ element—had left. Jones claimed that they were trying to (5)_____ and vilify° him. When he was not preaching his hours-long diatribes°, he was often (6)_____ and taciturn°, refusing to speak to anyone. Finally he announced that the Temple was moving to Guyana. There, he said, no one would be able to (7)_____ him and his mission.

After Jones and his followers left the country, former members of the Temple and relatives of those in Guyana began to fear that Temple members were being held against their will. They also said that members were being forced to keep up a(n) (8)_____ schedule of work with little sleep. Congressman Leo Ryan, some concerned relatives, and a few journalists went to visit Jonestown. When they arrived, Jones seemed (9)_____ enough. He encouraged them to wander through Jonestown. The people they saw seemed happy. But as Ryan and the others were leaving, two Temple families slipped notes to him in a stealthy° way. They said that they wanted to leave Jonestown, but Jones would not allow it. Ryan added the families to his party. As they started to board their plane, gunmen from the Temple opened fire. Five people, including Ryan, were killed.

As Ryan and the others were being shot, Jones gathered the community at Jonestown. He announced that the People's Temple would now commit "revolutionary suicide." Followers brought out tubs of a poisoned fruit drink. Parents fed the drink to their children, then took it themselves. By the time emergency workers reached the scene, the entire community—over nine hundred men, women, and children—had died. Jones died along with his followers.

As the news reports came out of Jonestown, people around the world were appalled° by such a (10)_____ loss of life. Probably no one but the dead themselves could explain what drove so many to kill themselves at the request of a madman.

Scores   Sentence Check 2 _____%   Final Check _____%

The box at the right lists twenty-five words from Unit Four. Using the clues at the bottom of the page, fill in these words to complete the puzzle that follows.

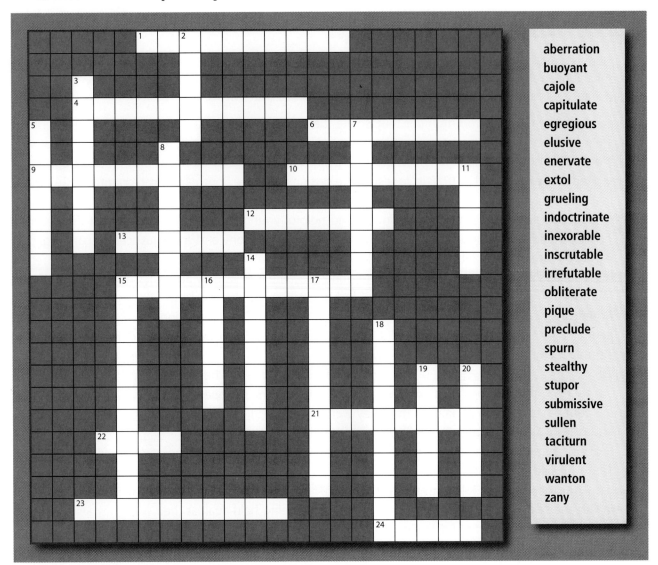

aberration
buoyant
cajole
capitulate
egregious
elusive
enervate
extol
grueling
indoctrinate
inexorable
inscrutable
irrefutable
obliterate
pique
preclude
spurn
stealthy
stupor
submissive
sullen
taciturn
virulent
wanton
zany

ACROSS

1. To give in
4. Impossible to disprove
6. Moving or acting in a cautious, deceptive way
9. To destroy or erase completely
10. Conspicuously bad
12. Hard to catch hold of or identify
13. Quietly resentful; bitter
15. To teach a specific body of doctrine or point of view
21. Habitually nontalkative
22. Wildly silly or comical
23. Not capable of being influenced or prevented
24. To praise highly

DOWN

2. A feeling of resentment or anger due to wounded pride
3. Very injurious; deadly
5. Able to float or rise
7. To weaken; rob of strength or energy
8. To make impossible in advance; prevent
11. To reject or refuse with scorn
14. Physically or mentally exhausting
15. Difficult to interpret or understand
16. To persuade with flattery
17. An oddity; something different from what is normal or expected
18. Obedient
19. A state of mental numbness; daze
20. Senseless

PART A

Choose the word that best completes each item and write it in the space provided.

_____ 1. When his guitar string broke during his performance, Marty did not lose his ___. He just smiled, calmly put on a new string, and continued to play.

    A. trepidation   B. composure   C. stupor   D. premonition

_____ 2. This hot weather ___ the polar bears at the zoo. Accustomed to cold weather, they are exhausted by the extreme heat.

    A. enervates   B. piques   C. precludes   D. cajoles

_____ 3. The statue has been ___ by years of exposure to the rain, snow, and wind.

    A. taciturn   B. egregious   C. marred   D. submissive

_____ 4. Since the Wilsons never travel anywhere without their cat and dog, they have to find hotels that are willing to ___ pets.

    A. extol   B. preclude   C. defame   D. accommodate

_____ 5. "When I first met Hal, his silence made me believe he was thinking deep thoughts," admitted Rhoda. "He's still ___, but I now suspect that he isn't really thinking at all."

    A. stealthy   B. clairvoyant   C. satirical   D. taciturn

_____ 6. "Somehow or other, I let my children ___ me into inviting seven of their best friends to sleep over on Friday night," Nadia confessed. "Why did I ever say 'yes' to such an idea?"

    A. cajole   B. obliterate   C. extol   D. indoctrinate

_____ 7. The Broadway show was a(n) ___ failure—not only did it close after its first performance, but more than half of the audience walked out before the third act.

    A. egregious   B. reverent   C. zany   D. cordial

_____ 8. When I shop for clothes, I need a true, honest friend to go with me, not a ___ who will say that everything I try on looks beautiful.

    A. premonition   B. sycophant   C. trepidation   D. composure

_____ 9. The school talent show is always a lot of fun. The faculty members put on ___ costumes—last year the chair of the English department dressed as a cabbage—and make fun of themselves.

    A. urbane   B. zany   C. sullen   D. discordant

_____ 10. I find it hard to be ___ to my sister-in-law, knowing how she criticizes me behind my back, but so far I've managed to be polite.

    A. wanton   B. grueling   C. officious   D. cordial

(Continues on next page)

_____ 11. Dennis was determined not to buy the vacuum cleaner, but he ___ when the salesman threw in a combination vegetable chopper and knife sharpener.

       A. spurned   B. precluded   C. capitulated   D. obliterated

_____ 12. When a bank teller didn't recognize him and asked for some identification, the rich client was furious. In a fit of ___, he withdrew his money and took it to a different bank.

       A. pique   B. premonition   C. stupor   D. aberration

_____ 13. The amusing 2002 movie *Catch Me If You Can* stars Leonardo DiCaprio as a(n) ___, identity-changing con man, always one step ahead of the FBI agent assigned to catch him.

       A. elusive   B. precocious   C. formidable   D. egregious

PART B

Write **C** if the italicized word is used **correctly**. Write **I** if the word is used **incorrectly**.

_____ 14. In order to make that plastic castle rest at the bottom of the fish tank, you'll have to weigh it down with something *buoyant,* like a stone.

_____ 15. "I'm the world's worst poker player," Will admitted. "I'm so *clairvoyant* that I never have a clue about what other players have in their hands."

_____ 16. Although I have only two minutes between algebra and Spanish, that's not a problem, because the two classes meet in *contiguous* classrooms.

_____ 17. Since neither my friend nor I had much money, we had dinner at a *prestigious* restaurant where we could just have a cheap hamburger.

_____ 18. After studying all night for her exam, Greta sat in class in a red-eyed *stupor,* unable to remember anything more than her own name.

_____ 19. The dentist keeps his radio tuned to a "smooth jazz" station, believing that patients are soothed by the quiet, *discordant* music.

_____ 20. Basic training in the Army is a *grueling* experience designed to toughen the new soldiers' bodies and minds with hard work and discipline.

_____ 21. Every kindergarten class seems to have at least one "boss," a child who is so *submissive* that the others naturally obey him or her.

_____ 22. Angry at having to clean her room rather than go out with her friends, Shelby stamped around the house with a *sullen* expression on her face.

_____ 23. Our cat and one of her kittens share an *aberration*—they each have six toes on each paw.

_____ 24. The supervisor *extolled* the maintenance worker for doing such a sloppy job of cleaning the floor.

_____ 25. Whistling happily and running up the steps two at a time, Jim was clearly filled with *trepidation.*

Score	(Number correct) _____ x 4 = _____%

PART A

On the answer line, write the word from the box that completes each item below. Use each word once.

A. debilitate	B. defame	C. formidable	D. indoctrinate	E. inscrutable
F. irrefutable	G. officious	H. partisan	I. preclude	J. premonition
K. satirical	L. virulent	M. wanton		

_____ 1. As soon as I heard my father's voice on the phone, I had a(n) ___ that he was about to tell me some bad news.

_____ 2. We say that a theory or argument is ___ when no one can disprove it.

_____ 3. Suzi wrote a(n) ___ essay on "The Joys of Surprise Quizzes," but her history teacher didn't realize that it was sarcastic. "I'm glad someone appreciates their value," he said.

_____ 4. Don't bother trying to get Uncle Ed to vote for your candidate. He is strictly ___—he has voted for the other party's candidates since 1986.

_____ 5. Being trapped without food and water for two days ___(e)d the hikers, leaving them as weak as newborn kittens.

_____ 6. Naomi's coworkers are tired of her ___ attitude. They say that she should just do her own job instead of worrying about how others are doing theirs.

_____ 7. "I'm sorry to have to cancel the party," said Mrs. Hendrix, "but Tommy's chicken pox ___(e)s it. We shouldn't have other children at the house."

_____ 8. The angry city councilman stormed into the newspaper office, claiming that the day's editorial had ___(e)d and embarrassed him.

_____ 9. If you ___ children at an early age with the idea that they must wear a seat belt, they are unlikely ever to give up the habit.

_____ 10. People working to aid the hungry often complain about the ___ waste by restaurants and supermarkets, which throw out enormous quantities of perfectly good food.

_____ 11. In fairy tales, heroes and heroines are often faced with ___ tasks, such as spinning straw into gold or counting the grains of sand on a beach.

_____ 12. As my instructor read my essay, her face was ___. I had no idea if she was pleased or disappointed.

_____ 13. The flu that swept over the town was so ___ that almost every family was affected. The schools closed, and most public meetings were canceled to try to halt the spread of the disease.

(Continues on next page)

PART B

Write **C** if the italicized word is used **correctly**. Write **I** if the word is used **incorrectly**.

_____ 14. From kindergarten on, Stan has always been a favorite with his teachers because he is so *incorrigible*.

_____ 15. At our annual dinner, we plan to *indict* several of the volunteers who have worked so hard to make our program a success.

_____ 16. Uncle Jake seems to take pride in being *parochial*. "I've never been outside the town I was born in, and I don't care about anything except what's right here," he says.

_____ 17. Builders, plumbers, electricians, and landscapers all worked around the clock in order to *thwart* plans to open the new supermarket on time.

_____ 18. Serafina *spurned* the job offer from a cigarette company. "I'm not going to help make something that sickens and kills people," she said.

_____ 19. Store detectives are trained to look for *stealthy* behaviors that could indicate someone is planning to shoplift.

_____ 20. Talking loudly or laughing during a church service is considered *reverent* behavior.

_____ 21. Michelle was embarrassed by her date's *urbane* behavior at the formal dinner. He showed up in a dirty sweatshirt and put his feet on the table.

_____ 22. Romeo and Juliet are two lovers in an unfortunate situation: their families are *inexorable* enemies, sworn to hate each other for all time.

_____ 23. The invading army *obliterated* the town, burning anything that remained standing.

_____ 24. Troy's limp is *congenital*. It's due to his twisting his ankle last week.

_____ 25. Because Matthew seemed so *precocious,* his parents and teachers decided it would be best if he repeated first grade.

Score   (Number correct) _____ x 4 = _____%

Enter your score above and in the **Vocabulary Performance Chart** on the inside back cover of the book.

PART A: Synonyms

In the space provided, write the letter of the choice that is most nearly the **same** in meaning as the **boldfaced** word.

_____ 1. **aberration**   A. an oddity   B. an expectation   C. an absence   D. a location

_____ 2. **accommodate**   A. to send away   B. to reply   C. to chase   D. to fit in

_____ 3. **cajole**   A. to prepare   B. to persuade   C. to correct   D. to torment

_____ 4. **clairvoyant**   A. intelligent   B. cautious   C. mind-reading   D. strong

_____ 5. **congenital**   A. local   B. creative   C. borrowed   D. inborn

_____ 6. **contiguous**   A. not matching   B. sharing a boundary   C. well-known   D. surprising

_____ 7. **defame**   A. to damage the good name of   B. to delay   C. to offer unwanted advice to   D. to reveal a secret

_____ 8. **discordant**   A. expensive   B. absent   C. lacking harmony   D. unjust

_____ 9. **egregious**   A. very friendly   B. silent   C. remarkably bad   D. tasteful

_____ 10. **extol**   A. to praise   B. to notice   C. to blame   D. to insist

_____ 11. **incorrigible**   A. quiet   B. unmanageable   C. having leadership qualities   D. creative

_____ 12. **indoctrinate**   A. to brainwash   B. to soothe   C. to try hard   D. to imitate

_____ 13. **inexorable**   A. easily moved   B. recent   C. genuine   D. inflexible

_____ 14. **irrefutable**   A. widespread   B. undeniable   C. washable   D. impossible

_____ 15. **marred**   A. damaged   B. improved   C. made taller   D. shrunk

_____ 16. **officious**   A. modern   B. meddlesome   C. well-planned   D. licensed

_____ 17. **partisan**   A. supporting a particular side   B. indecisive   C. not serious   D. hard-working

_____ 18. **preclude**   A. to separate   B. to deceive   C. to make impossible   D. to surprise

_____ 19. **premonition**   A. a forewarning   B. a rude comment   C. an excuse   D. a limit

_____ 20. **satirical**   A. mocking   B. complimentary   C. mistaken   D. foreign

_____ 21. **stupor**   A. absence   B. celebration   C. daze   D. joke

_____ 22. **sycophant**   A. a performer   B. a flatterer   C. an employee   D. a wine expert

_____ 23. **thwart**   A. to allow   B. to rehearse   C. to defeat   D. to complain

_____ 24. **virulent**   A. prepared   B. injurious   C. fake   D. fortunate

_____ 25. **wanton**   A. lacking   B. senseless   C. satisfied   D. careful

(Continues on next page)

PART B: Antonyms

In the space provided, write the letter of the choice that is most nearly **opposite** in meaning to the **boldfaced** word.

____ 26. **buoyant**   A. sinking   B. laughable   C. needed   D. dangerous

____ 27. **capitulate**   A. to welcome   B. to ignore   C. to pretend   D. to resist

____ 28. **composure**   A. luck   B. panic   C. politeness   D. mercy

____ 29. **cordial**   A. rude   B. frightened   C. awkward   D. confused

____ 30. **debilitate**   A. to select   B. to purify   C. to strengthen   D. to blame

____ 31. **elusive**   A. enlarged   B. harsh   C. safe   D. easily found

____ 32. **enervate**   A. to energize   B. to give in   C. to annoy   D. to push

____ 33. **formidable**   A. not legal   B. not demanding   C. hard to find   D. perfect

____ 34. **grueling**   A. slow-moving   B. honest   C. expensive   D. easy

____ 35. **indict**   A. to praise   B. to search for   C. to explain   D. to hide

____ 36. **inscrutable**   A. poorly planned   B. calm   C. able to be moved   D. easily understood

____ 37. **obliterate**   A. to observe closely   B. to build   C. to reason with   D. to fasten

____ 38. **parochial**   A. sophisticated   B. not decorated   C. unhealthy   D. exaggerated

____ 39. **pique**   A. honesty   B. pleasure   C. annoyance   D. effort

____ 40. **precocious**   A. fearful   B. mentally slow   C. very shy   D. sweet-tasting

____ 41. **prestigious**   A. flawless   B. needing repairs   C. lazy   D. having a poor reputation

____ 42. **reverent**   A. disrespectful   B. swollen   C. surprised   D. injured

____ 43. **spurn**   A. to prevent   B. to accept   C. to instruct   D. to speak quietly

____ 44. **stealthy**   A. quiet and sad   B. slow and careful   C. practical   D. open and direct

____ 45. **submissive**   A. disobedient   B. humorous   C. careless   D. relaxed

____ 46. **sullen**   A. fair   B. stubborn   C. cheerful   D. odd

____ 47. **taciturn**   A. rebellious   B. talkative   C. without expression   D. cruel

____ 48. **trepidation**   A. courage   B. anger   C. noisiness   D. good health

____ 49. **urbane**   A. expert   B. talkative   C. sorrowful   D. crude

____ 50. **zany**   A. insulting   B. serious   C. educated   D. sorry

Score   (Number correct) _____   x 2 = _____%

Enter your score above and in the **Vocabulary Performance Chart** on the inside back cover of the book.

Unit Five

Chapter 21

assiduous	fallacious
caustic	hypocrisy
chastise	insurgent
elucidate	placid
exalt	trite

Chapter 22

colloquial	judicious
crass	prerogative
discerning	tacit
hyperbole	tactless
incisive	whet

Chapter 23

ameliorate	negate
assent	potent
haphazard	rigorous
incontrovertible	spurious
intangible	therapeutic

Chapter 24

altercation	malevolent
circumspect	placate
deference	pugnacious
guile	tirade
impassive	volatile

Chapter 25

capricious	phenomenon
catharsis	rectify
discrepancy	resolution
ephemeral	retract
induce	serene

assiduous	fallacious
caustic	hypocrisy
chastise	insurgent
elucidate	placid
exalt	trite

Ten Words in Context

In the space provided, write the letter of the meaning closest to that of each **boldfaced** word. Use the context of the sentences to help you figure out each word's meaning.

1 assiduous
(ə-sĭj′o͞o-əs)
- *adjective*

- Our dog is an **assiduous** chewer. If we give him an old leather shoe, he will spend hours gnawing at it until he reduces it to a pile of scraps.
- Because Rafael has been an **assiduous** student this term, he will probably earn all A's.

___ *Assiduous* means   A. uncaring.   B. hard-working.   C. peaceful.

2 caustic
(kô′stĭk)
- *adjective*

- The writer Dorothy Parker was famous for her **caustic** wit. When she met a woman who had recently attempted suicide, Parker said, "Better luck next time."
- Cassie must have had a bad day. When I asked her how she was, her reply was **caustic**: "Oh, I'm just *wonderful*; now, if you'll excuse me, I'm going to lie down in the middle of traffic."

___ *Caustic* means   A. sarcastic.   B. careful.   C. old-fashioned.

3 chastise
(chăs′tīz′)
- *verb*

- The officer did not give Joe a ticket, but he did **chastise** him for driving with a burned-out headlight.
- The newspaper story **chastised** several city landlords for renting out filthy, unsafe apartments to poor families.

___ *Chastise* means   A. to admire.   B. to criticize.   C. to fear.

4 elucidate
(ĭ-lo͞o′sĭ-dāt′)
- *verb*

- To **elucidate** the stages of decision-making, the instructor drew a helpful chart on the chalkboard.
- When Mom told me her recipe for macaroni and cheese, I was only half listening. Later I asked her to **elucidate** some details, such as how much milk and flour to use.

___ *Elucidate* means   A. to understand.   B. to remember.   C. to make clear.

5 exalt
(ĭg-zôlt′)
- *verb*

- Some high schools **exalt** student athletes, making it seem that winning games is the most important thing in life.
- LaToya loves Siamese cats; in fact, she **exalts** them above all other pets.

___ *Exalt* means   A. to expect.   B. to praise.   C. to accompany.

6 fallacious
(fə-lā′shəs)
- *adjective*

- It would be **fallacious** to conclude that Norm and Lou are brothers just because they look alike. In fact, they're not related at all.
- Jerry's argument sounded good, but it was **fallacious**. He had based it on the wrong statistics.

___ *Fallacious* means   A. incorrect.   B. careful.   C. commonplace.

7 hypocrisy
(hĭ-pŏk′rĭ-sē)
- *noun*

- That candidate is guilty of **hypocrisy**. He promised to run a clean campaign, but all he's done so far is call his opponent names and tell lies about her.
- In order to avoid **hypocrisy**, simply remember the old saying, "Practice what you preach."

__ *Hypocrisy* means   A. falseness.   B. honesty.   C. prejudice.

8 insurgent
(ĭn-sûr′jənt)
- *noun*

- "If I lived under a dictatorship," Carmen confessed, "I think I would just keep quiet and try to stay out of trouble. I don't have the soul of an **insurgent**."
- As a young man, Uncle Kiril joined a group of **insurgents**. When their plot against the government was discovered, he had to flee for his life, and that's how he came to America.

__ *Insurgent* means   A. a rebel.   B. an elected official.   C. a candidate.

9 placid
(plăs′ĭd)
- *adjective*

- Jack and Cindy's first baby was restless and fussy, but their second baby was happy and **placid**.
- The two women who were waiting to hear if they had passed their driving test were very different. One was pacing up and down, a bundle of nerves, while the other was quietly reading a magazine and seemed quite **placid**.

__ *Placid* means   A. tense.   B. untroubled.   C. sad.

10 trite
(trīt)
- *adjective*

- "**Trite** but true—I love you!" was the poem accompanying the bouquet of roses.
- Tired of the **trite** expression "Have a nice day," Betty bought a T-shirt that said: "Don't tell me what kind of day to have."

__ *Trite* means   A. misunderstood.   B. original.   C. worn-out.

Matching Words with Definitions

Following are definitions of the ten words. Clearly write or print each word next to its definition. The sentences above and on the previous page will help you decide on the meaning of each word.

1. _____ To scold sharply

2. _____ To explain; clarify

3. _____ Based on error; mistaken

4. _____ Careful, hardworking, and thorough; diligent

5. _____ A person who revolts against established authority

6. _____ Peaceful; calm

7. _____ Overused and commonplace; stale

8. _____ To glorify; honor

9. _____ A pretense of having beliefs, feelings, or virtues that one does not actually possess; insincerity

10. _____ Sarcastic; biting; stinging

CAUTION: Do not go any further until you are sure the above answers are correct. Then you can use the definitions to help you in the following practices. Your goal is eventually to know the words well enough so that you don't need to check the definitions at all.

Sentence Check 1

Using the answer line provided, complete each item below with the correct word from the box. Use each word once.

| A. **assiduous** | B. **caustic** | C. **chastise** | D. **elucidate** | E. **exalt** |
| F. **fallacious** | G. **hypocrisy** | H. **insurgent** | I. **placid** | J. **trite** |

_____ 1. A good teacher can criticize her students' work without being ___; in other words, she does not attack the students with stinging sarcasm.

_____ 2. The police officer ___(e)d the driver for not wearing a seat belt.

_____ 3. Some ___s in the history class marched into the instructor's office and demanded an end to surprise quizzes. The instructor did not lose her composure°; she just laughed and told them to get back to their books.

_____ 4. The boys who washed the windows did such a(n) ___ job that they didn't leave a single speck of dust.

_____ 5. ___ expressions weaken a paper. One expert on writing even advises that if you have ever seen a phrase in print before, don't use it.

_____ 6. We assumed that Route 58 connects with Route 59. Unfortunately, our reasoning was ___; the two roads are nowhere near each other.

_____ 7. As our class discussed immigration reform, I found it hard to ___ my opinion. I think that the current laws are wrong, but I can't say exactly why.

_____ 8. It took all my self-control to look ___ during the job interview. Inside I was nervous and excited.

_____ 9. Shelly's ___ bothers me. She pretends to be very fond of her brother's girlfriend, but then she insults and defames° the poor girl behind her back.

_____ 10. Because Ralph wants his daughter to go to the state university, he ___s it above all other schools whenever they discuss colleges.

NOTE: Now check your answers to these items by turning to page 177. Going over the answers carefully will help you prepare for the next two practices, for which answers are not given.

Sentence Check 2

Using the answer lines provided, complete each item below with **two** words from the box. Use each word once.

_____
_____ 1–2. A careful writer makes ___ efforts to avoid ___, hackneyed°, overused words and phrases.

_____
_____ 3–4. Many people tend to admire and even ___ rebels, believing that they must be heroes. But whether a(n) ___ deserves praise depends on what he or she is rebelling against.

_____
_____ 5–6. It's ___ to assume that Sanjay has no worries just because he seems ___. A calm exterior may conceal anxiety, sadness, and even rage.

_____ 7–8. The play *Tartuffe* by Molière is about a wicked man who pretends to be very righteous. When people said the play was an attack on religion, the playwright tried to ___ his point: he explained that he was attacking not true religion, but religious ___.

_____ 9–10. "I don't like to ___ anyone," the boss always says. But her brusque° remarks about anything that someone has done wrong are often so ___ and wounding that she does seem to take pleasure in scolding people.

Final Check: *Helen Keller*

Here is a final opportunity for you to strengthen your knowledge of the ten words. First read the following selection carefully. Then fill in each blank with a word from the box at the top of the previous page. (Context clues will help you figure out which word goes in which blank.) Use each word once.

Most American schoolchildren know the story of Helen Keller—or at least they think they do. They know that Keller, who was born in 1880, became blind and deaf as a tiny child. They know she grew up wild and incorrigible°, unable to communicate, imprisoned in her dark world. They know she was befriended by a sagacious° teacher, Anne Sullivan, who taught her to speak, read, and write. For most people, those few scanty° facts sum up the Helen Keller story. She is often (1)_____(e)d as an unfortunate child who succeeded with the help of a dedicated teacher. *The Miracle Worker,* a famous play about Keller and Sullivan that was also made into a movie, (2)_____s these points.

But compared with Keller's full story, that version of her accomplishments is oversimplified and (3)_____. As an adult, she led a fascinating and controversial life as one of the best-known (4)_____s of her day. After graduating from college, she joined the American Socialist Party. She supported the communist revolution in Russia. She was a(n) (5)_____ worker for women's rights, leading marches of women demanding the vote. Through visiting slums, sweatshops, and hospitals, she learned that most disabled people did not have the opportunities she had as a child in a well-off family. She (6)_____(e)d political leaders for supporting a system in which poor people often became blind through industrial accidents and untreated disease. Then, she herself was criticized for her attacks. One newspaper editor was particularly (7)_____: he said that Keller's thinking was (8)_____ because of her disabilities, which precluded° her understanding things very well. In her reply, Keller pointed out that she had once met this editor, and she suggested that he was guilty of (9)_____ or duplicity°. "At the time [we met], the compliments he paid me were so generous that I blush to remember them," she wrote. "But now that I have come out for socialism he reminds me . . . that I am blind and deaf and especially liable to error. I must have shrunk in intelligence during the years since I met him." It is erroneous° to think of Keller as a(n) (10)_____, sweet symbol of victory over disability. She was a fiery spokeswoman for those who were as voiceless as she had once been.

| Scores | Sentence Check 2 _____% | Final Check _____% |

colloquial	judicious
crass	prerogative
discerning	tacit
hyperbole	tactless
incisive	whet

Ten Words in Context

In the space provided, write the letter of the meaning closest to that of each **boldfaced** word. Use the context of the sentences to help you figure out each word's meaning.

1 colloquial
(kə-lō′kwē-əl)
- *adjective*

● I enjoyed the lecturer's easygoing, **colloquial** style. He made the topic more interesting than a stiff, formal speaker could have done.

● Devan has two entirely different ways of talking: he uses **colloquial**, slangy words with his friends, but conventional, precise language at work.

__ *Colloquial* means   A. deceptive.   B. unclear.   C. informal.

2 crass
(krăs)
- *adjective*

● My brother enjoys a certain stand-up comic whom I find simply **crass**. I can't understand what's funny about being crude and insulting.

● The candidate lost the election after making a stupid joke about his opponent's weight. We were amazed at the damage one **crass** comment can do.

__ *Crass* means   A. humorless.   B. tasteless.   C. meaningless.

3 discerning
(dĭ-sûr′nĭng)
- *adjective*

● "That's an extremely **discerning** comment," the teacher said to Carmela. "Congratulations—you've been using your powers of observation."

● Mothers are the most **discerning** people on earth, as you'll agree if you've ever tried to hide anything from yours.

__ *Discerning* means   A. observant.   B. nasty.   C. bragging.

4 hyperbole
(hī-pûr′bə-lē)
- *noun*

● "My entire *life* will be *ruined* if you won't let me borrow your dress!" said my sister, causing me to laugh at her **hyperbole**.

● Marcella is a very dramatic person who uses a lot of **hyperbole** to express herself: a restaurant is never just "good"—it's "the most fabulous food in the universe"; her boyfriend isn't just "good-looking"—he's "divine beyond belief."

__ *Hyperbole* means   A. overstatement.   B. compliment.   C. accuracy.

5 incisive
(ĭn-sī′sĭv)
- *adjective*

● Ms. Martin is a great teacher. Her lectures are clear, **incisive**, and to the point.

● Sherlock Holmes, the fictional detective, is famous for his **incisive** mind. From just a few small clues, he makes brilliant deductions and solves the most difficult cases.

__ *Incisive* means   A. silly.   B. hesitant.   C. keen.

6 judicious
(jōō-dĭsh′əs)
- *adjective*

● Merle's decisions are **judicious**: he never does anything without careful thought.

● It was not **judicious** of Jen to stay up until 4 a.m. cramming for her exam. She was so exhausted when the test began that she couldn't remember the answers to the questions.

__ *Judicious* means   A. predictable.   B. wise.   C. exaggerated.

7 prerogative
(prĭ-rŏg′ə-tĭv)
- *noun*

● Just because you told the salesman you might buy the car doesn't mean you must buy it. You have the **prerogative** of changing your mind.

● A person suspected of a crime has the **prerogative** of refusing to answer questions unless his or her lawyer is present.

__ *Prerogative* means   A. a choice.   B. a duty.   C. a belief.

8 tacit
(tăs′ĭt)
- *adjective*

● Rosemary and her boyfriend aren't officially engaged, but they have a **tacit** understanding that they'll be getting married sooner or later.

● Most families seem to have a **tacit** agreement about who sits where at the dining table. Everyone always takes the same place, although the seating has never been discussed.

__ *Tacit* means   A. unusual.   B. unstated.   C. insensitive.

9 tactless
(tăkt′lĭs)
- *adjective*

● "If you don't want to eat the spinach quiche," Richard told his kids, "just say, 'No, thanks.' It's **tactless** to say, 'No, it's yucky.'"

● "How could you have been so **tactless**?" Marie said to Jim. "Even if it's true, you do *not* tell the hostess, 'We're really bored, so we're going home now.'"

__ *Tactless* means   A. long-winded.   B. insensitive.   C. intelligent.

10 whet
(wĕt *or* hwĕt)
- *verb*

● The opening scene of a TV drama must capture the audience's attention immediately, to **whet** viewers' interest in the story that is about to unfold.

● At newspaper stands in New York, the headlines are usually hidden from view. In London, however, headlines are boldly displayed. I wonder which system **whets** people's curiosity more.

__ *Whet* means   A. to arouse.   B. to account for.   C. to distract.

Matching Words with Definitions

Following are definitions of the ten words. Clearly write or print each word next to its definition. The sentences above and on the previous page will help you decide on the meaning of each word.

1. _____ Having keen insight; perceptive; clear-eyed

2. _____ Penetrating; clear and sharp; pointed

3. _____ Coarse; vulgar

4. _____ Related to informal speech or writing; conversational

5. _____ Showing good judgment; prudent; wise and careful

6. _____ Lacking skill or sensitivity in dealing with others

7. _____ Understood but not spoken; implied

8. _____ To excite or stimulate (the mind or appetite)

9. _____ A special right or privilege

10. _____ Obvious exaggeration, usually for effect or emphasis

CAUTION: Do not go any further until you are sure the above answers are correct. Then you can use the definitions to help you in the following practices. Your goal is eventually to know the words well enough so that you don't need to check the definitions at all.

Sentence Check 1

Using the answer line provided, complete each item below with the correct word from the box. Use each word once.

A. **colloquial**	B. **crass**	C. **discerning**	D. **hyperbole**	E. **incisive**
F. **judicious**	G. **prerogative**	H. **tacit**	I. **tactless**	J. **whet**

_____ 1. I can spend a long time reading the dictionary. Looking up one word ___s my curiosity about another, and the time passes without my noticing.

_____ 2. The play seemed very realistic: the stage set looked just like an ordinary apartment, and the dialog was ___—the characters used ordinary, commonplace words and phrases.

_____ 3. True, Aunt Myra can be irritating, but to call her "the most annoying person in the solar system" is ___.

_____ 4. The TV journalist is famous for her ___ questioning. Her sharp, pointed questions quickly reveal her subjects' real thoughts and feelings.

_____ 5. Before Uncle Trevor came to visit, we brought out the hideous painting he had given us and hung it up again. He's a(n) ___ man and would have noticed immediately if it was missing.

_____ 6. I love my older brother, but his ___ behavior at the wedding embarrassed me. He insisted on kissing every woman there and told loud, unfunny jokes.

_____ 7. The salesclerk seemed to make a(n) ___ assumption that I had a lot of money to spend on a coat. She lost interest when I said that I was on a tight budget.

_____ 8. It was rather ___ of Jon to brag about his great new job in front of Stan, who had just lost his. No wonder Stan walked away in a fit of pique°!

_____ 9. Years ago, schools used to hold "Sadie Hawkins Day" dances, to which girls had the ___ of inviting boys. But these days, girls don't need a special day to exercise that right.

_____ 10. Dropping out of school is seldom a(n) ___ decision, but many young people spurn° their opportunity to get an education and drop out anyway.

NOTE: Now check your answers to these items by turning to page 177. Going over the answers carefully will help you prepare for the next two practices, for which answers are not given.

Sentence Check 2

Using the answer lines provided, complete each item below with **two** words from the box. Use each word once.

_____
_____ 1–2. Lidia is not a very ___ woman. She never noticed when her own husband shaved off his beard, or when her son lost fifty pounds—and that's fact, not ___!

_____
_____ 3–4. Bart keeps trying to indoctrinate° us with his political views. It's his ___ to say whatever he wants, but his comments aren't original or ___; he just repeats whatever he hears on talk radio.

_____   5–6. In writing a paper, it is ___ to avoid ___ language. Although these casual
_____   phrases are fine for everyday conversation, they are usually considered out of
                                place in a student essay.

_____   7–8. The speaker intended to ___ his audience's interest by opening with a
_____   deliberately ___ remark. But his wanton° and egregious° vulgarity shocked
                                and angered his listeners.

_____   9–10. There was a(n) ___ agreement in the office never to mention the boss's
_____   speech impediment. But one day a(n) ___ visitor unintentionally thwarted°
                                the plan when he blurted out, "What a terrible stutter!"

Final Check: *Figures of Speech*

Here is a final opportunity for you to strengthen your knowledge of the ten words. First read the following selection carefully. Then fill in each blank with a word from the box at the top of the previous page. (Context clues will help you figure out which word goes in which blank.) Use each word once.

Authors often use figures of speech, and a(n) (1)_____ reader should be able to perceive and analyze these expressions. But figurative language is not the (2)_____ of only professional writers; fledgling° student writers are entitled to use it too. Here are a few examples.

(3)_____, or exaggeration, is a common figure of speech, as in this description of a bombastic° speaker: "The lecturer never used a word with fewer than ten syllables." Meiosis, or understatement, is its opposite—as when you get an A+ on a paper and say, "Not too bad." Simile and metaphor are very well known. In a simile, you state a comparison: "Jane is as thin as a toothpick." In a metaphor, however, the comparison is not stated but (4)_____: "Jane is a toothpick."

We all use euphemism to avoid sounding (5)_____ or unfeeling: "Jane had a nervous breakdown" is less caustic° and more sympathetic than "Jane went nuts." Dysphemism is the opposite of euphemism: it means being harsher than necessary, often for a humorous effect, as when you call a child "the little monster." Dysphemism appears in many (6)_____ and slang expressions, such as "bad" (meaning *good*) and "crazy" (meaning *wonderful*). Another type of dysphemism is deliberately using a vulgar, (7)_____ expression—such as an obscenity in a formal setting—to jolt and shock the audience.

Thoughtful, (8)_____ use of figures of speech can improve your writing. But don't pepper your papers with them, and don't expect them to work miracles: they won't turn a flabby, desultory° paper into a sharp, (9)_____ one, and they won't make an insipid°, plodding paper effervescent°. There are many other figurative expressions. If this brief review (10)_____s your appetite for more, try looking up *oxymoron, onomatopoeia,* and *paronomasia.*

Scores   Sentence Check 2 _____%   Final Check _____%

Enter your scores above and in the **Vocabulary Performance Chart** on the inside back cover of the book.

ameliorate	negate
assent	potent
haphazard	rigorous
incontrovertible	spurious
intangible	therapeutic

Ten Words in Context

In the space provided, write the letter of the meaning closest to that of each **boldfaced** word. Use the context of the sentences to help you figure out each word's meaning.

1 ameliorate
(ə-mēl′yə-rāt′)
- *verb*

- The precinct Outreach Committee was established to **ameliorate** troublesome police-community relations.
- Strained communication between parents and kids can often be **ameliorated** by just a few meetings with a family therapist.

__ *Ameliorate* means   A. to improve.   B. to make worse.   C. to end.

2 assent
(ə-sĕnt′)
- *verb*

- A doctor wrote a book advising parents to let their kids live on candy if that's what the kids wanted. Most parents would not **assent** to this proposal, though.
- When a motion is voted on in a formal meeting, the "ayes," or "yes" votes, are those who **assent**. The "nays," or "no" votes, are those who disagree.

__ *Assent* means   A. to express agreement.   B. to have a different opinion.   C. not to care.

3 haphazard
(hăp-hăz′ərd)
- *adjective*

- I never make a shopping list; I just wander through the grocery store, picking up items in a **haphazard** manner.
- Dan did a **haphazard** job of proofreading his term paper. Consequently, he caught some errors but missed many others.

__ *Haphazard* means   A. happy.   B. carefully planned.   C. unplanned.

4 incontrovertible
(ĭn-kŏn′trə-vûr′tə-bəl)
- *adjective*

- It's **incontrovertible** that Jeffrey is Paul's son; he looks exactly like his dad.
- Even in mathematics, there is not always one **incontrovertible** answer to a problem—sometimes two or more answers can be defended.

__ *Incontrovertible* means   A. unknown.   B. mistaken.   C. unquestionable.

5 intangible
(ĭn-tăn′jə-bəl)
- *adjective*

- Although Grandpa died with little money, he left us an **intangible** legacy: his strength, his warmth, and his honesty.
- As a child, I thought of Christmas in terms of the gifts I'd get. Now I focus on its **intangible** aspects—family closeness and sharing.

__ *Intangible* means   A. not permanent.   B. not important.   C. not touchable.

6 negate
(nĭ-gāt′)
- *verb*

- The jury awarded a million dollars to the accident victim, but the judge later **negated** that award, reducing it to only a few thousand.
- The board of elections had to **negate** the results of the mayoral race when it was discovered that many voting machines weren't working properly.

__ *Negate* means   A. to make invalid.   B. to demonstrate.   C. to confirm.

7 potent
(pōt′nt)
- *adjective*

● A child can easily overdose on pills meant to reduce pain and fever—they are **potent** medicines that need to be given carefully and in the right dosage.

● Alcohol is **potent** stuff—just as with drugs, one can die from an overdose.

__ *Potent* means   A. pure.   B. strong.   C. expensive.

8 rigorous
(rĭg′ər-əs)
- *adjective*

● There are several hiking trails in this area, ranging from easy ones for beginners to **rigorous** ones for experts.

● Erin is going through **rigorous** fitness training to get ready to run a marathon next month.

__ *Rigorous* means   A. easy.   B. difficult.   C. unfair.

9 spurious
(spyo͝or′ē-əs)
- *adjective*

● "I asked for real cream for my coffee," said the customer in the restaurant, "not some **spurious**, tasteless chemical substitute."

● When a supposed new work by Beethoven was discovered, music experts came from all over the world to decide if it was real or **spurious**.

__ *Spurious* means   A. false.   B. improved.   C. left over.

10 therapeutic
(thĕr′ə-pyo͞o′tĭk)
- *adjective*

● Liza had always heard that the "milk" in milkweed gets rid of warts, so she wrote to the Board of Health about it. The reply stated: "Its **therapeutic** properties, if any, have not been proved."

● Diego's insurance company would not pay for his surgery. The company ruled that the operation was experimental and not yet shown to be **therapeutic**.

__ *Therapeutic* means   A. dangerous.   B. magical.   C. healing.

Matching Words with Definitions

Following are definitions of the ten words. Clearly write or print each word next to its definition. The sentences above and on the previous page will help you decide on the meaning of each word.

1. _____ To make better

2. _____ Powerful

3. _____ Fake; counterfeit

4. _____ Careless; lacking a plan; lacking order

5. _____ To make ineffective; void; invalidate

6. _____ Challenging

7. _____ Serving to cure or heal

8. _____ Not material; not perceivable by touch; not concrete

9. _____ To agree

10. _____ Undeniable

CAUTION: Do not go any further until you are sure the above answers are correct. Then you can use the definitions to help you in the following practices. Your goal is eventually to know the words well enough so that you don't need to check the definitions at all.

Sentence Check 1

Using the answer line provided, complete each item below with the correct word from the box. Use each word once.

A. **ameliorate**	B. **assent**	C. **haphazard**	D. **incontrovertible**	E. **intangible**
F. **negate**	G. **potent**	H. **rigorous**	I. **spurious**	J. **therapeutic**

_____ 1. "You did a really ___ job of mowing the lawn," Mr. Dixon told his son. "Look—you left strips of tall grass all over the yard."

_____ 2. Exercise not only has salutary° physical effects, improving your health and fitness, but it also has a(n) ___ advantage: it raises your spirits.

_____ 3. Good study skills are a(n) ___ tool for any student, so schools that create study skills courses have made a judicious° curriculum decision.

_____ 4. Sandra wasn't sure she would make it through the ___ computer programming class, but when it was over, she felt very proud of herself.

_____ 5. When he was caught with the stolen jewels, the thief made up a(n) ___ story about having found them in an alley. He insisted he had nothing to do with the heist°.

_____ 6. Jerry is diffident° and shy with women, so he was nervous about asking Zoe to go out with him. He wasn't sure if she would ___ to the suggestion.

_____ 7. The evidence against the accused man is ___. Even his lawyers admit that he'll be indicted° and then found guilty.

_____ 8. "I said I'd let you have the car next weekend," Tom's mother said, "but I'll ___ that agreement if your behavior doesn't improve between now and then."

_____ 9. "This procedure is diagnostic, not ___," the doctor explained. "That is, it's used just to find out what's wrong with you, not to treat you."

_____ 10. "Settlement houses" such as the famous Hull House in Chicago were established to ___ conditions in the slums by providing social services to indigent° residents.

NOTE: Now check your answers to these items by turning to page 177. Going over the answers carefully will help you prepare for the next two practices, for which answers are not given.

Sentence Check 2

Using the answer lines provided, complete each item below with **two** words from the box. Use each word once.

_____
_____   1–2. Ghost stories grip our imagination partly because ghosts are ___ but also ___: how can creatures that are just thin air be so powerful?

_____
_____   3–4. To do well on a difficult, ___ exam, you need to plan and organize your studying. An unplanned, ___ approach will not get you a good grade.

_____   5–6. The evidence against the defendant seemed ___—beyond dispute—but his lawyer intended to call a surprise witness whose testimony would ___ the prosecution's supposedly irrefutable° case.
_____

_____   7–8. "Snake oil," worthless stuff with no ___ effects, was sold in traveling medicine shows as a cure-all. Now the term "snake oil" refers to any kind of phony, ___ claim.
_____

_____   9–10. "I can't ___ to your proposal to cut tuition in half," the college president told the protesting students. "It might ___ your finances, but it would wreck the school's budget, and the college might have to close its doors."
_____

Final Check: *When Is a Treatment Therapy?*

Here is a final opportunity for you to strengthen your knowledge of the ten words. First read the following selection carefully. Then fill in each blank with a word from the box at the top of the previous page. (Context clues will help you figure out which word goes in which blank.) Use each word once.

When a news item appears about a health insurer's refusal to pay for "experimental" medical treatment, people often wonder exactly what this means. The answer is that an experimental procedure is being contrasted with a(n) (1)_____ treatment, which offers a good chance of recovery or improvement: it will cure patients or (2)_____ their condition. In addition, to be considered a therapy, a treatment must be safe. For instance, a(n) (3)_____ medicine may have equally strong, but unwanted, side effects that can lessen or even (4)_____ its benefits.

How does a new, experimental treatment become established as therapy? This is not a(n) (5)_____ process: it does not happen by chance but involves a lengthy period of (6)_____ research. The research is usually done first with animals and then with large numbers of people. The scientists conducting the research on humans must first elucidate° the procedure and any possible risks. Once they understand what's involved, the humans, of course, must (7)_____ to being experimental subjects: this is the meaning of the well-known term "informed consent." The scientists who test a treatment must also be objective and dispassionate°. They disregard (8)_____ effects such as "giving the patient hope." Instead, they look for solid, (9)_____ evidence of physical results, and they are not swayed by (10)_____, untenable° claims of nonexistent cures.

Only a treatment that performs well on this formidable° test has real promise, so insurers that are wary of "experiments" are not necessarily being unreasonable or whimsical°. After all, it's their prerogative° to make decisions that involve matters of such gravity° as the health of their clients.

Scores	Sentence Check 2 _____%	Final Check _____%

Enter your scores above and in the **Vocabulary Performance Chart** on the inside back cover of the book.

altercation	malevolent
circumspect	placate
deference	pugnacious
guile	tirade
impassive	volatile

Ten Words in Context

In the space provided, write the letter of the meaning closest to that of each **boldfaced** word. Use the context of the sentences to help you figure out each word's meaning.

1 altercation
(ôl′tər-kā′shən)
- *noun*

● The **altercation** between the store clerk and customer began when the customer accused the clerk of shortchanging him.

● The party guests were embarrassed when they heard their host and hostess having a bitter **altercation** in the kitchen.

__ *Altercation* means   A. an embrace.   B. a task.   C. a quarrel.

2 circumspect
(sûr′kəm-spĕkt′)
- *adjective*

● Tory's two brothers are feuding. Tory has wisely decided to be **circumspect** and consider every aspect of the situation before becoming involved.

● Someone was stealing money from the cash register, but the boss chose to be **circumspect** and not make an accusation without weighing the consequences.

__ *Circumspect* means   A. careful.   B. honest.   C. aggressive.

3 deference
(dĕf′ər-əns)
- *noun*

● A few generations ago, a young person was expected to stand up when an older person entered the room. That kind of **deference** is rare nowadays.

● In **deference** to his parents' wishes, Alan agreed not to get his eyebrow pierced until he was over twenty-one.

__ *Deference* means   A. defiance.   B. courteous respect.   C. a difference of opinion.

4 guile
(gīl)
- *noun*

● The older boy used **guile** to decide who would get the last piece of pie. He told his little brother, "We'll flip a coin for it. Heads, I win; tails, you lose."

● Psalm 24 in the Bible says: "Keep thy tongue from evil, and thy lips from speaking **guile**."

__ *Guile* means   A. deceit.   B. nonsense.   C. truthfulness.

5 impassive
(ĭm-păs′ĭv)
- *adjective*

● No one could tell what the judges were thinking during the competition—they had trained themselves to remain **impassive**.

● How could you remain **impassive** during that heartbreaking movie? I cried so much I used up a box of tissues.

__ *Impassive* means   A. expressing horror.   B. expressing love.   C. expressing no feelings.

6 malevolent
(mə-lĕv′ə-lənt)
- *adjective*

● The ancient Egyptian tomb of Tutankhamen was said to be haunted by a **malevolent** spirit—a curse would fall on anyone who entered it.

● Early religions typically believed in many gods. Some gods were good and kind, but others were **malevolent** and would cause harm if they were displeased.

__ *Malevolent* means   A. friendly.   B. visible.   C. evil.

7 placate
(plā′kāt′)
- verb

● José had not finished his homework, but he was able to **placate** his teacher by offering to do it at lunchtime.

● In ancient times, people tried to keep volcanoes from erupting by offering food and gifts to **placate** the "volcano god."

__ *Placate* means   A. to anger.   B. to calm.   C. to fight.

8 pugnacious
(pŭg-nā′shəs)
- adjective

● There are two **pugnacious** children in the class who constantly start fights on the playground.

● Although Max is a professional boxer, he is not **pugnacious** in his private life. In fact, he is gentle and considerate.

__ *Pugnacious* means   A. quarrelsome.   B. curious.   C. funny.

9 tirade
(tī′rād′)
- noun

● The meeting of the school board was interrupted by a long **tirade** from a parent who wanted to express his fury about the amount of homework his son had to do.

● The history instructor, whose lectures were usually scholarly and calm, startled the class one day with a heated **tirade** about the Vietnam war.

__ *Tirade* means   A. a dialog.   B. an angry speech.   C. a theory.

10 volatile
(vŏl′ə-tl)
- adjective

● Bipolar disorder is a psychiatric condition that makes people extremely **volatile**. They have periods of excitement and giddy cheerfulness but then fall into a deep depression.

● Jean is difficult to get along with because her moods are so **volatile**. One day she's on top of the world; the next day she's in the depths of despair.

__ *Volatile* means   A. insensitive.   B. indirect.   C. changeable.

Matching Words with Definitions

Following are definitions of the ten words. Clearly write or print each word next to its definition. The sentences above and on the previous page will help you decide on the meaning of each word.

1. _____ A heated argument

2. _____ Considering all the circumstances related to an action or a decision; prudent; cautious

3. _____ To soothe or pacify, especially by making concessions

4. _____ A long, passionate, critical speech

5. _____ Slyness and cunning; trickery

6. _____ Tending to change suddenly or violently; unstable

7. _____ A courteous yielding to another's wishes

8. _____ Having or showing ill will; malicious; spiteful

9. _____ Eager and ready to fight

10. _____ Showing no emotion

CAUTION: Do not go any further until you are sure the above answers are correct. Then you can use the definitions to help you in the following practices. Your goal is eventually to know the words well enough so that you don't need to check the definitions at all.

Sentence Check 1

Using the answer line provided, complete each item below with the correct word from the box. Use each word once.

| A. **alteration** | B. **circumspect** | C. **deference** | D. **guile** | E. **impassive** |
| F. **malevolent** | G. **placate** | H. **pugnacious** | I. **tirade** | J. **volatile** |

_____ 1. Steve was ___ about the fact that he was looking for a new job. He went about the process quietly, not wanting his current employer to notice.

_____ 2. The newspaper story warned of a band of thieves who used ___ to charm and befriend elderly people, get into their homes, and then rob them.

_____ 3. Lamar will never be a good poker player, because he can't keep his face ___. If he gets a good hand, he looks delighted; if the hand is bad, he frowns, looks somber°, and shakes his head.

_____ 4. The two children were friendly with each other until they both wanted to play with the toy truck. Then there was a fierce ___ over who would get it.

_____ 5. I never speak to my neighbor if I can avoid it. He is so ___ that he can take offense and start a fight over the most innocent remark.

_____ 6. Alana and Len postponed their wedding in ___ to his parents, who were about to leave on a world cruise they'd been planning for years.

_____ 7. The French have a saying about their ___ climate: "If you don't like our weather, wait ten minutes." That's because the weather in France often does seem to change that quickly.

_____ 8. Invited to give a talk about the work his drug rehabilitation center was doing, the director instead presented a harsh, virulent° ___ about cuts in state funding.

_____ 9. After Kim was served a main dish that had bits of glass in it, the restaurant manager tried to ___ her by giving her a gift certificate for a free meal.

_____ 10. Ferocious animals are not ___. They act out of instinct, not from any spiteful desire to hurt.

NOTE: Now check your answers to these items by turning to page 177. Going over the answers carefully will help you prepare for the next two practices, for which answers are not given.

Sentence Check 2

Using the answer lines provided, complete each item below with **two** words from the box. Use each word once.

_____
_____ 1–2. June tried to remain stoic° and ___ during her father's angry ___, but finally she could no longer hide her feelings and burst into tears.

_____
_____ 3–4. The crowd at the game seemed ___. There was a lot of rough kidding, and though some of it was good-natured, the fans looked as if they might turn mean and ___ at any moment.

_____   5–6. The poisoner in the movie was ___ but also ___. She concealed her
_____   warped, evil plans by posing as a prim, proper librarian and remaining as
                                  unobtrusive° as possible.

_____   7–8. "In ___ to our neighbors," said a sign at the sidewalk café, "let's not make
_____   too much noise." Nearby residents had complained, and the owner wanted to
                                  ___ them by heeding° their concerns.

_____   9–10. To end a long, grueling° ___ with his roommate, Adam resorted to ___ and
_____   hypocrisy°. "I guess you're right," he said, not meaning a word of it.

Final Check: _Hawks and Doves_

Here is a final opportunity for you to strengthen your knowledge of the ten words. First read the following
selection carefully. Then fill in each blank with a word from the box at the top of the previous page.
(Context clues will help you figure out which word goes in which blank.) Use each word once.

Are you a hawk or a dove? According to some scientists who study behavior, a "hawk" is a

fighter, a(n) (1)_____ individual who meets every issue head-on. Hawks are

not necessarily (2)_____: they don't wish evil on other people. But they are

(3)_____: in a conflict, they tend to react angrily—to "explode"—and they are not

likely to back down. They may use words, in an abusive (4)_____, or they may use

physical violence, or both.

A "dove" is cautious and (5)_____. Doves want to avoid trouble. If a(n)

(6)_____ arises, they will try to stop it or at least keep the quarrel from getting any

worse. They'll try to (7)_____ their opponents by being soothing, soft-spoken, and

submissive°, and by listening with polite (8)_____. Doves aren't necessarily angels:

they sometimes use (9)_____ and duplicity° to obtain their own ends; and their

unemotional, (10)_____ reaction may be part of a plan of deceit. Usually, though,

they are sincere about being peaceable and about their willingness to acquiesce° in another's wishes or

capitulate° to another's demands.

Of course, people cannot be divided neatly into these two categories, and most of us probably show

some dovish traits as well as some hawkish traits. But the question above is a fair one. Think about yourself

and about people you know: On the whole, are you peace-loving, conciliatory° doves—or warlike, irascible°

hawks?

| Scores | Sentence Check 2 _____% | Final Check _____% |

Enter your scores above and in the **Vocabulary Performance Chart** on the inside back cover of the book.

capricious	phenomenon
catharsis	rectify
discrepancy	resolution
ephemeral	retract
induce	serene

Ten Words in Context

In the space provided, write the letter of the meaning closest to that of each **boldfaced** word. Use the context of the sentences to help you figure out each word's meaning.

1 capricious
(kə-prĭsh′əs)
- *adjective*

- It's understandable when a child says "I want to be a firefighter" one day and "I want to be a doctor" the next, but it's strange for an adult to be so **capricious**.
- The actress is so spoiled and **capricious** that she'll order an entire new wardrobe, then decide she doesn't like any of it and throw all the clothes away.

___ *Capricious* means   A. impulsive.   B. wicked.   C. intelligent.

2 catharsis
(kĕ-thär′sĭs)
- *noun*

- Some therapists advise their clients to punch and kick pillows. The idea is that the patients can experience **catharsis** by releasing their anger in this way.
- People in some families never raise their voices, while others seem to need to achieve **catharsis** by yelling at each other occasionally.

___ *Catharsis* means   A. confusion.   B. letting out feelings.   C. love.

3 discrepancy
(dĭ-skrĕp′ən-sē)
- *noun*

- After a **discrepancy** was found in the accounts, an investigation revealed that one of the bookkeepers had been stealing.
- The police solved the homicide case by asking all the suspects to account for their movements on the night of the killing. There was a **discrepancy** in one person's story—half an hour was missing—and he turned out to be the killer.

___ *Discrepancy* means   A. a reduction.   B. an increase.   C. a difference.

4 ephemeral
(ĭ-fĕm′ər-əl)
- *adjective*

- "Cooking is an **ephemeral** art," said Mom. "You create something beautiful, people gobble it up, and in minutes, it's gone."
- One theory about fireworks is that they fascinate us because they are so **ephemeral**: they burst and fade away almost immediately.

___ *Ephemeral* means   A. worthless.   B. impossible to explain.   C. brief.

5 induce
(ĭn-dōos′)
- *verb*

- The hypnotist claimed to be able to **induce** a trance in any volunteer.
- Whatever **induced** you to do your Bugs Bunny imitation at that very formal dinner?

___ *Induce* means   A. to cause.   B. to prevent.   C. to predict.

6 phenomenon
(fĭ-nŏm′ə-nŏn′)
- *noun*

- "Déjà vu" is a common **phenomenon**. It is the sensation, when hearing or seeing something for the first time, that one has heard or seen it before.
- A comet was a terrifying **phenomenon** in earlier times. No one knew what comets were, so when one appeared in the sky, people saw it as a sign of disaster.

___ *Phenomenon* means   A. something noticed.   B. something imaginary.   C. something that fails.

7 rectify
(rĕk′tə-fī′)
- *verb*

- According to an old story, when Abraham Lincoln was a store clerk, he shortchanged a customer by a nickel, then walked miles to her house to **rectify** the situation.
- I put a cup of salt instead of a cup of sugar into the cake batter. There's no way to **rectify** the mistake; I'll have to throw the whole mess out.

___ *Rectify* means   A. to repeat.   B. to discuss.   C. to correct.

8 resolution
(rĕz′ə-lōō′shən)
- *noun*

- By increasing the police force, installing better street lights, and starting neighborhood watch programs, the new mayor demonstrated her **resolution** to make the city a safer place to live.
- When Jane's brother made a nasty remark about her husband, Jane forgot her **resolution** not to lose her temper.

___ *Resolution* means   A. a question.   B. a solemn promise.   C. a repetition.

9 retract
(rĭ-trăkt′)
- *verb*

- Jane says she will never speak to her brother again unless he will **retract** his insult to her husband.
- No one can trust Harry's promises: he **retracts** them as soon as he makes them.

___ *Retract* means   A. to withdraw.   B. to strengthen.   C. to remember.

10 serene
(sə-rēn′)
- *adjective*

- On a day like this, when the ocean is so smooth and **serene**, it is hard to imagine that it can be rough and stormy.
- Shaken and upset after her accident, Jolene sat very still and had a cup of tea to try to make herself feel **serene** again.

___ *Serene* means   A. quiet and at peace.   B. anxious.   C. angry.

Matching Words with Definitions

Following are definitions of the ten words. Clearly write or print each word next to its definition. The sentences above and on the previous page will help you decide on the meaning of each word.

1. _____ A fact or event that can be observed; something unusual or remarkable

2. _____ To persuade or influence; cause to happen

3. _____ Changeable; acting on impulses; unpredictable

4. _____ To remedy; make right

5. _____ A lack of agreement, as between facts; an inconsistency

6. _____ Emotional release

7. _____ Peaceful; calm; placid°

8. _____ Lasting for only a short time; fleeting

9. _____ To take back

10. _____ Determination; a firm decision; a vow

CAUTION: Do not go any further until you are sure the above answers are correct. Then you can use the definitions to help you in the following practices. Your goal is eventually to know the words well enough so that you don't need to check the definitions at all.

Sentence Check 1

Using the answer line provided, complete each item below with the correct word from the box. Use each word once.

A. **capricious**	B. **catharsis**	C. **discrepancy**	D. **ephemeral**	E. **induce**
F. **phenomenon**	G. **rectify**	H. **resolution**	I. **retract**	J. **serene**

_____   1. Whatever ___(e)d you to invite Seth and Reuben to the same small dinner party? Don't you know that they are bitter enemies?

_____   2. "I'm not a callous° person—I feel bad about what happened, and I'd like to ___ it," said our neighbor. "How much will it cost to fix the window my kids broke with their baseball?"

_____   3. After a rough day at work, what makes you feel ___ again? For some people, the answer is a brisk walk; others prefer a hot bath or a brief nap.

_____   4. When Leon gets his monthly bank statement, there is usually a(n) ___ between it and his own records. The gap isn't large—just five or ten dollars—but it's almost always there.

_____   5. After years of being impassive° and holding back her anger, Mimi achieved ___ by writing her father a long, furious letter listing all the ways he had marred° her life—and then burning it.

_____   6. An old French song describes the joys of love as ___, but the sorrows of love as lasting a lifetime.

_____   7. "I said I would marry you," Marie told Hank. "But now that I know how you've lied to me, I ___ that promise."

_____   8. Superstitions are a puzzling ___. What is it that makes otherwise well-informed and sensible people step aside to avoid walking under a ladder?

_____   9. Having decided that TV was taking up too much of her life, Angie made a(n) ___ not to watch it for a week.

_____   10. Tina seems to take pleasure in being ___. One day she says she loves school; the next day she says she hates it. On Tuesday she decides that she likes being single; on Wednesday she's upset that she's not married.

NOTE: Now check your answers to these items by turning to page 177. Going over the answers carefully will help you prepare for the next two practices, for which answers are not given.

Sentence Check 2

Using the answer lines provided, complete each item below with **two** words from the box. Use each word once.

_____
_____   1–2. To escape the stress and turbulence° of city life, my parents retired to a quiet, ___ small town. Now they say nothing would ___ them to leave that placid° spot.

_____
_____   3–4. Her next-door neighbor's cold, unfriendly attitude was a puzzling ___ to Lucy. She made a(n) ___ to ask him directly if she had somehow offended him.

_____   5–6. The heat in our apartment building is ___: we're either too hot or too cold.
_____   The owner is afraid that only an expensive new boiler can ___ the situation.

_____   7–8. People who have a "near-death" experience often describe it as a(n) ___
_____   that leaves them feeling purified. But the effect is usually ___: it soon fades,
                            and they return to their old ways of life.

_____   9–10. "I hated to ___ my promise to buy the kids new bicycles," Nikki explained,
_____   "but there was a large ___ between what the bikes cost and what I could
                            afford to pay."

Final Check: *New Year's Resolutions*

Here is a final opportunity for you to strengthen your knowledge of the ten words. First read the following selection carefully. Then fill in each blank with a word from the box at the top of the previous page. (Context clues will help you figure out which word goes in which blank.) Use each word once.

Breathes there the man, with soul so dead (to quote Sir Walter Scott), who never to himself has said, "This year I resolve to . . ."? Probably not. Every year, everyone seems to make at least one New Year's (1)_____. It's a recurring (2)_____: no matter how little success we've had in quitting smoking or getting more exercise in the months just past, we still believe in the therapeutic° power of a promise to begin on January 1. We have a touching faith that expressing our determination will somehow (3)_____ us to ameliorate° our behavior, will lead us to (4)_____ whatever is wrong with our lives. And perhaps making these promises also serves as a(n) (5)_____: we feel cleaner and purer, (6)_____ and at peace with the world.

However, we seem to overlook a few incontrovertible° facts. For one thing, most New Year's vows prove to be (7)_____. It's amazing how soon we forget them and return to our former depravity°. This may be because so many of them are (8)_____: we make a whimsical° or quixotic° promise on the spur of the moment without thinking, "Can I really *do* this?" or even "Do I really *want* to do this?" Thus (if we consider the matter at all), we will usually see a huge (9)_____ between our goals and what we actually achieve. Interestingly, though, no one ever seems to (10)_____ a resolution. You've probably never said, "No, I take it back. I *won't* lose ten pounds this year." And although time after time, our New Year's goals turn out to be elusive°, we keep on setting them, in the fallacious° belief that this time, we'll succeed in reaching them.

This year, I resolve to read some Scott, instead of just quoting him.

Scores   Sentence Check 2 _____%   Final Check _____%

The box at the right lists twenty-five words from Unit Five. Using the clues at the bottom of the page, fill in these words to complete the puzzle that follows.

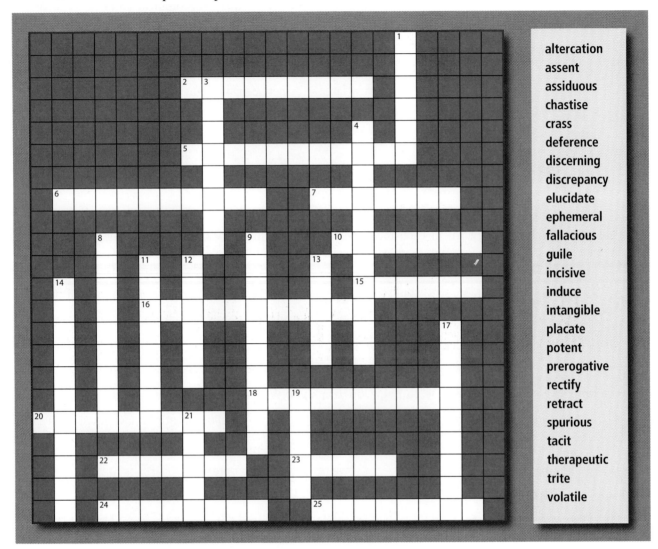

altercation
assent
assiduous
chastise
crass
deference
discerning
discrepancy
elucidate
ephemeral
fallacious
guile
incisive
induce
intangible
placate
potent
prerogative
rectify
retract
spurious
tacit
therapeutic
trite
volatile

ACROSS

2. Careful, hardworking, and thorough
5. A special right or privilege
6. Based on error; mistaken
7. To correct; make right
10. To take back
15. To agree
16. A heated argument
18. Not material
20. A courteous yielding to another's wishes
22. To soothe or pacify
23. Understood but not spoken
24. Penetrating; pointed
25. Tending to change suddenly or violently

DOWN

1. To persuade or influence; cause to happen
3. Fake
4. A lack of agreement, as between facts; inconsistency
8. To explain; clarify
9. Having keen insight; clear-eyed
11. To scold sharply
12. Powerful
13. Slyness and cunning
14. Serving to cure or heal
17. Lasting for only a short time; fleeting
19. Overused and commonplace
21. Coarse; vulgar

PART A

Choose the word that best completes each item and write it in the space provided.

_____ 1. To his horror, the bank teller realized that there was a $4,000 ___ between the money in his drawer and what his records showed he should have.

      A. phenomenon   B. deference   C. discrepancy   D. catharsis

_____ 2. The job applicant's letters of recommendation were very impressive. They ___ her as a model employee whom any company would be lucky to hire.

      A. exalted   B. induced   C. assented   D. placated

_____ 3. The peaceable old hound lay quietly on the porch, gazing ahead with a sweet, ___ expression.

      A. capricious   B. crass   C. placid   D. malevolent

_____ 4. The movie about a kindly man who murders in a moment of panic poses an interesting question: does one horrible act ___ a lifetime of good works?

      A. negate   B. elucidate   C. whet   D. rectify

_____ 5. The boys certainly did a(n) ___ job of shoveling the sidewalk. A few places are cleared, but others are still covered with snow and ice.

      A. serene   B. haphazard   C. assiduous   D. discerning

_____ 6. Old-time doctors used to recommend that their patients visit the seashore, believing that salty sea breezes were ___.

      A. spurious   B. insurgent   C. impassive   D. therapeutic

_____ 7. _Gaslight_ is a chilling movie about an evil man who uses ___ to convince his wife that she is insane.

      A. tirade   B. phenomenon   C. guile   D. hyperbole

_____ 8. The town council is a(n) ___ force in our city. Its members are effective leaders who get things done.

      A. potent   B. tactless   C. impassive   D. volatile

_____ 9. When Rena fell into debt, her husband criticized her for careless spending. Later, when she learned he was even more in debt, she was angry at his ___.

      A. phenomenon   B. prerogative   C. hypocrisy   D. resolution

_____ 10. It took Darryl only half an hour to put his daughter's new toy together incorrectly, but it took him three hours to ___ his error.

      A. chastise   B. exalt   C. rectify   D. induce

(Continues on next page)

_____ 11. Why is Chuck such a bully? No one else in his family is the least bit ___, but he is constantly looking for a fight.

        A. pugnacious   B. serene   C. assiduous   D. colloquial

_____ 12. The "bad guy" in many Disney movies is actually a(n) ___ female. *Snow White* has a wicked queen; *Sleeping Beauty* has an evil fairy, Maleficent; and *The Little Mermaid* has Ursula the Sea Witch.

        A. judicious   B. ephemeral   C. malevolent   D. intangible

_____ 13. A visit to the art museum ___ my interest in learning more about Frida Kahlo, a fascinating Mexican artist who did many self-portraits while confined to her bed by illness.

        A. ameliorated   B. chastised   C. negated   D. whetted

PART B

Write **C** if the italicized word is used **correctly**. Write **I** if the word is used **incorrectly**.

____ 14. For the first time in years, our whole family was together for Thanksgiving. It was a wonderful *altercation*, with everyone laughing and talking and telling old family stories.

____ 15. The neighbor *assented* angrily when the children asked if they could retrieve their baseball from his yard, saying, "Don't even think of stepping on my property!"

____ 16. That couple has a *tacit* understanding that whoever doesn't make dinner washes the dishes. They've never discussed it; they just started it when they got married, and they've continued that way.

____ 17. Beware of workmen who come to your door and offer to pave your driveway with materials they have "left over from another job." The story is probably *spurious,* and you'll end up losing money.

____ 18. "I'm too embarrassed to tell Kathleen I lost the ring she lent me," Cindy said to Kathleen's husband. "Could you tell her? You're so *tactless*—you'll make her understand and forgive me."

____ 19. It was strange to finally meet my pen pal. After all those years of imagining what she'd be like, suddenly there she was, solid and *intangible*.

____ 20. With so many bills waiting to be paid, it was *judicious* of Kenneth to spend his entire paycheck on a new leather jacket.

____ 21. Although Susan is usually very gentle with her children, she *chastises* them sharply if they do something that could endanger themselves or others.

____ 22. Don't ever put butter on a burn. Although butter was once believed to relieve the pain, it could actually *ameliorate* the injury.

____ 23. No matter how many times I see a rainbow, I still find it a fascinating *phenomenon*. What a wonderful display of light and color!

____ 24. It's hard to know how upset Lee really is about her fight with Bob. She says, "This is the worst thing that ever happened to me," but since she always uses *hyperbole*, I'm not sure how serious she is.

____ 25. Finding Rebekah nervously pacing the floor at 3 a.m., her housemate asked worriedly, "Why are you so *serene*? What's the matter?"

Score   (Number correct) _____ x 4 = _____%

PART A

On the answer line, write the word from the box that completes each item below. Use each word once.

A. **assiduous**	B. **capricious**	C. **catharsis**	D. **caustic**	E. **circumspect**
F. **colloquial**	G. **elucidate**	H. **fallacious**	I. **incontrovertible**	J. **insurgent**
K. **prerogative**	L. **tirade**	M. **trite**		

_____ 1. The link between cigarette smoking and lung cancer is not merely suspected—it is a(n) ___ fact.

_____ 2. When Chen struck out at the company softball game, everyone was polite about it except the office sourpuss. "Nice work, loser," he said in a(n) ___ tone of voice.

_____ 3. Spring is often a(n) ___ season, with the weather changing hour to hour from summery heat to autumn chill.

_____ 4. When someone asks you "How are you?" do you usually give the expected but ___ answer—"Fine"—or do you describe how you really are?

_____ 5. I had to rewrite my entire paper after I realized that my reasoning was ___—I had drawn the wrong conclusions from some of my facts.

_____ 6. The revolution was begun by a few ___s who had come to believe that the king was evil and corrupt and had to be overthrown.

_____ 7. No one in the office had ever heard Howard raise his voice, so everyone was astonished when he delivered an angry ___ to a client who was being rude and abusive to the receptionist.

_____ 8. Will Rogers, a famous humorist in the 1920s and 1930s, was beloved for his informal, ___ style. He had been a cowboy, and he talked in plain language that everyone could understand and enjoy.

_____ 9. The congregation was so moved by the powerful preacher that many of them wept and prayed aloud. Afterward, churchgoers seemed exhausted by the ___ they had experienced.

_____ 10. It's not "luck" that makes Juan a success at his job. It's old-fashioned effort—he's a very ___ worker.

_____ 11. Because Angie's approach is so ___, her friends often ask her for advice. She listens carefully and considers every detail before making a suggestion.

_____ 12. Don't cut the birthday cake! It is the ___ of the guest of honor to cut the first slice.

_____ 13. I couldn't figure out what the little girl's drawing was supposed to be, so I said "Tell me about it," hoping that she would ___ the meaning of the brown squiggles and purple stripes.

(Continues on next page)

PART B

Write **C** if the italicized word is used **correctly**. Write **I** if the word is used **incorrectly**.

_____ 14. My grandmother is the most *volatile* person I know. Nothing seems to affect her mood, which is always calm and peaceful.

_____ 15. The Porters are so *crass* that their home is always open to anyone who needs a place to stay and some friendly assistance for a few days.

_____ 16. In Japan, students are expected to show their teacher a good deal of *deference,* accepting his or her statements and never arguing.

_____ 17. When I play Monopoly with my little sister, I give her too much of my money so that she can win and the game can finally end. She's so *discerning* that she never notices.

_____ 18. The doctor's *impassive* face as she sat down to tell me my test results told me nothing—the news could have been either good or tragic.

_____ 19. Becoming a restaurant chef may sound like fun, but it's not easy. The courses at most restaurant schools are *rigorous*—many people drop out without completing the work.

_____ 20. Realizing that the clerk had not heard her request, Dinah *retracted* her question again, more loudly.

_____ 21. I groaned when I saw that Dr. Latham was teaching my American history class. His lectures are so *incisive* that I have to struggle to stay awake.

_____ 22. In order to *placate* the neighbors after our dog dug up their garden, we spent a Saturday repairing the damage and even bought them some new garden tools.

_____ 23. The movie was not only terrible but also *ephemeral,* lasting for nearly three long, boring hours.

_____ 24. Dorrie has made up her mind to stay in school until she graduates. "Nothing would *induce* me to leave without my diploma," she declares.

_____ 25. Matt has too much *resolution* to decide what he wants to do next. He keeps waffling among ideas: College? The military? Vocational school? A job?

Score   (Number correct) _____ x 4 = _____%

PART A: Synonyms

In the space provided, write the letter of the choice that is most nearly the **same** in meaning as the **boldfaced** word.

_____ 1. **altercation**   A. a bruise   B. a widely-known fact   C. a luxury   D. a fight

_____ 2. **assiduous**   A. hard-working   B. doubtful   C. sly   D. messy

_____ 3. **catharsis**   A. a medical procedure   B. a journey   C. an emotional release   D. a period of solitude

_____ 4. **circumspect**   A. busy   B. tolerant   C. prudent   D. lazy

_____ 5. **deference**   A. self-righteousness   B. confusion   C. dislike   D. respect

_____ 6. **discerning**   A. argumentative   B. undersized   C. dishonest   D. perceptive

_____ 7. **discrepancy**   A. an announcement   B. an observation   C. an inconsistency   D. an explanation

_____ 8. **hypocrisy**   A. insincerity   B. cleanliness   C. bad temper   D. generosity

_____ 9. **incisive**   A. legal   B. boring   C. penetrating   D. swift

_____ 10. **incontrovertible**   A. sad   B. undeniable   C. blameless   D. never tiring

_____ 11. **induce**   A. accuse   B. leave alone   C. set free   D. bring about

_____ 12. **insurgent**   A. an instructor   B. a rebel   C. an assistant   D. an annoyance

_____ 13. **intangible**   A. flawless   B. from another country   C. rare; nearly extinct   D. not able to be touched

_____ 14. **negate**   A. to make strong   B. to make ineffective   C. to make fun of   D. to make larger

_____ 15. **phenomenon**   A. a tradition   B. a religious belief   C. a story with a moral   D. an event

_____ 16. **potent**   A. lengthy   B. humble   C. bitter   D. strong

_____ 17. **prerogative**   A. a special privilege   B. a way of life   C. a habit   D. an absence

_____ 18. **rectify**   A. to collapse   B. to carry   C. to correct   D. to connect

_____ 19. **resolution**   A. supplies   B. self-importance   C. wastefulness   D. determination

_____ 20. **retract**   A. to take back   B. to be careful   C. to take for granted   D. to worry

_____ 21. **serene**   A. talkative   B. lonely   C. peaceful   D. greedy

_____ 22. **tacit**   A. sarcastic   B. rapid   C. implied   D. polite

_____ 23. **therapeutic**   A. unknown   B. loosely connected   C. curative   D. modern

_____ 24. **tirade**   A. a refusal to speak   B. a plea   C. an exclamation   D. an angry speech

_____ 25. **whet**   A. to disgust   B. to stimulate   C. to bore   D. to listen

(Continues on next page)

PART B: Antonyms

In the space provided, write the letter of the choice that is most nearly **opposite** in meaning to the **boldfaced** word.

____ 26. **ameliorate**   A. to remove   B. to worsen   C. to repeat   D. to steal

____ 27. **assent**   A. to refuse   B. to pretend   C. to insist   D. to construct

____ 28. **capricious**   A. steady   B. worried   C. strong   D. famous

____ 29. **caustic**   A. forceful   B. unusual   C. boring   D. kindly

____ 30. **chastise**   A. to give directions to   B. to confuse   C. to grasp   D. to praise

____ 31. **colloquial**   A. spoken by one person   B. formal   C. lengthy   D. humorous

____ 32. **crass**   A. tasteful   B. enlarged   C. noisy   D. absurd

____ 33. **elucidate**   A. to forget   B. to make confusing   C. to add to   D. to lose

____ 34. **ephemeral**   A. permanent   B. vicious   C. honest   D. friendly

____ 35. **exalt**   A. to waste time   B. to ridicule   C. to search for   D. to plan for

____ 36. **fallacious**   A. far away   B. harmless   C. truthful   D. graceful

____ 37. **guile**   A. honesty   B. stubbornness   C. ability   D. action

____ 38. **haphazard**   A. talkative   B. highly educated   C. carefully planned   D. lonely

____ 39. **hyperbole**   A. understatement   B. translation   C. excuse   D. betrayal

____ 40. **impassive**   A. forgiving   B. pushy   C. musical   D. emotional

____ 41. **judicious**   A. colorful   B. foolish   C. talented   D. abnormal

____ 42. **malevolent**   A. foreign-born   B. well-meaning   C. complicated   D. smooth

____ 43. **placate**   A. to irritate   B. to befriend   C. to allow   D. to destroy

____ 44. **placid**   A. excited   B. loyal   C. stubborn   D. careless

____ 45. **pugnacious**   A. wise   B. peaceful   C. mentally slow   D. useful

____ 46. **rigorous**   A. amusing   B. based on false information   C. unstable   D. easy

____ 47. **spurious**   A. genuine   B. common   C. generous   D. insulting

____ 48. **tactless**   A. recent   B. sensitive   C. unfair   D. positive

____ 49. **trite**   A. bad-smelling   B. original   C. lengthy   D. graceful

____ 50. **volatile**   A. wealthy   B. proud   C. numerous   D. stable

Score   (Number correct) _____   x 2 = _____%

Unit Six

abstemious	eclectic
abstruse	extraneous
astute	hardy
aversion	intractable
diminutive	soporific

Ten Words in Context

In the space provided, write the letter of the meaning closest to that of each **boldfaced** word. Use the context of the sentences to help you figure out each word's meaning.

1 abstemious
(ăb-stē′mē-əs)
- *adjective*

- Kori is **abstemious** when it comes to chocolate. She rarely has any, and when she does, it's never more than one or two small pieces.
- We say that an **abstemious** person who eats very little "eats like a bird"—but in fact, birds eat almost all the time.

___ *Abstemious* means   A. self-indulgent.   B. moderate in eating and drinking.   C. sophisticated.

2 abstruse
(ăb-stroōs′)
- *adjective*

- The scholarship winner was so bright that as a high-school freshman, she was already taking university-level courses in **abstruse** subjects, such as biochemistry and ancient Greek philosophy.
- The Swedish art film was too **abstruse** for me—it was full of symbols and references that I couldn't understand.

___ *Abstruse* means   A. hard to comprehend.   B. absurd.   C. elementary.

3 astute
(ə-stoōt′)
- *adjective*

- How kind of you to give me a sweater, and how **astute** of you to have noticed that sea-green is my favorite color!
- If you were a little more **astute**, you would have noticed that Betsy and Eli are not getting along well—they didn't say a word to each other during dinner.

___ *Astute* means   A. surprised.   B. shrewdly observant.   C. courageous.

4 aversion
(ə-vûr′zhən)
- *noun*

- Dad has such an **aversion** to answering machines that he hangs up as soon as he hears a recorded message.
- Denise has an **aversion** to dresses and skirts. She wears only pants.

___ *Aversion to* means   A. a strong distaste for.   B. a strong preference for.   C. a knowledge of.

5 diminutive
(dǐ-mǐn′yə-tǐv)
- *adjective*

- Kiran's income last year seemed so **diminutive** that he assumed he wouldn't have to pay taxes. He was wrong.
- When I saw a display of eighteenth-century costumes at the museum, I was surprised at their small size. Our ancestors must have been **diminutive** people!

___ *Diminutive* means   A. impossible to measure.   B. sizable.   C. little.

6 eclectic
(ĭ-klěk′tĭk)
- *adjective*

- "We're having an **eclectic** dinner tonight," Kris announced. "First wonton soup, then Swedish meatballs, and then Pennsylvania Dutch shoofly pie for dessert!"
- The concert program was **eclectic**: the songs came from America, Germany, Italy, Spain, and Japan; and they included selections from musical comedy, grand opera, and children's songs.

___ *Eclectic* means   A. lacking in diversity.   B. varied.   C. lengthy.

7 extraneous
(ĭk-strā′nē-əs)
- *adjective*

- If you want to tell a joke well, don't include a lot of **extraneous** remarks, such as "OK, here comes the funny part" or "Wait, I didn't tell that part right."
- On the famous old TV show *Dragnet,* the detective, Sergeant Joe Friday, often said, "All we want are the facts, ma'am," to prevent witnesses from wasting his time with **extraneous** comments and ideas.

__ *Extraneous* means   A. unrelated.   B. excellent.   C. important.

8 hardy
(här′dē)
- *adjective*

- Although they are small, Shetland ponies are **hardy**, able to survive the long, cold winters of their native Shetland Islands.
- Farm children had to be **hardy**; they were expected to work long hours in the fields.

__ *Hardy* means   A. healthy and sturdy.   B. delicate.   C. hardhearted.

9 intractable
(ĭn-trăk′tə-bəl)
- *adjective*

- Doria came home from her job at the daycare center looking worn out. "The kids were really **intractable** today," she said. "We just couldn't get them to calm down and behave."
- Mules are notoriously **intractable**. You've probably heard the expression "as stubborn as a mule."

__ *Intractable* means   A. unclassifiable.   B. uncontrollable.   C. unrecognizable.

10 soporific
(sŏp′ə-rĭf′ĭk)
- *adjective*

- If you're having trouble sleeping, try a glass of warm milk, which is supposed to be **soporific**.
- Raquel plays tapes of soft, dreamy music in her baby's room at naptime. She hopes the music will have a **soporific** effect.

__ *Soporific* means   A. causing anger.   B. causing excitement.   C. causing drowsiness.

Matching Words with Definitions

Following are definitions of the ten words. Clearly write or print each word next to its definition. The sentences above and on the previous page will help you decide on the meaning of each word.

1. _____ Difficult to understand; deep

2. _____ An intense dislike

3. _____ Coming from many sources

4. _____ Not essential; irrelevant

5. _____ Clever; perceptive

6. _____ Causing sleep

7. _____ Tough; strong

8. _____ Self-denying; exercising restraint in appetites or behavior

9. _____ Difficult to manage; hard to control; unruly

10. _____ Extremely small

CAUTION: Do not go any further until you are sure the above answers are correct. Then you can use the definitions to help you in the following practices. Your goal is eventually to know the words well enough so that you don't need to check the definitions at all.

Sentence Check 1

Using the answer line provided, complete each item below with the correct word from the box. Use each word once.

A. **abstemious**	B. **abstruse**	C. **astute**	D. **aversion**	E. **diminutive**
F. **eclectic**	G. **extraneous**	H. **hardy**	I. **intractable**	J. **soporific**

_____ 1. Many birds fly south in the winter, but some ___ species, such as cardinals and chickadees, stay to add color and life to the cold northern landscape.

_____ 2. At first, our puppy seemed ___; we couldn't teach him to obey. But a professional trainer showed us how to control him with praise and rewards.

_____ 3. Cho used to love olives, but once she ate so many of them that she got sick. Since then, she has had a real ___ to olives—she can't even stand to look at one, and nothing can induce° her to try them again.

_____ 4. When there's a death in the family, parents shouldn't try to hide it from the kids. Even young children can be ___ enough to see that something is wrong.

_____ 5. Grandmother was a(n) ___ woman, not even five feet tall, but she had the strength of a much larger person.

_____ 6. Our pastor wants to inspire people, but his sermons are so long and boring that they have a(n) ___ effect instead—all they inspire is a stupor°.

_____ 7. "You need to edit your report," Ms. Hawkins told the student. "You've got some good, useful information here, as well as some incisive° ideas, but they're buried under paragraphs of ___ data."

_____ 8. Please be ___ in using the Scotch tape—we've got only one roll to wrap all these presents.

_____ 9. Trying to impress his intelligent new girlfriend, Al pretended to be reading books on ___ subjects such as quantum physics and chaos theory.

_____ 10. Joel is a great dinner guest because his interests are so ___; no matter what the topic is, he can talk about it intelligently and amusingly.

NOTE: Now check your answers to these items by turning to page 177. Going over the answers carefully will help you prepare for the next two practices, for which answers are not given.

Sentence Check 2

Using the answer lines provided, complete each item below with **two** words from the box. Use each word once.

_____
_____ 1–2. Vaughn is a(n) ___ man who has a(n) ___ to any kind of excess: he doesn't smoke or drink, he never overeats, and he limits his spending.

_____
_____ 3–4. The ___ chapter in the chemistry text had a(n) ___ effect on Yasmin. As she tried to peruse° the difficult material, she had to struggle to stay awake.

_____
_____ 5–6. Mildew is a very ___ form of life. In damp weather, this potent° fungus can start to grow on shower curtains and walls and soon becomes ___: it's almost impossible to control.

_____   7–8. A bonsai is a(n) ___ tree that is made tiny by special cultivation. When
_____   her parents got one, three-year-old Lani was ___ enough to see where it
belonged: she put it contiguous° to the front porch of her dollhouse.

_____   9–10. The readings in the course were ___: old and new, from many cultures, by
_____   both women and men. But they all had the same theme—growing up—with
no peripheral° or ___ topics.

Final Check: *Weird Facts*

Here is a final opportunity for you to strengthen your knowledge of the ten words. First read the following
selection carefully. Then fill in each blank with a word from the box at the top of the previous page.
(Context clues will help you figure out which word goes in which blank.) Use each word once.

"The world is so full of a number of things, I'm sure we should all be as happy as kings." These
lines were written by the poet Robert Louis Stevenson more than a hundred years ago. The world *is*
full of a number of things, many of them strange, some of them wonderful, some funny, some nearly
unbelievable. Some are basic to everyone's education; others are (1)_____
but still fun to know. Here is a(n) (2)_____ collection of facts, taken from
fields including science, psychology, and just plain silliness:

● Albert Einstein was known as one of the most discerning°, (3)_____ thinkers
  of all time. He had a remarkable understanding of such (4)_____ topics as
  time and space. Yet when Einstein was nine years old, he still couldn't speak fluently. His parents
  thought he might have a learning disability.

● If you're going into an area where there are lots of mosquitoes, be (5)_____
  about eating bananas. Assiduous° research has found that mosquitoes are attracted to people who
  have recently eaten this fruit.

● You probably know already that the penguin must be a(n) (6)_____ bird to
  survive in the fierce cold of Antarctica. Did you know, though, that a penguin can jump six feet in
  the air?

● Donald Duck comics were banned in Finland because Donald doesn't wear pants.

● In the movie *E.T.: The Extraterrestrial,* the sound of E.T. walking was made by a woman squishing her
  hands in Jell-O.

● The famous psychiatrist Sigmund Freud had such a(n) (7)_____ to ferns
  that he could not stay in the same room with one.

● There are more plastic flamingos in the United States than real ones.

● When opossums "play possum," they are not actually playing. Oddly enough, terror has a(n)
  (8)_____ effect on possums. Fright makes them go to sleep.

● A duck's quack does not echo. (No one knows the reason for this phenomenon°.)

● Mosquitoes have teeth. Since mosquitoes are so tiny, imagine how (9)_____
  their teeth must be!

● Snakes are occasionally born with two heads. A two-headed snake is extremely
  (10)_____. Not only is it pugnacious° toward other animals, but its two
  heads fight each other for food.

● Thomas Edison was afraid of the dark. (Do you suppose that's why he invented the light bulb?)

Scores   Sentence Check 2 _____%   Final Check _____%

abstract	iconoclast
archaic	laudable
engender	painstaking
erudite	pompous
fervor	renown

Ten Words in Context

In the space provided, write the letter of the meaning closest to that of each **boldfaced** word. Use the context of the sentences to help you figure out each word's meaning.

1 abstract
(ăb′străkt′)
- *adjective*

- For a person who has been blind since birth, color is just an **abstract** idea.
- A couple may believe in the **abstract** idea of "commitment," but they find out what true commitment is only when they face difficult experiences together.

___ *Abstract* means   A. vague.   B. absurd.   C. temporary.

2 archaic
(är-kā′ĭk)
- *adjective*

- Computer software is changing so rapidly that a program bought just two years ago is already **archaic**.
- Marriage vows used to include the bride's promise to obey her husband. Today many couples consider this **archaic** and leave it out of the ceremony.

___ *Archaic* means   A. old-fashioned.   B. necessary.   C. permanent.

3 engender
(ĕn-jĕn′dər)
- *verb*

- An introductory music course in school can **engender** a lifelong love of music.
- Ken's rivalry with his cousin was **engendered** long ago, when they were in the same kindergarten class and competed to see who would learn the alphabet first.

___ *Engender* means   A. to endanger.   B. to complete.   C. to begin.

4 erudite
(ĕr′yə-dīt′)
- *adjective*

- Zahra has earned several graduate degrees, although no one else in her family went to college. Her parents are proud of their **erudite** daughter.
- You don't have to be **erudite** to enjoy action movies—they are designed to entertain you, not make you think.

___ *Erudite* means   A. unskilled.   B. learned.   C. kindhearted.

5 fervor
(fûr′vər)
- *noun*

- Before the game, the coach talked to her players with great **fervor**, making them feel excited and determined to win.
- You can tell that Christy really loves the piano by the **fervor** with which she practices.

___ *Fervor* means   A. fear.   B. humor.   C. passion.

6 iconoclast
(ī-kŏn′ə-klăst′)
- *noun*

- Many people regard Steve Jobs, founder of Apple, as a brilliant **iconoclast** for the way he overthrew established beliefs about the personal computer industry.
- It's always risky to have Grandma and Jeff in the same room. Grandma is a very traditional Italian Catholic, while Jeff is an **iconoclast** who makes jokes about the Pope and questions the teachings of Catholicism.

___ *Iconoclast* means   A. a conservative.   B. a rebel.   C. a criminal.

7 laudable
(lô′də-bəl)
- *adjective*

- The work of the Prom Committee was really **laudable**. As people entered the ballroom and saw the magnificent decorations, many burst into applause.
- The congresswoman has demonstrated a **laudable** concern for the voters, who have shown their appreciation by reelecting her twice.

__ *Laudable* means   A. admirable.   B. insufficient.   C. undesirable.

8 painstaking
(pānz′tā′kĭng)
- *adjective*

- The **painstaking** effort that went into the century-old patchwork quilt is hard to imagine. There are thousands of tiny patches, each stitched patiently by hand.
- Providing footnotes and a bibliography for a paper is **painstaking** work. Don't leave this task until the last minute, but start working on it from the beginning.

__ *Painstaking* means   A. causing harm.   B. done with great care.   C. very enjoyable.

9 pompous
(pŏm′pəs)
- *adjective*

- The ship's captain was so **pompous** that he would not eat at the same table with his officers. Instead, he sat in solitary splendor at a special table set with the ship's best china.
- "Do you expect me to stand in line with all these people to buy a concert ticket?" the man asked in a **pompous** voice. "Don't you realize who I am and how valuable my time is?"

__ *Pompous* means   A. self-important.   B. modest.   C. cruel.

10 renown
(rĭ-noun′)
- *noun*

- The artist Vincent van Gogh was unknown in his lifetime, but after his death, he gained great **renown**.
- Throughout our neighborhood, Mrs. Lewis has won **renown** for her fabulous chocolate-chip cookies.

__ *Renown* means   A. criticism.   B. reality.   C. fame.

Matching Words with Definitions

Following are definitions of the ten words. Clearly write or print each word next to its definition. The sentences above and on the previous page will help you decide on the meaning of each word.

1. _____ Having or showing wide knowledge

2. _____ Great warmth or intensity of emotion

3. _____ To cause or produce; bring into existence

4. _____ Worthy of praise; deserving admiration

5. _____ Showing much care, effort, and hard work; diligent

6. _____ Having an inflated idea of one's own importance; arrogant

7. _____ Widespread honor and praise; acclaim

8. _____ Someone who attacks traditional ideas; someone who considers nothing sacred

9. _____ No longer current; out-of-date

10. _____ Theoretical; not applied; not practical

CAUTION: Do not go any further until you are sure the above answers are correct. Then you can use the definitions to help you in the following practices. Your goal is eventually to know the words well enough so that you don't need to check the definitions at all.

Sentence Check 1

Using the answer line provided, complete each item below with the correct word from the box. Use each word once.

A. **abstract**	B. **archaic**	C. **engender**	D. **erudite**	E. **fervor**
F. **iconoclast**	G. **laudable**	H. **painstaking**	I. **pompous**	J. **renown**

_____ 1. Today's children have been brought up with cell phones. To them, their grandmother's old-fashioned rotary dial telephone looks positively ___.

_____ 2. We are lucky to have such a(n) ___ speaker with us today. Dr. Volkmer holds three doctoral degrees and has taught at some of the world's most prestigious° universities.

_____ 3. Year after year, the town pageant was very traditional until its new director—a real ___—decided to wrap the actors in aluminum foil and have them speak their lines in rap style. His predecessor°, in a letter to the editor, chastised° him for desecrating° the production.

_____ 4. I knew that Tai would feel strongly about our change of plans, but I didn't expect him to respond with such ___. His emotional tirade° lasted half an hour.

_____ 5. Dave and his brother Barry are very different. Dave is down-to-earth and practical, while Barry loves to discuss ___ concepts like infinity and time.

_____ 6. Little things can often ___ long-standing hostility. My aunts were on bad terms for years because one of them turned down a dinner invitation from the other. They were never able to rectify° this injury to their cordial° relationship.

_____ 7. The new biography of Emily Dickinson won high praise. "The author's ___ research has revealed many details about the poet that were not previously known," one reviewer wrote.

_____ 8. After winning a diminutive° part in a Broadway show, the actor became so ___ and supercilious° that he wouldn't speak to his old friends. "I don't have time for little people," he said.

_____ 9. That restaurant enjoys such ___ that it's almost impossible to get a reservation there—the tables are booked months in advance.

_____ 10. "It's ___ to go out and help clean up the neighborhood streets," Mother told us, "but it would also be praiseworthy for you to clean up your rooms."

NOTE: Now check your answers to these items by turning to page 177. Going over the answers carefully will help you prepare for the next two practices, for which answers are not given.

Sentence Check 2

Using the answer lines provided, complete each item below with **two** words from the box. Use each word once.

_____ 1–2. Is it ___ for parents to say "yes" every time their kids ask for something? I _____ don't think it's praiseworthy at all; it will just ___ in the children a sense that the world owes them a living.

_____ 3–4. The lecturer was certainly ___, but despite her vast knowledge, she was hard
_____ to follow because her talk was too ___. She spoke about intangible° theories
and abstruse° principles without ever giving concrete, specific examples.

_____ 5–6. Marya gained ___ as a(n) ___ in third grade, when she drew a moustache and
_____ an eye patch on Washington's picture in the auditorium. Today she's still
known as a rebel and a heretic°.

_____ 7–8. In the movie, the stiff, formal, ___ young businessman suddenly falls in love,
_____ and he sweeps the heroine off her feet with his passionate, eloquent° ___.

_____ 9–10. Completing the crossword puzzle took hours of ___ work because many of
_____ the answers were ___ words—terms so old they weren't in my dictionary.

Final Check: *The Scholar*

Here is a final opportunity for you to strengthen your knowledge of the ten words. First read the following
selection carefully. Then fill in each blank with a word from the box at the top of the previous page.
(Context clues will help you figure out which word goes in which blank.) Use each word once.

New students at a university are usually cognizant° of an important fact about the faculty:
that these people are more than just teachers—they are scholars. But some students with narrow,
parochial° outlooks have formed a mistaken notion of scholarship: they think of a scholar as stuffy and
(1)_____, as having only impractical, (2)_____ ideas and being out
of touch with reality. They dismiss scholarship as (3)_____, something left over
from the distant, stagnant° past. The truth is quite different, though.

Scholarship has three aspects, each (4)_____ and admirable. First, there is learning.
Scholars are (5)_____: they know all about their own field, and often a great deal else.
Second is teaching. Scholars are expected to pass their knowledge along to the next generation. They also
hope to whet° students' interest in their field by conveying their own (6)_____ for the
subject—and eventually to (7)_____, in their most astute° students, a similar passion
and commitment. Third, scholars are expected to make a contribution to their subject, to add to the body
of knowledge. This involves rigorous°, (8)_____, often lengthy research and writing.
This writing cannot be haphazard° or colloquial°; scholars are expected to present their findings in an
organized, formal framework. Also, scholars must write clearly enough to make their otherwise inscrutable°
subject matter understandable.

So, to recapitulate°, scholars may win (9)_____ for their knowledge, for inspired
teaching, for exemplary° writing—or for all three. Occasionally, such fame is a source of controversy: a
scholar whose approach is highly original may become known as a(n) (10)_____ and
may set off an intellectual revolution. Look around you—is there such a rebel on your campus?

| Scores | Sentence Check 2 _____% | Final Check _____% |

Enter your scores above and in the **Vocabulary Performance Chart** on the inside back cover of the book.

convivial	paradigm
equanimity	profusion
lassitude	recalcitrant
listless	resigned
mollify	surmise

Ten Words in Context

In the space provided, write the letter of the meaning closest to that of each **boldfaced** word. Use the context of the sentences to help you figure out each word's meaning.

1 convivial
(kən-vĭv′ē-əl)
- *adjective*

● Dawn and Freddy's date at the candlelit restaurant was not as romantic as they hoped. They had to shout at each other to be heard over the loud laughter and singing of the **convivial** group at the next table.

● The emcee at my cousin's wedding was too **convivial**. He hugged all the women and dragged couples onto the dance floor instead of letting them sit and talk.

__ *Convivial* means   A. dull.   B. argumentative.   C. sociable.

2 equanimity
(ē′kwə-nĭm′ĭ-tē)
- *noun*

● We can usually react to misfortune with **equanimity** when it happens to someone else. When it happens to us, we tend to be much more distressed.

● Tracy gave a birthday party for her four-year-old son and ten of his little friends without losing her **equanimity**. However, she spent the next day in bed, weakly sipping tea.

__ *Equanimity* means   A. equality.   B. calmness.   C. grief.

3 lassitude
(lăs′ĭ-tōod′)
- *noun*

● **Lassitude**, a strange drowsiness or lack of vigor, is one symptom of spring fever.

● It used to be thought that people in southern climates were naturally lazy. In fact, their apparent **lassitude** was caused by a widespread disease, malaria.

__ *Lassitude* means   A. illness.   B. tiredness.   C. resistance.

4 listless
(lĭst′lĭs)
- *adjective*

● Children who seem **listless** on school mornings, complaining of pains or nausea, may actually have "school phobia." They're not really sick; they're afraid.

● Depression often goes undiagnosed in the elderly because people assume—mistakenly—that being **listless** and weary is just part of being old.

__ *Listless* means   A. without energy.   B. lonely.   C. refusing to obey.

5 mollify
(mŏl′ə-fī′)
- *verb*

● Theo is furious when anyone disagrees with him. We've learned to **mollify** him by saying, "You're right. We were just tossing ideas around."

● When Ruben forgot to show up for their date, Jillian was enraged. But she was **mollified** when he sent her candy and flowers and begged her to forgive him.

__ *Mollify* means   A. to mislead.   B. to calm down.   C. to reject.

6 paradigm
(păr′ə-dīm′)
- *noun*

● The Constitution of the United States became a **paradigm** for several emerging democracies, which based their own governments on it.

● The "disease model" of mental disturbance—seeing it as comparable to physical illness—has been a **paradigm** for other conditions, such as addiction.

__ *Paradigm* means   A. a pattern to follow.   B. a puzzle to solve.   C. a descendant.

7 profusion
(prə-fyōō′zhən)
- *noun*

- If you're hungry, get off the highway at the next exit. You'll find a **profusion** of fast-food restaurants there.
- When Paco returned from his summer vacation, he found his yard overgrown with a **profusion** of weeds.

__ *Profusion* means   A. a large quantity.   B. a shortage.   C. a probability.

8 recalcitrant
(rĭ-kăl′sĭ-trənt)
- *adjective*

- As other shoppers watched with amusement, a father tried to persuade his child to climb out of the dress rack she was hiding in, while the **recalcitrant** child cried, "No—you climb in!"
- A truly **recalcitrant** person would not do well in the army—soldiers must be willing to follow orders.

__ *Recalcitrant* means   A. disobedient.   B. disappointed.   C. dishonest.

9 resigned
(rĭ-zīnd′)
- *adjective*

- Scott had become **resigned** to being the shortest boy in his class, but during the summer, he grew four inches.
- Although Nina has never learned to like spinach, she has become **resigned** to eating it once in a while.

__ *Resigned to* means   A. refusing to believe in.   B. agreeing to without protest.   C. eager about.

10 surmise
(sər-mīz′)
- *verb*

- Archaeologists in the year 2998, digging up the ruins of a baseball stadium, find a hand-lettered banner: KILL THE UMPIRE! They write: "We **surmise** that this place was used for human sacrifices."
- Arriving for dinner on December 25, Uncle Jake looked at the tree with its ornaments, the holly, and the brightly wrapped gifts. "I **surmise**," he said thoughtfully, "that it must be Christmas."

__ *Surmise* means   A. to express surprise.   B. to deny.   C. to suppose.

Matching Words with Definitions

Following are definitions of the ten words. Clearly write or print each word next to its definition. The sentences above and on the previous page will help you decide on the meaning of each word.

1. _____ A lack of energy or interest; weariness; fatigue

2. _____ To soothe the temper of

3. _____ An abundance; a rich supply

4. _____ Stubbornly refusing to obey

5. _____ To infer; guess

6. _____ Unresisting; passively accepting; accepting as inevitable

7. _____ An example that serves as a model for others

8. _____ The quality of staying calm and even-tempered

9. _____ Fond of social pleasures; merry; festive

10. _____ Lacking energy or interest; sluggish

CAUTION: Do not go any further until you are sure the above answers are correct. Then you can use the definitions to help you in the following practices. Your goal is eventually to know the words well enough so that you don't need to check the definitions at all.

Sentence Check 1

Using the answer line provided, complete each item below with the correct word from the box. Use each word once.

A. convivial	B. equanimity	C. lassitude	D. listless	E. mollify
F. paradigm	G. profusion	H. recalcitrant	I. resigned	J. surmise

_____ 1. The biology teacher's ___ was tested when a lab rat escaped from its cage and ran up the teacher's pant leg. He attempted to remain calm, but the beads of sweat on his forehead revealed his trepidation°.

_____ 2. For months after his father's death, Kareem felt ___: he was uninterested in his usual activities and seemed incapable of exerting any effort.

_____ 3. Each spring the meadow is filled with a(n) ___ of wildflowers.

_____ 4. Johanna's ___ neighbor gives a party every weekend.

_____ 5. Ray has trouble keeping a job because he tends to be ___. He doesn't understand that a worker has to assent° to and carry out the boss's orders.

_____ 6. The leader of the insurgents° never grew ___ to being in jail. Every day, his resolution° to escape and rejoin the rebel forces grew stronger.

_____ 7. "I'm handing out a sample research paper," said the instructor. "You can use its footnotes and references as a(n) ___ for your own."

_____ 8. There's a good reason why we feel so sleepy after Thanksgiving dinner. Turkey is soporific°—it contains a chemical that produces ___ in many people.

_____ 9. The Hoof 'n' Claw Restaurant advertised a special lobster dinner and then ran out of lobster. The manager tried to ___ the angry customers by offering them free steaks.

_____ 10. No one is answering the phone at my neighbor's house, and the newspapers are piling up on his porch. I ___ that he is on vacation.

NOTE: Now check your answers to these items by turning to page 177. Going over the answers carefully will help you prepare for the next two practices, for which answers are not given.

Sentence Check 2

Using the answer lines provided, complete each item below with **two** words from the box. Use each word once.

_____
_____   1–2. Most people experience ___ during a heat wave—they have little energy. But for me, cold weather, rather than hot weather, has a debilitating° effect: I feel ___ and enervated° when it's freezing out.

_____
_____   3–4. To avoid a(n) ___ of different methods for teaching gifted children, the board of education developed one model program that would serve as a(n) ___ for all schools statewide.

_____
_____   5–6. When his fiancée broke off their engagement, Joe reacted with stoic° ___. "I had a premonition° this would happen," he said calmly, "and I'm ___ to it."

_____   7–8. The ___ people in the upstairs apartment do a lot of entertaining, but to ___
_____   their neighbors, they try to keep the noise to a minimum.

_____   9–10. Bill keeps getting into trouble in the navy by refusing to obey orders. I ___
_____   that he must also have been ___ as a child.

Final Check: *A Case of Depression*

Here is a final opportunity for you to strengthen your knowledge of the ten words. First read the following selection carefully. Then fill in each blank with a word from the box at the top of the previous page. (Context clues will help you figure out which word goes in which blank.) Use each word once.

Gina is known to her friends as an outgoing, (1)_____ person who responds with exuberance° to any invitation: "Sounds like fun! Let's go!" So when Gina stopped going to parties, movies, and nights out last year, it seemed strange. "You go," she would tell her friends. "I'm tired. I just don't feel like it."

"She's just a little blue," her friends told one another. "She'll snap out of it." But she didn't. Weeks turned into months, and Gina's (2)_____ attitude persisted. She had no appetite, and she told her friends that she couldn't sleep. They were concerned, but Gina didn't appear to have enough energy to worry. She seemed (3)_____ to the idea that she would spend the rest of her life as a morose°, tired recluse°. Luckily, her friends kept insisting that she see a doctor. To (4)_____ them, she agreed.

Despite her (5)_____, Gina made an appointment and dragged herself to it. Her doctor quickly confirmed what her friends had (6)_____(e)d: Gina was suffering from serious depression. He suggested that she try an antidepressant medication. At first Gina was (7)_____—she stubbornly insisted that she should be able to "tough it out" on her own. Her doctor listened and then said something that made sense to her. "Nobody goes through life in a state of total (8)_____," he said. "Ups and downs are perfectly normal. But the kind of depression that you're experiencing is not normal. It's an aberration°, and it's not something you can control. It's a sign that something's gone wrong with the chemistry of your brain. The (9)_____ I like to use is diabetes: If you were diabetic, it would be erroneous° to think you should 'tough it out' without insulin."

There is a(n) (10)_____ of antidepressant medications available these days, and it took a few tries to find the one that worked well for Gina. But a few weeks into her treatment, she realized that the dark cloud of depression had lifted. She was once again eagerly looking forward to all life had to offer. Today she continues to take her medication, knowing that it is something her body needs. "I had a disease called depression," she tells anyone who asks. "But it didn't have me."

Scores	Sentence Check 2 _____%	Final Check _____%

Enter your scores above and in the **Vocabulary Performance Chart** on the inside back cover of the book.

ambivalence	incipient
anomaly	nefarious
biased	prodigious
credulous	servile
despot	temper

Ten Words in Context

In the space provided, write the letter of the meaning closest to that of each **boldfaced** word. Use the context of the sentences to help you figure out each word's meaning.

1 ambivalence
(ăm-bĭv′ə-ləns)
- *noun*

● Ramona and Felipe have broken their engagement three times now. If they feel such **ambivalence** about getting married, why do you think they stay together?

● Many people approach a job change with **ambivalence**. They want the new job's challenges and rewards, but they dislike giving up the security of the old job.

___ *Ambivalence* means   A. conflicting feelings.   B. ambition.   C. ignorance.

2 anomaly
(ə-nŏm′ə-lē)
- *noun*

● Dena's poor score on the math test was an **anomaly**; she usually does very well in math.

● A colored diamond is an **anomaly**; most diamonds are colorless or bluish-white.

___ *Anomaly* means   A. an annoyance.   B. a source of anxiety.   C. an abnormality.

3 biased
(bī′əst)
- *adjective*

● Studies show that names influence how we react to other people. For instance, a group of teenaged boys expected that any girl named "Michelle" would be attractive, while they were **biased** against anyone named "Hulga."

● Every human group seems to be **biased** against some other group. For example, the French tell jokes about the Belgians, and people in Quebec make fun of people from Newfoundland.

___ *Biased* means   A. having a good opinion.   B. having an opinion beforehand.   C. having no opinion.

4 credulous
(krĕj′ə-ləs)
- *adjective*

● Maya reads her horoscope every day but insists that she's not **credulous**. "It's just for fun," she says. "I never take it seriously."

● **Credulous** Dwayne believed his girlfriend when she told him she was an actress. In fact, the only part she ever had was in a health play in third grade, as a radish.

___ *Credulous* means   A. too trustful.   B. too skeptical.   C. not paying attention.

5 despot
(dĕs′pət)
- *noun*

● During the American Revolution, the British king, George III, was seen as an unjust **despot**, but history has dealt more kindly with him in recent years.

● Some parents are harsh **despots** who make their children obey their commands, while others are lenient and easygoing.

___ *Despot* means   A. an elected official.   B. an oppressive ruler.   C. a revolutionary.

6 incipient
(ĭn-sĭp′ē-ənt)
- *adjective*

● Are Kenyon and Rasheedah just friends, or is there an **incipient** romance developing?

● "Precancerous" cells are an **incipient** tumor—a cancer that may be starting to develop.

___ *Incipient* means   A. coming to an end.   B. coming into existence.   C. fully grown.

7 nefarious
(nə-fâr′ē-əs)
- *adjective*

- The name of Jack the Ripper, whose **nefarious** murders shocked nineteenth-century England, has become almost a synonym for a brutal killer.
- The movie, about a **nefarious** plot by terrorists to kidnap a bus full of schoolchildren, had us on the edge of our seats.

___ *Nefarious* means   A. praiseworthy.   B. amusing.   C. evil.

8 prodigious
(prə-dĭj′əs)
- *adjective*

- This week the lottery prize is a **prodigious** amount of money—almost a hundred million dollars.
- It takes a **prodigious** supply of patience to put together a 5,000-piece jigsaw puzzle.

___ *Prodigious* means   A. huge.   B. unknown.   C. small.

9 servile
(sûr′vīl *or*
(sûr′vəl)
- *adjective*

- In the play, Roberto portrayed a fawning, **servile** hotel clerk who would do anything to please the hotel's clients.
- The spoiled celebrity likes to surround herself with **servile** people who do whatever she wants and constantly tell her how fabulous she is.

___ *Servile* means   A. bossy.   B. acting like a slave.   C. powerful.

10 temper
(tĕm′pĕr)
- *verb*

- "**Temper** justice with mercy"—a phrase from Milton's *Paradise Lost*—suggests that we need to remember to be kind, even when we are punishing someone.
- The saying "God **tempers** the wind to the shorn lamb" means that God lightens the burdens of weaker people, so that they don't have to suffer as much.

___ *Temper* means   A. to reinforce.   B. to tone down.   C. to continue.

Matching Words with Definitions

Following are definitions of the ten words. Clearly write or print each word next to its definition. The sentences above and on the previous page will help you decide on the meaning of each word.

1. _____ Prejudiced; having a preconceived opinion

2. _____ Mixed feelings; uncertainty; indecisiveness

3. _____ Beginning; early; in the earliest stages (of)

4. _____ Humbly obedient

5. _____ To reduce in intensity, especially by mixing in some other quality; moderate; soften

6. _____ Someone who rules with absolute power; a tyrant

7. _____ Enormous

8. _____ Very wicked; villainous

9. _____ Tending to believe too readily; easily convinced

10. _____ Something different, odd, or peculiar

CAUTION: Do not go any further until you are sure the above answers are correct. Then you can use the definitions to help you in the following practices. Your goal is eventually to know the words well enough so that you don't need to check the definitions at all.

Sentence Check 1

Using the answer line provided, complete each item below with the correct word from the box. Use each word once.

A. ambivalence	B. anomaly	C. biased	D. credulous	E. despot
F. incipient	G. nefarious	H. prodigious	I. servile	J. temper

_____ 1. Sandra is very funny, but she needs to ___ her humor with kindness—sometimes her jokes can hurt others.

_____ 2. Amy feels some ___ about spending the holidays alone in her new apartment. On the one hand, she thinks celebrating there will make her new place feel more like home. On the other hand, she will miss her family.

_____ 3. There are two kinds of waiters I dislike: the zany° ones who keep making jokes and the sycophants° who, hoping for a bigger tip, are overly humble and ___.

_____ 4. In our neighborhood, almost everyone drives a battered second-hand car. Cecil's shiny new Corvette is a real ___.

_____ 5. Jen takes an aspirin at the first sign of a(n) ___ headache. Lin, by contrast, resists taking medicine even when she's really sick.

_____ 6. It's silly to be ___ against all red-haired people just because you had one bad date with a redhead. You should try to overcome your aversion° to redheads.

_____ 7. The thriller was the kind of book you can't put down—it traced a(n) ___ plan by a malevolent° scientist to turn his neighbors into zombies.

_____ 8. "Sorry," said Professor Chiu. "I am not ___ enough to believe that aliens from a flying saucer flew away with your term paper."

_____ 9. Shelley's famous poem "Ozymandias" is about a cruel ___ whose statue lies broken and whose kingdom has vanished in the desert sands. Its tacit° message is that all of us, even pompous° tyrants, are ephemeral°—nothing can survive the inexorable° forces of nature and time.

_____ 10. Thomas Jefferson was a man of ___ talent. Not only was he President of the United States, but he was also an inventor, an erudite° and eloquent° writer, and an architect.

NOTE: Now check your answers to these items by turning to page 177. Going over the answers carefully will help you prepare for the next two practices, for which answers are not given.

Sentence Check 2

Using the answer lines provided, complete each item below with **two** words from the box. Use each word once.

_____
_____ 1–2. The people's attitude toward the ___ who ruled them was one of ___. They hated him for his cruelty, but they also felt reverent° toward him for making their nation rich and powerful.

_____   3–4. Uriah Heep is a famous fictional villain created by the novelist Charles
_____   Dickens. The evil Heep conceals his ___ plans by acting very ___: he
                           constantly describes himself as "humble."

_____   5–6. The report was ___: the authors included only the evidence supporting
_____   their theory and left out the contrary evidence that would have negated° its
                           findings. But although the report was spurious°, ___ people simply accepted
                           it without examining the facts.

_____   7–8. The term "child prodigy" describes a(n) ___: someone who is very young but
_____   already shows ___ knowledge, talent, or skill in a particular area. Mozart, a
                           piano virtuoso° at age 6, is an example.

_____   9–10. People are always looking for ways to ___ the effects of a(n) ___ cold. Some
_____   swear by certain vitamins and herbs to keep the cold from getting worse.

Final Check: *Scientific Discoveries*

Here is a final opportunity for you to strengthen your knowledge of the ten words. First read the following selection carefully. Then fill in each blank with a word from the box at the top of the previous page. (Context clues will help you figure out which word goes in which blank.) Use each word once.

Students in a biology class were arguing about some recent developments in science and what they might mean to the world.

"I love science, so I am (1)_____ in favor of scientific discoveries. I tend to think they are laudable° and wonderful," said Ms. Kirschfeld, the teacher. "But even I feel some (2)_____ about certain discoveries and how they might be used. For instance, scientists have been able to clone animals that are exact copies of other animals. There is a(n) (3)_____ amount of research being conducted on cloning. What are some results that this profusion° of research could engender°?"

"Cloning scares me," said Eileen. "Imagine some evil (4)_____ who wants a country full of people who will do exactly what he tells them to do. He could clone a population of (5)_____ citizens who obeyed his every command."

"But cloning is just one part of a field that is full of wonderful discoveries," said Nguyen. "Every day, scientists are learning more about how they can eliminate certain diseases and disorders, like Down syndrome or sickle-cell anemia, which are caused by a(n) (6)_____ in the genes. And other (7)_____ breakthroughs are on the way. Imagine a person who is badly burned and needs a skin graft, or someone who needs a heart transplant. Someday, scientists might be able to grow skin or a heart from the person's own genetic material."

"Don't be so (8)_____," Brad said. "You have too much faith that any discovery will be put only to good use. But evil people often have (9)_____ plans for new discoveries. As Eileen said, some nut could decide to produce an army of submissive° people who would do anything he wanted."

"Clearly, these discoveries have good and bad possibilities," said Ms. Kirschfeld. "Let's hope that scientists will be circumspect° and (10)_____ their fervor° about what they are learning with caution about its future use."

Scores	Sentence Check 2 _____%	Final Check _____%

Enter your scores above and in the **Vocabulary Performance Chart** on the inside back cover of the book.

arduous	eulogy
ascetic	gratuitous
blithe	raze
deprecate	tawdry
didactic	unimpeachable

Ten Words in Context

In the space provided, write the letter of the meaning closest to that of each **boldfaced** word. Use the context of the sentences to help you figure out each word's meaning.

1 arduous
(är′jo͞o-əs)
- *adjective*

● According to an ancient story, the hero Hercules had to perform twelve **arduous** tasks, including killing a serpent with nine heads.

● By the time she finished the fifth bridesmaid's gown, Martha wished she had not taken on the **arduous** task of making all the dresses for her daughter's wedding.

__ *Arduous* means A. effortless.   B. demanding great effort.   C. useless.

2 ascetic
(ə-sĕt′ĭk)
- *adjective*

● Monks live a very **ascetic** life. Their rooms, for example, have plain white walls, a single bed, and one hard-backed chair.

● Many religious people believe in being **ascetic**. They feel that too many luxuries and possessions get in the way of their relationship with God.

__ *Ascetic* means A. self-denying.   B. selfish.   C. lazy.

3 blithe
(blīth)
- *adjective*

● In the play *Blithe Spirit*, a lighthearted ghost haunts her former husband.

● The students were in a **blithe** mood after their teacher canceled the midterm exam.

__ *Blithe* means A. bitter.   B. tragic.   C. joyful.

4 deprecate
(dĕp′rĭ-kăt′)
- *verb*

● Some writers **deprecate** television as a harmful influence, calling it a "vast wasteland" and a "plug-in drug." But despite these warnings, people keep watching.

● The Italian chef on television **deprecated** store-bought pasta, saying it tasted like cardboard. "Make your own fresh pasta!" she urged. "You'll love it."

__ *Deprecate* means A. to condemn.   B. to appreciate.   C. to describe.

5 didactic
(dī-dăk′tĭk)
- *adjective*

● Students are sometimes in college for reasons that have little to do with its **didactic** function: they care less about learning than about pleasing their parents, finding a husband or wife, "making contacts," and so on.

● Tests and examinations are not given just to annoy students. They have a **didactic** purpose as part of the learning process.

__ *Didactic* means A. twofold.   B. educational.   C. secret.

6 eulogy
(yo͞o′lə-jē)
- *noun*

● In Shakespeare's play *Julius Caesar,* the famous **eulogy** for Caesar begins like this: "Friends, Romans, countrymen: lend me your ears . . ."

● In a touching children's book called *The Tenth Good Thing about Barney,* a little boy creates a **eulogy** for his dead cat, listing ten things he loved about the cat.

__ *Eulogy* means A. a statement of praise.   B. an attack.   C. a plan.

7 gratuitous
(grə-tōō′ĭ-təs)
- *adjective*

● In some very good movies, violence is an important part of the story, but many other movies include **gratuitous** violence just to sell tickets.

● Mark makes a lot of **gratuitous** comments about how much money he has. Even if money isn't the topic of conversation, he wants everyone to know he is rich.

__ *Gratuitous* means   A. showing gratitude.   B. unnecessary.   C. unclear.

8 raze
(rāz)
- *verb*

● More than a dozen homes were **razed** to make way for the new shopping mall.

● The children spent hours building houses out of popsicle sticks, **razing** them with a toy bulldozer, then building them again.

__ *Raze* means   A. to build.   B. to repair.   C. to wreck.

9 tawdry
(tô′drē)
- *adjective*

● Katia has no taste in clothes and always chooses something **tawdry**. Her gold prom dress was trimmed with red and purple feathers and covered with silver spangles.

● The restaurant looked **tawdry**: the pink velvet curtains were grimy; the white carpet was stained; the crystal chandelier—actually plastic—was covered with dust.

__ *Tawdry* means   A. old-fashioned.   B. sleazy.   C. elegant.

10 unimpeachable
(ŭn′ĭm-pē′chə-bəl)
- *adjective*

● Janos said, "My mother's parenting has been **unimpeachable**. You can tell she was an excellent parent simply by the fact that I have turned out so well."

● "I expect your conduct on the playing field to be **unimpeachable**," the coach told the team. "Everything you do should bring credit and honor to the school."

__ *Unimpeachable* means   A. without fault.   B. difficult to judge.   C. inadequate.

Matching Words with Definitions

Following are definitions of the ten words. Clearly write or print each word next to its definition. The sentences above and on the previous page will help you decide on the meaning of each word.

1. _____ Cheerful and lighthearted

2. _____ Difficult to do; strenuous

3. _____ Designed to teach; instructive

4. _____ Uncalled for; without any good reason

5. _____ Practicing self-denial; austere

6. _____ To tear down completely; demolish

7. _____ Tastelessly showy; cheap and gaudy; vulgar

8. _____ A spoken or written tribute, especially to someone who has died

9. _____ Blameless; beyond reproach; beyond criticism

10. _____ To express disapproval of; criticize

CAUTION: Do not go any further until you are sure the above answers are correct. Then you can use the definitions to help you in the following practices. Your goal is eventually to know the words well enough so that you don't need to check the definitions at all.

Sentence Check 1

Using the answer line provided, complete each item below with the correct word from the box. Use each word once.

A. arduous	B. ascetic	C. blithe	D. deprecate	E. didactic
F. eulogy	G. gratuitous	H. raze	I. tawdry	J. unimpeachable

_____ 1. Although the older children were upset about moving, their four-year-old sister was her usual ___ self. She said, "This will be fun!"

_____ 2. Student teachers take some classes in specific subjects, such as math, and some in ___ methods, such as "Teaching the Elementary-School Child."

_____ 3. Readers are beginning to object to the newspaper's ___ use of photographs of crime scenes. Several times a week, the paper unnecessarily splashes some gruesome photo across the front page.

_____ 4. Before the invention of the modern printing press, publishing books was a(n) ___ and painstaking° task—it required copying every word by hand.

_____ 5. The work of the Widget Department has been ___. In the latest shipment of 633,521 widgets, there was not a single defect.

_____ 6. At the music teacher's funeral, one student spoke the ___, and then several others offered a musical tribute, singing some of her favorite choruses.

_____ 7. For his wedding, Bert wore a powder-blue tuxedo with fake leopard lapels. "It may be ___," he said, "but it's more fun than quiet good taste."

_____ 8. A big crowd gathered to watch the demolition crew ___ the old department store. It was strange to see the huge building crumble like a house of cards.

_____ 9. The Walkers have adopted a(n) ___ lifestyle in order to remember the many people in the world who are hungry. They often have only a little rice and some beans for dinner.

_____ 10. Dr. Krankheit ___s prescribing antibiotics for every case of the sniffles. "Let nature take its course," he says.

NOTE: Now check your answers to these items by turning to page 177. Going over the answers carefully will help you prepare for the next two practices, for which answers are not given.

Sentence Check 2

Using the answer lines provided, complete each item below with **two** words from the box. Use each word once.

_____
_____ 1–2. I don't ___ the town council's decision to ___ the old theater—I'm resigned° to the fact that some old buildings must come down. But I do feel ambivalence° about it; I wish we could preserve more landmarks from our past.

_____
_____ 3–4. A speaker may make "asides"—extraneous° comments that seem to be off the main point. Don't assume, however, that these are ___ and can be ignored; they may have a(n) ___ purpose.

_____

_____

5–6. Eleanor's brother delivered an eloquent° ___ at her funeral. He said she had been a(n) ___ spirit; her joyfulness and levity° would always remain with her family and friends.

_____

_____

7–8. "Your performance on this ___ assignment has been ___," the instructor told the research group. "You achieved perfection on a formidable° task."

_____

_____

9–10. Cognizant° of her own affinity° for ___, cheap-looking furnishings, Lorna hired a decorator for her new apartment. But his taste was so ___ that she now thinks the place looks stark and bare.

Final Check: *Saint Francis of Assisi*

Here is a final opportunity for you to strengthen your knowledge of the ten words. First read the following selection carefully. Then fill in each blank with a word from the box at the top of the previous page. (Context clues will help you figure out which word goes in which blank.) Use each word once.

Saints are generally thought of as, well, saintly. It's easy to surmise° that anyone who became a saint must have been born that way. But such congenital° holiness was not true of the man who became known as Saint Francis of Assisi.

Francis was born into a wealthy family in Assisi, Italy, in the year 1182. A convivial°, fun-loving young man, he was known as the life of the party. He neglected his studies, enjoyed practical jokes, and ran around with a fast crowd. Serving as a soldier at the age of twenty, he was captured and held as a prisoner of war. After he was released, he was seriously ill for many months. When he recovered, Francis had changed. He (1)_____(e)d his former frivolous° life and renounced° its meaningless, (2)_____ pleasures. He began to be more concerned about doing good, and so he decided to rebuild an old church that had been (3)_____(e)d. When Francis's father learned of this, he objected. In turn, Francis gave up any claim to his father's prodigious° wealth. He sold his property, even gave away his shoes, and began the (4)_____ life of a barefoot monk. He wandered through Italy, caring for the poor. He spoke with all he met, telling them that money and possessions were (5)_____, and extolling° the blessings of the spirit. Throughout his travels, he impressed people with his joyous presence. His (6)_____ personality attracted many followers, and eventually he founded the Franciscan order of monks and the Poor Clares, an order of nuns. Francis preached to thousands in his lifetime, teaching them to love and care for the poor; but while his talks were (7)_____, they were never dull. He was a natural teacher, preaching even to the birds, whom he called "my little sisters," and reminding them always to praise and exalt° God. According to legend, Francis was so kind to animals that wild rabbits ran to him for protection.

Francis's faith in God was so strong that he once undertook a(n) (8)_____ forty-day fast on a mountain, where he prayed and meditated. Such acts brought him renown° as a man of (9)_____ goodness, simplicity, and love. He died at the age of 45 and was declared a saint by the Catholic Church two years later. After Francis's death, the artist Giotto painted a famous picture of the joyful saint preaching to the birds—a tribute more fitting than any spoken (10)_____ for the modest man who called himself "little brother Francis."

Scores   Sentence Check 2 _____%   Final Check _____%

Enter your scores above and in the **Vocabulary Performance Chart** on the inside back cover of the book.

The box at the right lists twenty-five words from Unit Six. Using the clues at the bottom of the page, fill in these words to complete the puzzle that follows.

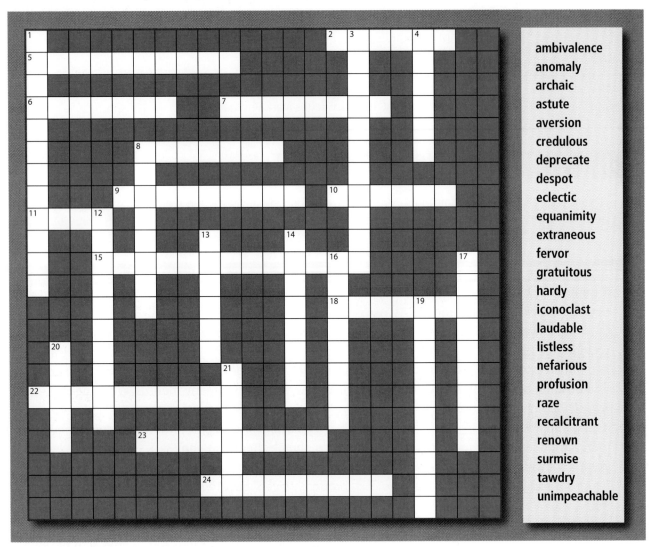

ambivalence
anomaly
archaic
astute
aversion
credulous
deprecate
despot
eclectic
equanimity
extraneous
fervor
gratuitous
hardy
iconoclast
laudable
listless
nefarious
profusion
raze
recalcitrant
renown
surmise
tawdry
unimpeachable

ACROSS

2. Cheap and gaudy
5. Not essential; irrelevant
6. No longer current; out-of-date
7. Coming from many sources
8. Something different or odd
9. Very wicked
10. Someone who rules with absolute power; a tyrant
11. To tear down completely
15. Blameless
18. To infer; guess
22. Uncalled for; without good reason
23. An abundance; rich supply
24. To express disapproval of; criticize

DOWN

1. Stubbornly refusing to obey
3. Mixed feelings
4. Widespread honor and praise; acclaim
8. An intense dislike
12. The quality of staying calm
13. Great warmth or intensity of emotion
14. Worthy of praise; deserving admiration
16. Lacking energy or interest; sluggish
17. Easily convinced
19. Someone who attacks traditional ideas
20. Tough; strong
21. Clever; perceptive

PART A

Choose the word that best completes each item and write it in the space provided.

_____ 1. Although the new supervisor is ___ and young-looking, he quickly earned the respect of everyone in the office.

    A. tawdry   B. diminutive   C. extraneous   D. eclectic

_____ 2. "This book," wrote the critic, "could be sold as a sleeping aid—it is that ___."

    A. soporific   B. unimpeachable   C. recalcitrant   D. credulous

_____ 3. Instead of having the preacher deliver the usual ___, friends of the woman who had died took turns speaking about her and her wonderful qualities.

    A. eulogy   B. paradigm   C. profusion   D. despot

_____ 4. Spring came suddenly this year. One week, it seemed, the earth was dead and dull, but the next week, there was a(n) ___ of wildflowers.

    A. paradigm   B. iconoclast   C. eulogy   D. profusion

_____ 5. When you write a paper, stick to your point. Don't introduce any ___ topics.

    A. extraneous   B. nefarious   C. didactic   D. diminutive

_____ 6. Hoping to sound ___ to his date, Len spent the afternoon reading the *Wall Street Journal,* the *New York Times,* and some articles in the encyclopedia.

    A. hardy   B. credulous   C. erudite   D. incipient

_____ 7. "Dost thou take this woman to be thy lawfully wedded wife?" the preacher asked. Amused by the ___ language, the couple couldn't help giggling.

    A. recalcitrant   B. soporific   C. archaic   D. resigned

_____ 8. "Are you comfortable? Can I get you something to eat? You're looking awfully pretty today. Would you like a pillow for your head?" my brother asked me, making me very suspicious. Why was he being so ___?

    A. resigned   B. incipient   C. listless   D. servile

_____ 9. To me, geese always look ___, strutting around with their chests puffed out and their heads held high in the air.

    A. servile   B. credulous   C. gratuitous   D. pompous

_____ 10. The discovery of life on another planet would ___ tremendous excitement among both scientists and the general population.

    A. deprecate   B. surmise   C. raze   D. engender

(Continues on next page)

_____ 11. Tanya likes her bleached-blond hair, but her grandmother thinks it makes her look ___. "Nice girls don't dye their hair," she says.

        A. erudite   B. prodigious   C. listless   D. tawdry

_____ 12. People are arguing about what to do with the beautiful but run-down old town hall: ___ it and build a new one, or spend a lot of money restoring it?

        A. surmise   B. temper   C. engender   D. raze

_____ 13. To many of his students, Professor Oppenheimer was the ___ of a teacher: kind, wise, generous, and insightful.

        A. iconoclast   B. profusion   C. paradigm   D. despot

PART B

Write **C** if the italicized word is used **correctly**. Write **I** if the word is used **incorrectly**.

_____ 14. Try to get to the refreshment table before my *abstemious* uncle does. He'll eat anything that isn't nailed down.

_____ 15. Holidays at Mrs. Miller's house are always exactly the same. She's such an *iconoclast*— everything has to be done according to old family traditions.

_____ 16. Jaime has very *eclectic* tastes in music. His CD collection contains everything from Mozart to old-time country music to hip-hop to reggae.

_____ 17. I like to order a very spicy curry in my favorite Indian restaurant, but I also like to *temper* its fiery heat with a side order of cool plain yogurt.

_____ 18. The Wilsons were delighted by their son's engagement to a girl they all loved. "We're not losing a son," said Mr. Wilson. "We're gaining the most *nefarious* daughter we could have ever hoped for."

_____ 19. The doctor tried to calm the frightened child, but everything he said only *mollified* her, making her shriek and cry even more.

_____ 20. The second-grade teacher noticed an *incipient* dislike developing between two boys who sat beside each other, so she changed the seating arrangement to keep the problem from going any further.

_____ 21. Unlike some flowers, such as marigolds, which are tough and easy to grow, orchids are *hardy* and need very delicate care in order to do well.

_____ 22. Fans cheered when the boxer knocked his opponent down, but then booed when he delivered a *gratuitous* punch to the fallen man.

_____ 23. An amusing children's song tells the story of Pierre, a boy whose answer to any question is "I don't care." He responds with the same *fervor*—saying "I don't care"—even when a lion asks "Shall I eat you up?" And so the lion does.

_____ 24. This morning Roseanne worked silently at her desk, frowning and snapping "Yes" or "No" when anyone asked her a question. I have no idea what's making her so *blithe*.

_____ 25. Mrs. Kopeckne conducts most employee interviews at her workplace. But when her niece applied for a job, Mrs. K. asked a colleague to do the interview: "If Rachael is hired, I don't want anyone saying it was because I was *biased* in her favor."

Score   (Number correct) _____ x 4 = _____%

PART A

On the answer line, write the word from the box that completes each item below. Use each word once.

A. anomaly	B. arduous	C. ascetic	D. astute	E. despot
F. didactic	G. equanimity	H. listless	I. painstaking	J. prodigious
K. recalcitrant	L. surmise	M. unimpeachable		

_____ 1. Reading through the want ads for live-in baby sitters, Cara was attracted to one that said, "Are you friendly and cheerful? Is your honesty ___? Do you want to become a member of a loving family?"

_____ 2. Tamika did a(n) ___ job of braiding her sister's hair. Her hours of long, careful work showed—every braid was perfect and beautiful.

_____ 3. When a usually energetic child becomes ___, parents often suspect that he or she is getting sick.

_____ 4. Paul Bunyan, a hero of American folktales, was known for his ___ appetite. Breakfast for Paul might be three dozen eggs, six pounds of bacon, and all the bread a bakery could produce in a day.

_____ 5. I know it's silly to think of a machine as having human motives, but I still believe my computer is ___. Sometimes it seems to say, "I won't obey that command, and there's nothing you can do to make me."

_____ 6. Children's TV shows like *Sesame Street* are designed to be both entertaining and ___, keeping kids amused as they learn colors, numbers, and ABCs.

_____ 7. Good parenting is ___ work. No one should have a baby without realizing that the job of being a parent is a difficult one.

_____ 8. As he waited to hear whether he'd gotten a part in a Broadway play, the young actor had trouble maintaining his ___—one minute he'd feel cheerful and confident, and the next he was in despair.

_____ 9. Ivan the Terrible was a(n) ___ in sixteenth-century Russia. This ruler was so violent and power-mad that he would slaughter an entire village if he thought one resident was disloyal.

_____ 10. My father's eyes are a(n) ___—one is brown and the other is blue.

_____ 11. A(n) ___ person and a person who loves luxury are not suited as housemates. One is trying to scale down his or her standard of living, while the other is trying to raise it.

_____ 12. The teacher was so amused by my excuse for not handing in my paper that he gave me a compliment. "Anyone ___ enough to see that I'd enjoy an excuse like that is also smart enough to write a good paper," he said.

_____ 13. We make all kinds of assumptions every day. For instance, when we see the lights on in a friend's house, we ___ that the friend is at home.

(Continues on next page)

PART B

Write **C** if the italicized word is used **correctly**. Write **I** if the word is used **incorrectly**.

_____ 14. Just before leaving for her job interview, Eva felt *ambivalence* about what she was wearing. She liked her suit but wondered if the skirt was too short. She asked herself if her floral print dress would have been a better choice.

_____ 15. Although she is behind in the race, the candidate is *resigned* to losing. She will work desperately to earn votes until Election Day arrives.

_____ 16. Charles is a writer of such *renown* that hardly anyone has ever heard of him or his books.

_____ 17. That little boy's *aversion* to spinach is so great that he can't even bear to see it on the table, much less taste it.

_____ 18. The dance was a disaster. The guests were so *convivial* that they stood silently against the wall, ignoring one another all evening.

_____ 19. At present I have just an *abstract* idea of the house I'd like to build some day. To get a more realistic idea of what it would be like, I'd have to work with an architect and draw up some plans.

_____ 20. The judge spoke sternly to the convicted man. "Your offenses against the community are so *laudable* that I am going to give you the most severe punishment available to me."

_____ 21. The instructions for the children's new board game were so *abstruse* that the kids gave up in frustration and went outside to ride their bikes.

_____ 22. You have to be pretty *credulous* to believe some of the stories in the tabloids: "Blind Man Can Smell Colors" or "Aliens Built Mount Rushmore."

_____ 23. Silver is a beautiful horse, but he is too *intractable* for anyone but the most experienced riders to control.

_____ 24. Theresa worked hard on her dinner party, and her appreciative guests *deprecated* her efforts, praising the food and decorations to the skies.

_____ 25. Even on the phone, Wes's depression is obvious. His voice is full of *lassitude*, making him sound sad, tired, and sick.

Score   (Number correct) _____   x   4 = _____%

PART A: Synonyms

In the space provided, write the letter of the choice that is most nearly the **same** in meaning as the **boldfaced** word.

_____ 1. **abstract**   A. theoretical   B. clear   C. made up of many parts   D. common

_____ 2. **abstruse**   A. brightly colored   B. confined   C. complicated   D. broken

_____ 3. **anomaly**   A. a vegetarian   B. an oddity   C. a weakness   D. a preventive measure

_____ 4. **astute**   A. shy   B. recent   C. violent   D. clever

_____ 5. **aversion**   A. hatred   B. explanation   C. nuisance   D. absence

_____ 6. **despot**   A. a tyrant   B. a piece of furniture   C. a period of rest   D. a comrade

_____ 7. **didactic**   A. intended to deceive   B. educational   C. cheerful   D. sympathetic

_____ 8. **eclectic**   A. handed down over generations   B. not provable
C. from multiple sources   D. from one source

_____ 9. **engender**   A. to prove   B. to force   C. to cause   D. to defeat

_____ 10. **equanimity**   A. calmness   B. aggressiveness   C. weight   D. vision

_____ 11. **eulogy**   A. a tribute   B. a visit   C. an excuse   D. a loss

_____ 12. **fervor**   A. disturbance   B. passion   C. illness   D. insight

_____ 13. **lassitude**   A. talent   B. eagerness   C. resistance   D. weariness

_____ 14. **mollify**   A. to resent   B. to lie to   C. to soothe   D. to destroy

_____ 15. **paradigm**   A. something abnormal   B. a pleasant surprise   C. an ideal   D. a trick

_____ 16. **prodigious**   A. huge   B. perfect   C. expert   D. annoyed

_____ 17. **raze**   A. to allow   B. to rebuild   C. to withdraw   D. to destroy

_____ 18. **recalcitrant**   A. worthless   B. stubborn   C. excited   D. reckless

_____ 19. **renown**   A. fame   B. absence   C. location   D. waste

_____ 20. **resigned**   A. furious   B. unresisting   C. valuable   D. curious

_____ 21. **soporific**   A. suspicious   B. teasing   C. amusing   D. causing sleep

_____ 22. **surmise**   A. to hide   B. to guess   C. to refuse   D. to attack

_____ 23. **tawdry**   A. useless   B. without cause   C. cheap and vulgar   D. lasting a long time

_____ 24. **temper**   A. to excite   B. to explain   C. to tone down   D. to pull back

_____ 25. **unimpeachable**   A. blameless   B. bearing fruit   C. hairless   D. common

(Continues on next page)

PART B: Antonyms

In the space provided, write the letter of the choice that is most nearly **opposite** in meaning to the **boldfaced** word.

_____ 26. **abstemious**   A. unrestrained   B. self-important   C. peaceful   D. observant

_____ 27. **ambivalence**   A. the ability to use either the left or the right hand   B. generosity
                              C. acceptance   D. decisiveness

_____ 28. **archaic**   A. very large   B. hidden   C. up-to-date   D. violent

_____ 29. **arduous**   A. brief   B. graceful   C. romantic   D. easy

_____ 30. **ascetic**   A. unknown   B. self-indulgent   C. pleasant   D. loose

_____ 31. **biased**   A. open-minded   B. normal   C. stubborn   D. not decorated

_____ 32. **blithe**   A. empty   B. easily broken   C. depressed   D. not complete

_____ 33. **convivial**   A. lazy   B. honest   C. unsociable   D. talented

_____ 34. **credulous**   A. unstable   B. respected   C. highly educated   D. disbelieving

_____ 35. **deprecate**   A. to complain   B. to approve of   C. to look for   D. to reduce

_____ 36. **diminutive**   A. amusing   B. huge   C. wealthy   D. narrow

_____ 37. **erudite**   A. protected   B. ignorant   C. legal   D. jealous

_____ 38. **extraneous**   A. complicated   B. essential   C. thorough   D. frantic

_____ 39. **gratuitous**   A. level   B. necessary   C. proud   D. forced

_____ 40. **hardy**   A. varied   B. fragile   C. bossy   D. numerous

_____ 41. **iconoclast**   A. a talkative person   B. an athlete   C. a traditionalist   D. a supervisor

_____ 42. **incipient**   A. fully developed   B. badly planned   C. without reason   D. stubborn

_____ 43. **intractable**   A. obedient   B. scarce   C. excited   D. restless

_____ 44. **laudable**   A. dull   B. worried   C. careless   D. deserving blame

_____ 45. **listless**   A. easily angered   B. energetic   C. fair   D. moist

_____ 46. **nefarious**   A. bored   B. well-dressed   C. grateful   D. saintly

_____ 47. **painstaking**   A. careless   B. bad-tempered   C. distrustful   D. angry

_____ 48. **pompous**   A. humble   B. aggressive   C. hard-working   D. sarcastic

_____ 49. **profusion**   A. lack of interest   B. scarcity   C. obedience   D. arrogance

_____ 50. **servile**   A. sickly   B. worried   C. faithful   D. proud

Score   (Number correct) _____ x 2 = _____%

Enter your score above and in the **Vocabulary Performance Chart** on the inside back cover of the book.

A. Limited Answer Key

IMPORTANT NOTE: Be sure to use this answer key as a learning tool only. You should not turn to this key until you have considered carefully the sentence in which a given word appears.

Used properly, the key will help you to learn words and to prepare for the activities and tests for which answers are not given. For ease of reference, the title of the "Final Check" passage in each chapter appears in parentheses.

Chapter 1 (Blue Jeans)

Sentence Check 1

1. opulence	6. supplant
2. unassailable	7. incessant
3. voluminous	8. proximity
4. sagacious	9. fledgling
5. affinity	10. hackneyed

Chapter 2 (Do Opposites Attract?)

Sentence Check 1

1. brusque	6. effervescent
2. indefatigable	7. progeny
3. nonchalance	8. voracious
4. morose	9. misanthrope
5. stoic	10. dispassionate

Chapter 3 (What Are You Stingy About?)

Sentence Check 1

1. coalesce	6. surreptitious
2. exemplary	7. writhe
3. incidental	8. prodigal
4. parsimonious	9. insolvent
5. decadence	10. exuberance

Chapter 4 (Loony but True)

Sentence Check 1

1. frivolous	6. torpor
2. heist	7. unscathed
3. clemency	8. lampoon
4. brevity	9. respite
5. querulous	10. reproach

Chapter 5 (Writing a Better Paper)

Sentence Check 1

1. jargon	6. vacillate
2. levity	7. dearth
3. substantiate	8. meander
4. eloquent	9. unobtrusive
5. peripheral	10. copious

Chapter 6 (Bad Translations)

Sentence Check 1

1. cognizant	6. commiserate
2. hindrance	7. scrutinize
3. lavish	8. kindle
4. appall	9. expedient
5. negligent	10. ludicrous

Chapter 7 (Memory Aids)

Sentence Check 1

1. Irresolute	6. equivocal
2. untenable	7. rescind
3. contract	8. duplicity
4. Vilify	9. stagnant
5. clamor	10. uniform

Chapter 8 (A Formula for Teaching)

Sentence Check 1

1. apocryphal	6. irascible
2. garbled	7. desultory
3. loquacious	8. paucity
4. opaque	9. recapitulate
5. affable	10. obtuse

Chapter 9 (The One-Room Schoolhouse)

Sentence Check 1

1. profane
2. cacophony
3. accolade
4. assuage
5. gravity
6. censure
7. edifice
8. infraction
9. somber
10. diatribe

Chapter 10 (Galileo)

Sentence Check 1

1. languish
2. blasphemy
3. renounce
4. enmity
5. erroneous
6. garner
7. heretic
8. incite
9. recluse
10. peruse

Chapter 11 (Isadora Duncan)

Sentence Check 1

1. virtuoso
2. vitriolic
3. insipid
4. ingratiate
5. disparage
6. peerless
7. propriety
8. catalyst
9. aesthetic
10. whimsical

Chapter 12 (Miles Standish)

Sentence Check 1

1. rebuff
2. devious
3. efface
4. garrulous
5. ponderous
6. dissonance
7. amicable
8. static
9. predecessor
10. immutable

Chapter 13 (Men, Women, and Talk)

Sentence Check 1

1. articulate
2. belittle
3. diffident
4. laconic
5. acquiesce
6. delineate
7. scanty
8. subjugate
9. conciliatory
10. bombastic

Chapter 14 (Is Human Nature Good or Evil?)

Sentence Check 1

1. meager
2. salutary
3. anarchy
4. suppress
5. depravity
6. authoritarian
7. turbulence
8. predilection
9. temerity
10. quixotic

Chapter 15 (The Strange Case of X)

Sentence Check 1

1. steadfast
2. desecrate
3. heed
4. indigent
5. evanescent
6. callous
7. provincial
8. usurp
9. supercilious
10. paragon

Chapter 16 (The Salem Witches)

Sentence Check 1

1. buoyant
2. marred
3. satirical
4. pique
5. irrefutable
6. inexorable
7. enervate
8. incorrigible
9. partisan
10. parochial

Chapter 17 (Fashion Show)

Sentence Check 1

1. capitulate
2. zany
3. sycophant
4. premonition
5. prestigious
6. urbane
7. Stupor
8. cajole
9. reverent
10. egregious

Chapter 18 (Math Anxiety)

Sentence Check 1

1. congenital
2. extol
3. composure
4. inscrutable
5. trepidation
6. precocious
7. virulent
8. elusive
9. formidable
10. aberration

Chapter 19 (The Roma)

Sentence Check 1

1. obliterate
2. taciturn
3. stealthy
4. debilitate
5. contiguous
6. clairvoyant
7. spurn
8. accommodate
9. preclude
10. officious

Chapter 20 (The Jonestown Tragedy)

Sentence Check 1

1. discordant
2. indict
3. defame
4. sullen
5. grueling
6. thwart
7. indoctrinate
8. wanton
9. submissive
10. cordial

Chapter 21 (Helen Keller)

Sentence Check 1

1. caustic
2. chastise
3. insurgent
4. assiduous
5. Trite
6. fallacious
7. elucidate
8. placid
9. hypocrisy
10. exalt

Chapter 22 (Figures of Speech)

Sentence Check 1

1. whet
2. colloquial
3. hyperbole
4. incisive
5. discerning
6. crass
7. tacit
8. tactless
9. prerogative
10. judicious

Chapter 23 (When Is a Treatment Therapy?)

Sentence Check 1

1. haphazard
2. intangible
3. potent
4. rigorous
5. spurious
6. assent
7. incontrovertible
8. negate
9. therapeutic
10. ameliorate

Chapter 24 (Hawks and Doves)

Sentence Check 1

1. circumspect
2. guile
3. impassive
4. altercation
5. pugnacious
6. deference
7. volatile
8. tirade
9. placate
10. malevolent

Chapter 25 (New Year's Resolutions)

Sentence Check 1

1. induce
2. rectify
3. serene
4. discrepancy
5. catharsis
6. ephemeral
7. retract
8. phenomenon
9. resolution
10. capricious

Chapter 26 (Weird Facts)

Sentence Check 1

1. hardy
2. intractable
3. aversion
4. astute
5. diminutive
6. soporific
7. extraneous
8. abstemious
9. abstruse
10. eclectic

Chapter 27 (The Scholar)

Sentence Check 1

1. archaic
2. erudite
3. iconoclast
4. fervor
5. abstract
6. engender
7. painstaking
8. pompous
9. renown
10. laudable

Chapter 28 (A Case of Depression)

Sentence Check 1

1. equanimity
2. listless
3. profusion
4. convivial
5. recalcitrant
6. resigned
7. paradigm
8. lassitude
9. mollify
10. surmise

Chapter 29 (Scientific Discoveries)

Sentence Check 1

1. temper
2. ambivalence
3. servile
4. anomaly
5. incipient
6. biased
7. nefarious
8. credulous
9. despot
10. prodigious

Chapter 30 (Saint Francis of Assisi)

Sentence Check 1

1. blithe
2. didactic
3. gratuitous
4. arduous
5. unimpeachable
6. eulogy
7. tawdry
8. raze
9. ascetic
10. deprecate

B. Dictionary Use

It isn't always possible to figure out the meaning of a word from its context, and that's where a dictionary comes in. Following is some basic information to help you use a dictionary.

How to Find a Word

A dictionary contains so many words that it can take a while to find the one you're looking for. But if you know how to use guidewords, you can find a word rather quickly. *Guidewords* are the two words at the top of each dictionary page. The first guideword tells what the first word is on the page. The second guideword tells what the last word is on that page. The other words on a page fall alphabetically between the two guidewords. So when you look up a word, find the two guidewords that alphabetically surround the word you're looking for.

● Which of the following pairs of guidewords would be on the page with the word *disparage*?

disport / dissociate   **disentangle / diskette**   **dislike / displease**

The answer to this question and the questions that follow are given on the next page.

How to Use a Dictionary Listing

A dictionary listing includes many pieces of information. For example, here is a typical listing. Note that it includes much more than just a definition.

grum•ble (grŭm′bəl) *v.* **-bled, -bling.** To mutter discontentedly.
— *n.* A muttered complaint. —**grum′bler** *n.* —**grum′bly** *adj.*

Key parts of a dictionary entry are listed and explained below.

Syllables. Dots separate dictionary entry words into syllables. Note that *grumble* has one dot, which breaks the word into two syllables.

● To practice seeing the syllable breakdown in a dictionary entry, write the number of syllables in each word below.

mis•an•thrope _____   **res•o•lu•tion** _____   **in•de•fat•i•ga•ble** _____

Pronunciation guide. The information within parentheses after the entry word shows how to pronounce the entry word. This pronunciation guide includes two types of symbols: pronunciation symbols and accent marks.

Pronunciation symbols represent the consonant and vowel sounds in a word. The consonant sounds are probably very familiar to you, but you may find it helpful to review some of the sounds of the vowels—*a, e, i, o,* and *u.* Every dictionary has a key explaining the sounds of its pronunciation symbols, including the long and short sounds of vowels.

Long vowels have the sound of their own names. For example, the *a* in *pay* and the *o* in *no* both have long vowel sounds. Long vowel sounds are shown by a straight line (called a *macron*) above the vowel.

In many dictionaries, the *short vowels* are shown by a curved line (called a *breve*) above the vowel. Thus the *u* in the first syllable of *grumble* is a short *u*. The pronunciation chart on the inside front cover of this book indicates that the short *u* has the sound of *u* in *up*. It also indicates that the short *a* has the sound of *a* in *apple*, that the short *e* has the sound of *e* in *end*, and so on.

● Which of the words below have a short vowel sound? Which has a long vowel sound?

drink _____   **flight** _____   **stand** _____

Another pronunciation symbol is the *schwa* (ə), which looks like an upside-down *e*. It stands for certain rapidly spoken, unaccented vowel sounds, such as the *a* in *above*, the *e* in *item*, the *i* in *easily*, the *o* in *gallop*, and the *u* in *circus*. More generally, it has an "uh" sound, like the "uh" a speaker says when hesitating. Here are three words that include the schwa sound:

com•mence•ment (kə-měns′mənt)   **ex•tro•vert** (ěk′strə-vûrt)   **buoy•ant** (boi′ənt)

● Which syllable in *grumble* contains the schwa sound, the first or the second? _____

Accent marks are small black marks that tell you which syllable to emphasize, or stress, as you say a word. An accent mark follows *grum* in the pronunciation guide for *grumble,* which tells you to stress the first syllable of *grumble*. Syllables with no accent mark are not stressed. Some syllables are in between, and they are marked with a lighter accent mark.

● Which syllable has the stronger accent in *supercilious*? _____

su•per•cil•i•ous (soo′pər-sĭl′ē-əs)

Parts of speech. After the pronunciation key and before each set of definitions, the entry word's parts of speech are given. The parts of speech are abbreviated as follows:

noun—*n.*   pronoun—*pron.*   adjective—*adj.*   adverb—*adv.*   verb—*v.*

● The listing for *grumble* shows that it can be two parts of speech. Write them below:

_____   _____

Definitions. Words often have more than one meaning. When they do, each meaning is usually numbered in the dictionary. You can tell which definition of a word fits a given sentence by the meaning of the sentence. For example, the verb *discriminate* has two definitions: **1.** To make a clear distinction. **2.** To make distinctions on the basis of preference or prejudice.

● Show with a check ( ) which definition (1 or 2) applies in each sentence below:

The directors of the Acme Company have been accused of discriminating against women. 1 __ 2 __

Colorblind people cannot discriminate between red and green.   1 __ 2 __

Other information. After the definitions in a listing in a hardbound dictionary, you may get information about the *origin* of a word. Such information about origins, also known as *etymology,* is usually given in brackets. And you may sometimes be given one or more synonyms or antonyms for the entry word. *Synonyms* are words that are similar in meaning to the entry word; *antonyms* are words that are opposite in meaning.

Which Dictionaries to Own

You will find it useful to own two recent dictionaries: a small paperback dictionary to carry to class and a hardbound dictionary, which contains more information than a small paperback version. Among the good dictionaries strongly recommended are both the paperback and the hardcover editions of the following:

The American Heritage Dictionary
The Random House College Dictionary
Webster's New World Dictionary

Answers to the Dictionary Questions

Guidewords: *dislike/displease*   Accent: stronger accent on third syllable *(cil)*
Number of syllables: 3, 4, 6   Parts of speech: verb and noun
Vowels: *drink, stand* (short); *flight* (long)   Definitions: 2; 1
Schwa: second syllable of *grumble*

C. Topics for Discussion and Writing

NOTE: The first three items for each chapter are intended for discussion; the last two, for writing. Feel free, however, to either talk or write about any of the items.

Chapter 1 (Blue Jeans)

1. If you could live anywhere in the world, what place would you choose? Does your **affinity** for that location have to do with its geographical features, weather, cultural opportunities, or other factors?

2. Think of a time you have been trapped in close **proximity** to an **incessant** talker. How did you cope with the situation?

3. Depending upon one's personality, certain luxuries have more or less appeal. For instance, you might love the idea of owning a yacht or a **voluminous** designer handbag, but have no interest in a huge mansion or a Ferrari. What are some forms of **opulence** that especially appeal to you? What are some you would gladly do without?

4. What's one **hackneyed** phrase you'd be happy to never hear again? Which phrase or expression could **supplant** it? Write about why you dislike the stale, trite phrase, and suggest one or more alternatives that would express its meaning in a more original way.

5. Write about an important decision you have made recently. Looking back on that decision, do you now feel it was a **sagacious** one? Why or why not?

Chapter 2 (Do Opposites Attract?)

1. What are some techniques parents can use in order to encourage their **progeny** to become **voracious** readers?

2. Do you know someone who seems constantly **morose**, managing to see the dark side of even the happiest situation? Describe this person, giving examples of his or her negative reactions. By contrast, do you know another person, perhaps someone with an **effervescent** personality, who always manages to look on the bright side? Again, describe this person, giving examples.

3. What person do you know that could best be described as a **misanthrope**? How does he or she demonstrate that quality? Perhaps the person is a "loner," someone who really seems to dislike being with other people; or maybe he or she is someone who refuses to get involved in long conversations, preferring to be **brusque**. What, in your opinion, might have caused this person to become so unfriendly?

4. When you're upset about something, who would you rather talk to: a friend who will always tell you you're right, or someone who will be honest and **dispassionate**? Write about the pros and cons of both kinds of responses.

5. Write about a situation in which you tried to appear **stoic** or pretended **nonchalance**, but were really feeling something quite different. Why did you hide your true feelings?

Chapter 3 (What Are You Stingy About?)

1. Of all your relatives, which one do you consider the most **exemplary**? What qualities of that person do you find particularly admirable?

2. Some people find the current fad for reality shows a sign of society's **decadence**, declaring that we are, in the words of one writer, "amusing ourselves to death." Others think our involvement with these shows is **incidental**—nothing to be concerned about. What is your opinion of reality shows? Are they harmless entertainment, or something more troubling?

3. In their **exuberance**, excited little kids sometimes blurt out remarks that would be better left unsaid. What are some honest, perhaps funny or shocking (but ill-advised) remarks you've heard from high-spirited youngsters?

4. We all have incidents in our past that, when remembered, make us **writhe** with embarrassment. Write an account of such an incident from your life (or the life of someone you know). Are there any lessons that can be learned from this embarrassing incident?

5. In writing, compare and contrast two people of your acquaintance: one who is **prodigal** in spending, maybe even at the risk of becoming **insolvent**—and another who is **parsimonious**. Give examples of the spending habits of each.

Chapter 4 (Loony but True)

1. Comedians and talk-show hosts love to **lampoon** public figures, seizing upon those people's weaknesses and making them seem as ridiculous as possible. Few well-known people manage to get through their careers **unscathed** by such humorous criticism. Who are some public figures that are currently targets of this treatment? What are the comedians and talk-show hosts saying about them?

2. Celebrities are sometimes **querulous** about their treatment by comedians and the press, complaining that it is unfair, simply because they're famous, to single them out for criticism and ridicule. Do you agree that celebrities deserve better treatment than the negative or **frivolous** remarks found in gossip columns or on late-night TV? Or is such unwanted attention the price of fame?

3. Electronic entertainment—from TV to video games to social networking—is often blamed for making young people inactive and overweight. What are some ways parents, schools, and others can rouse kids from this electronic **torpor**? What can be done to encourage kids to give themselves a **respite** from passive entertainment—and become active again?

4. Write about a time that you received a **reproach** you did not think was deserved. By contrast, write about a time you were shown **clemency** when you *did* deserve criticism. How did each incident make you feel about yourself and the other person involved?

5. Think of a movie or TV show you've seen that involved a successful or attempted **heist**. Then write a review of this movie or show, telling why you thought it was (or was not) worth seeing. Include your opinion regarding whether this theft could occur in real life.

Chapter 5 (Writing a Better Paper)

1. Laughter and joking can be wonderful things, but in some situations, **levity** seems out of place. When have you observed, or experienced, misplaced levity? Have you, for instance, even been overcome with laughter at a solemn event? Explain.

2. Some people do not use a **copious** amount of words—when they speak, they come straight to the point. Others are inclined to **meander** from subject to subject, wandering off on **peripheral** topics until you've forgotten what the main point was. What people do you know who fit into that second category? Do you find their wandering conversational style charming, funny, irritating, or something else?

3. Think of a public figure whom you consider especially **eloquent**. Discuss that person's speaking style, explaining what it is about it that you find particularly impressive. For example, does the person avoid **jargon** or clichés? overused) trite

4. Sometimes the things we like best about our communities are small, ordinary details. Write about some **unobtrusive** aspect of your community that you like. Perhaps, for instance, it is a little hole-in-the-wall restaurant, or a small lot where kids play ball, or some other location that is easily overlooked, but that you think deserves recognition. Be sure to **substantiate** your opinion with plenty of specific details.

5. Write about an occasion when you **vacillated** over making a decision. (Maybe you're trying to decide about something right now!) Explain why the decision was (or is) so hard to make. If you finally made a choice, say whether you think it turned out to be the right one.

Chapter 6 (Bad Translations)

1. What do you think of the way your local TV station covers stories of crimes and other tragedies? Some viewers are **appalled** by the way reporters will ask bereaved people, "What happened? How do you feel?" On the other hand, perhaps the victims appreciate the way the TV reporters **commiserate** with them, saying things like "I'm so sorry; this is a terrible time for you." Do you think TV crews generally do a good job of covering tragic stories? Why or why not?

2. A genie comes to you and says, "I am giving you a wish. You may have one **lavish** gift for yourself. But there are limits. The gift has to be available for purchase at a mall. In other words, no new house, no trip, no car." The genie's words **kindle** in you the desire for one particular extravagant gift. What would it be, and why would this be the gift you wanted?

3. Think of a time that you were very angry. Now, consider this: Therapists often say that anger is a "top layer" emotion—it's one that is easy to feel, but often hides other feelings, such as hurt, fear, or embarrassment. As you think of the time you were angry, **scrutinize** your feelings and see if there were other emotions going on. Describe what happened and the anger you felt. Then continue with "In addition to anger, I was feeling _____ (name those other emotions)."

4. It's easy to see the faults of others. It's often harder to see our own. Write about a fault that you are **cognizant** you possess. For example, you might be **negligent** about starting a paper well before it's due, or you sometimes do the **expedient** thing instead of the right thing. How does that fault affect you? What might you do to overcome it?

5. Write about one single goal that is important in your life. As you see it now, what will be the biggest **hindrance** to your reaching that goal? How do you plan to deal with that obstacle?

Chapter 7 (Memory Aids)

1. If these houses cost the same, which would you choose: a brand-new four-bedroom house in a housing development where the houses were exactly **uniform**, each on a one-quarter-acre lot; or an older three-bedroom house that sat by itself on a large wooded lot, but that needed repairs? Why?

2. Under what circumstances might you deliberately say something **equivocal**? Think of situations where you would consider saying something that could be interpreted in more than one way. What would be the advantages—and the disadvantages—of your vague statements?

3. Teens sometimes use networking sites like Facebook and MySpace to bully and **vilify** one another, posting cruel comments and rumors about fellow teens. Why do you think they do this? How might they be made to stop hurting others in this way?

4. Write about a time you have been the victim of another person's **duplicity**. Did the person lie to you? Cheat you? **Rescind** an offer or a promise that you had already accepted? How did you respond?

5. Imagine that you have a relative, age 45, who feels that her career is **stagnant** and going nowhere. She would like to go to nursing school, but she's **irresolute**; she keeps saying, "I'd love it, but I'd be 50 before I got my degree." You think her position is **untenable** and that she should grab the opportunity to have a more satisfying career. Write an e-mail to her, explaining why she should apply to nursing school, including specific reasons to make your argument as convincing as possible.

Chapter 8 (A Formula for Teaching)

1. "Urban legends" are defined as "**apocryphal** stories involving incidents of the recent past, often including elements of humor and horror." Such stories spread quickly, thanks to **loquacious** people, and are generally told as if they were true. Classic urban legends include stories of deep-fried rats being served at fried-chicken restaurants, poisonous snakes hiding in rolled-up department store carpets, and vanishing hitchhikers who may have been ghosts. What stories have you heard that you suspect may be urban legends? **Recapitulate** one of these stories. How might you determine if the story is actually true?

2. Some people can be overly friendly—for example, starting conversations with total strangers, or inviting to their homes people they have just met. Do you know anyone who you think is *too* **affable**? What are the risks involved in such behavior?

3. What is a situation that is guaranteed to make you **irascible**? Is it waiting in line? Being caught in traffic? Receiving an important message that has somehow been **garbled** by whoever wrote it down? Describe a situation that is sure to bring out your inner grump.

4. Even the best students find certain subjects **opaque**. What is a class you've taken that was so difficult you felt absolutely **obtuse**? Write about the subject and what made it so hard to understand.

5. Who do you know who you would say suffers from a **paucity** of common sense? Write about this person. In your description, be sure to include some examples of his or her foolish behavior.

Chapter 9 (The One-Room Schoolhouse)

1. Consider some of the world's great **edifices**—the pyramids of Egypt; the Eiffel Tower in Paris; the Opera House in Sydney, Australia; etc. Of all the world's great buildings, which would you most like to visit? Why?

2. If you were in charge of discipline at your school, what are some **infractions** you would punish severely? What are others you would consider of lesser **gravity** and so would not take as seriously? What would make the difference to you?

3. When you are in a **somber** mood and want to lift your spirits, what do you do? What are some activities that you know can **assuage** your sad feelings?

4. Counselors sometimes recommend that when you're very angry, you write a letter to the person you're angry with. You're encouraged to make the letter a real **diatribe**, full of every hateful thing you've ever wanted to say to the person. Then, you burn the letter. If you were to write such a letter, who would receive it? (The recipient may be either real or imaginary.) What are some of the things you'd say? Write the letter, being specific about what the person has said or done to deserve your **censure**.

5. If you were to give out a "Greatest Person Award" to someone you know, who would receive that **accolade**, and why? Write about this person, providing examples that show why he or she deserves such praise.

Chapter 10 (Galileo)

1. Famous people sometimes become **recluses**, withdrawing mostly or completely from the public view. Examples of such celebrities include actress Greta Garbo, author J.D. Salinger, wealthy businessman Howard Hughes, and entertainer Michael Jackson. What do you think could drive a well-known person to **renounce** society in favor of a solitary life?

2. Anyone who has ever tried to buck the system or fight for change is likely, at some point, to be labeled a **heretic**. Who are some modern-day heretics that you know of? They might be active in local or national politics, religion, science, or another area. Do you support what they're doing, or do you consider them troublemakers? Explain.

3. When it comes to dealing with products that requires assembly, people seem to fall into two categories: those that carefully **peruse** the instructions before beginning to put the product together, and those that just dive in, figuring that they'll **garner** whatever information they need as they go along. Which category do you fall into? Are you usually successful in your efforts?

4. Think of a time that you developed a real feeling of **enmity** toward somebody. The person might be someone you know personally, a public figure, or perhaps someone you've just heard about through an acquaintance. Write about that experience, explaining what happened to **incite** your strong feelings of dislike. Did you ever get over your dislike of the person, or has it persisted to this day?

5. Write about a time when you formed an **erroneous** first impression of someone. Perhaps you initially found someone cold and unfriendly, but later learned the person was warm and caring. What do you think led to your mistaken first impression? How did you learn that it wasn't accurate?

Chapter 11 (Isadora Duncan)

1. Depending upon your own interests, you probably admire a variety of athletes, actors, musicians, or other well-known people. Of those celebrities, who would you say best deserves to be described as **peerless**—so talented that he or she is beyond compare? Provide some examples of why you consider this person such a **virtuoso**.

2. While "bullying" is often thought of as involving physical roughness, it is just as likely to involve harsh criticism and **vitriolic** remarks. How much of a problem was (or is) verbal bullying at your school? In what ways did kids **disparage** one another? Were adults of any help in stopping the bullying?

3. Take a look around the room in which you are sitting right now. How would you rate it in terms of **aesthetic** appeal? Is it attractive and pleasant to be in? What would you change to make it look more beautiful?

4. When we prepare a meal for company, we want to **ingratiate** ourselves with the guests, so we normally try to make the food tasty and attractive. But as an experiment, try designing a meal that is as **insipid** as possible. What are the most bland, boring, tasteless dishes you could serve? Write a description of that meal.

5. Imagine that you had an unlimited budget to design your own bedroom. The only requirement is that you make the room as unusual as possible. You could design it to look like a spaceship, for instance, or an Egyptian pyramid, or a treehouse. Let your imagination go wild, and write a description of your **whimsical** room.

Chapter 12 (Miles Standish)

1. One of the good things about Facebook and other social networks is that you may hear from old friends you've lost track of. On the other hand, you may also hear from people whom you don't particularly like or want to "friend." What do you do in that second situation? Do you openly **rebuff** the person by saying "no" to the friend request, or do you feel obligated to be **amicable** and say "yes"? Or is there a third, perhaps more **devious**, way to handle the situation that allows you to avoid the person but still seem friendly?

2. A common bit of advice about dating is "Don't talk too much about your ex-boyfriend or girlfriend." On the other hand, it's not realistic to expect people to completely **efface** their memories of former romantic partners. If you were starting to date someone, what would you want to know about your **predecessor**—the person's former boyfriend or girlfriend? Are there good reasons to want to hear these details?

3. When it comes to music, how do the different generations in your household get along? Do you and the older (or younger) people find each other's music boring, or mere **dissonance**? Are the words "That is not music; that is just noise" ever heard in your house? Or do you manage to find some music that you all enjoy?

4. There is an old saying, "Nothing in life is certain but death and taxes." And yet there are some things in life that appear unchanging and **static**. Write—seriously or humorously—about aspects of your life and your world that seem **immutable**. You might write, for instance, that Dad will always burn the grilled chicken, that Cousin Rob will always want to borrow money, and that your sister will always date losers.

5. When you're on public transportation and find yourself sitting beside a nonstop talker, how do you react? Do you simply ignore the talker, or do you use some other technique? Write about possible strategies for dealing with an extremely **garrulous** seatmate.

Chapter 13 (Men, Women, and Talk)

1. Imagine that you have been assigned to live alone for a week in a small, bare room. You will be provided with a chair, a table, a bed, clothing, and food. You are allowed to bring only four possessions. Which four would you bring? Why did you choose these? And how would you feel about spending a week alone with such scanty possessions?

2. Who do you consider the most articulate teacher you have ever had? Describe this teacher, making sure you delineate what made that person an unusually good communicator.

3. Think about a time when, to avoid an unpleasant situation, you acquiesced to someone else's wishes. How did you feel afterward? In general, is it better to be conciliatory and let the other person "win"—or to refuse to be belittled and insist on getting your own way? What are the advantages and disadvantages of each?

4. How wordy and overblown can you be? Select a common proverb such as one of these: "Never put off to tomorrow what you can do today"; "An ounce of prevention is worth a pound of cure"; "All work and no play makes Jack a dull boy"; "Two wrongs don't make a right." Now rewrite that proverb in as bombastic a way as you can.

5. On the other hand, can you be laconic? Rewrite this famous opening line (taken from Charles Dickens' novel *A Tale of Two Cities*) in as few words as possible:

    It was the best of times, it was the worst of times, it was the age of wisdom, it was the age of foolishness, it was the epoch of belief, it was the epoch of incredulity, it was the season of Light, it was the season of Darkness, it was the spring of hope, it was the winter of despair, we had everything before us, we had nothing before us, we were all going direct to heaven, we were all going direct the other way.

Chapter 14 (Is Human Nature Good or Evil?)

1. Some parents and children are involved in a movement called "unschooling." Unlike home schooling, "unschooling" involves no adult-planned lessons at all. Instead, children are encouraged to follow their own predilections and learn—or not learn—from doing whatever they like. Unschooling is a reaction against the authoritarian style of education, where schools and teachers make rules for students to follow. Do you think unschooling could be a workable way to educate children? Or is it a quixotic idea—nice in theory, but not practical?

2. You've probably encountered at least one teacher whose classroom was calm and peaceful, as well as at least one whose efforts to control the class were so meager that the classroom was a scene of anarchy, with no one seeming to be in charge. In your opinion, what makes a teacher an effective disciplinarian? If you were to advise the second teacher, what methods would you suggest to bring the turbulence under control?

3. When we hear of some unspeakable crime, it's tempting to think of the perpetrator, "That person is completely evil." But do you believe in absolute evil—in other words, that some people are simply born bad? Or when a person demonstrates some awful depravity, do you tend to think there must be some other underlying reason—extreme mental illness, perhaps, or abuse in the person's background? Support your opinion with examples from history or from recent and current events.

4. Just about everyone has had the experience of wanting to laugh at the wrong time. Think of a time when you were nearly overcome with laughter, but had to suppress it. Write about where you were, what amused you so, and what you did to try to force yourself not to laugh.

5. There is an old saying, "Fools rush in where angels fear to tread." In other words, people sometimes act with temerity when it is not very wise for them to do so. When have you done something rash and impulsive and not very sensible? Write about that incident and whether or not you regretted your actions afterward.

Chapter 15 (The Strange Case of X)

1. It's often difficult to know how to respond when people on the street ask for money. When someone is obviously **indigent** and perhaps hungry, it seems **callous** not to help. On the other hand, are there reasons *not* to **heed** the pleas of people who ask for handouts? Explain.

2. Are you a dog person—or a cat person? Dog people often say cats are **supercilious** creatures, unfriendly and scornful. Dogs, they insist, are loyal, **steadfast** companions. Cat people, on the other hand, may view dogs as drooling, messy creatures that are too **provincial** to use a litter box. Argue the case for your favorite pet!

3. Think of an activity you used to enjoy but are not interested in any more—perhaps a sport you no longer play, a former favorite TV show, or a neglected hobby. Why do you think this activity no longer appeals to you? What other activities have **usurped** its place?

4. If you could magically become a top performer in some field, what would that field be? Would you choose to be a **paragon** of athletic performance; a superb singer or musician or actor; a successful businessperson; a Nobel-Prize-winning scientist? Or is your fantasy to be a model of perfection in some other area? Write a description of yourself as a top achiever of some sort.

5. What kind of dreamer are you? Do your dreams tend to be vivid, leaving strong, lasting memories? Or are your dreams more often **evanescent**, leaving behind only faint impressions? Write a description of your "dream style," including at least one recent example.

Chapter 16 (The Salem Witches)

1. What are some examples of entertainment you have enjoyed that could be described as **satirical**? You might name a movie, TV show, book, or program produced for the Internet. What aspect of human foolishness or vice do they poke fun at?

2. Many people feel that global climate change is **irrefutable**—that the evidence is too strong to be doubted. Others are **inexorable** in their belief that global climate change is a myth; that any changes we witness are part of the natural weather cycle. What's your opinion?

3. Children can be delightful people. They can also be **incorrigible**. Describe one you know who falls into that second category. In what ways is this child uncontrollable or unmanageable?

4. Write about a time that your pride was hurt—perhaps by a critical remark from someone. How long did your fit of **pique** last? How did you express your resentment?

5. How would you describe yourself politically—as a liberal, a conservative, a middle-of-the-roader, or something else? Are you "rubbed the wrong way" by people who have **partisan** views that are different from your own? Write about how relationships can be **marred** when people hold opposing political beliefs.

Chapter 17 (Fashion Show)

1. What is a place you have visited that has given you a **reverent** feeling? Perhaps it was a place of great natural beauty, or a place you consider holy, or a place associated with a person or event that you greatly respect. Describe that place and the feelings of awe it inspired.

2. It's not unusual to hear people say after a misfortune, "I knew something bad was going to happen." Do you believe such **premonitions** are actually possible? Why or why not?

3. What's the worst movie you've ever seen? It shouldn't be just a bad movie, but one whose awfulness was so **egregious** that the movie was unforgettable. Were there any **prestigious** actors in the movie, or was it acted by unknowns? What factors made the movie so very dreadful?

4. What kind of comedy movies do you prefer? Do you like **zany**, slapstick movies that rely on physical humor and gross-out jokes—or more **urbane**, sophisticated comedies whose humor comes from clever dialog? Write about your preference, including recent examples of each type.

5. You have to clean your room, which is a real mess. You hate to clean your room. Fortunately, you have a younger brother or sister whom you can sometimes **cajole** into doing unpleasant tasks for you. Write a dialog between the two of you in which you persuade your sibling to do the cleaning. When your sibling **capitulates**, indicate how you would reward him or her for giving in to your request.

Chapter 18 (Math Anxiety)

1. What is a class that you approached with **trepidation**, because you expected the subject matter to be difficult? Once you actually began the class, was the subject matter as **inscrutable** as you expected, or less puzzling?

2. Members of families often share certain traits—anything from "We're all good at softball" to "We hate anchovies." Because of this, a family member who does not share that trait—for example, one sister who loves anchovies—may stand out as an oddity. In what way are you such a family **aberration**? How do you not fit in with the others?

3. From your observation, would you say that a child is born with a certain personality, or is personality formed by the child's environment? In other words, is personality **congenital**, or does it develop in response to what goes on in the child's world? Explain.

4. Usually, humility is a good thing. But now, we'd like you to **extol** something about yourself. Write about a good quality or feature that you possess. Maybe it's your skill as a cook, or your singing voice, or your beautiful eyes, or your ability to give good advice. Praise that quality or feature to the skies!

5. Sometimes when we are trying to be serious and dignified, something unexpected happens which makes it extremely difficult to keep our **composure**. Write a lighthearted account of a time you were trying to be calm and composed, but faced a **formidable** challenge to doing so. What finally happened?

Chapter 19 (The Roma)

1. Imagine that you are talking to a fortune-teller. How would you finish this sentence? "If you are *really* clairvoyant, you'll tell me . . ."

2. How would you describe the people living contiguous to your house or apartment? Are any of them officious—always getting involved in your business? Or are they more taciturn people who quietly keep to themselves? Give examples.

3. When vegetarians, vegans, and other people who limit what they will eat go to other people's homes, should the hosts accommodate them by providing special dishes? Or is it up to the guests to provide their own food? Discuss.

4. Many people are concerned about the effects of electronic entertainment (TV, video games, computers, etc.) on children. Some worry that spending hours sitting in front of a screen debilitates kids, making them inactive, overweight and unhealthy. Others go further, saying that electronic entertainment obliterates kids' creativity and imagination, making them unable to think for themselves. Which of these points of view do you agree with? Write about what *you* think electronic entertainment does to (or for) kids, giving evidence for your opinion.

5. Imagine that you are a store detective, in charge of preventing shoplifting. As you observe shoppers, what sort of stealthy behaviors alert you to a possible shoplifter? Other than simply watching people, what are other actions you would take in order to preclude shoplifting? Write a guide for newly hired store detectives. In it, describe typical shoplifting behavior, and then recommend appropriate actions the detectives could take to prevent this crime.

Chapter 20 (The Jonestown Tragedy)

1. Being famous would certainly have its advantages. But if you were famous, you would be under constant pressure to be cordial to strangers who felt that they knew you. It would be grueling to have photographers constantly around trying to catch you in unflattering situations. In your opinion, would being famous be worth the trouble? Why or why not?

2. When you were a kid, which of your friends would you say had the most discordant home life? Describe a typical visit to the friend's home, showing the lack of harmony between family members. How did your friend react to the arguments? Did he or she become quiet and sullen, or loud and argumentative?

3. When (or if) you have children, will you expect them to be submissive—easy to indoctrinate and quick to obey your instructions? Or will it be OK if they ask questions and even argue with you? Explain which parenting style you favor and why you prefer it.

4. Think of a time when two of your friends were angry with each other. Write about their argument. What did each indict the other for? Did you feel that one was to blame, or did they share the blame equally?

5. Sadly, some people seem to be truly their own worst enemy. They engage in wanton behavior that is self-destructive, and thwart the efforts of others to help them. Write about someone you know who fits this description. Do you have any theories about why he or she behaves this way?

Chapter 21 (Helen Keller)

1. Do you get e-mails from friends warning you of viruses, hoaxes, crimes, and another alarming topics? Many of these forwarded e-mails are fallacious—filled with half-truths or sometimes outright lies. Is it worthwhile to try to elucidate the truth about these e-mails to the sender, or is it better to just ignore them?

2. Give some recent examples of what you consider hypocrisy on the part of public figures. Be specific about the difference you perceive between each person's words and actions. Do you think these people should be publicly chastised for their insincerity? Why or why not?

3. Of all the trite phrases out there, the one that seems to annoy people most is "Have a nice day." If you were in a particularly irritable mood, what is a caustic response you might make to that phrase?

4. Think about the vacation site you would prefer—a quiet cabin at the edge of a placid lake with no neighbors, a beach house in a town with lots of entertainment, or somewhere else. How would you spend your time there? Write about the type of vacation "escape" that most appeals to you.

5. Of your friends in school, which one is the most assiduous student? Write a description of that person, giving examples of his or her diligent work and study habits.

Chapter 22 (Figures of Speech)

1. The purpose of a movie trailer is to whet viewers' interest in seeing the movie. In your opinion, what makes a good (or bad) movie trailer? What are some particularly good (or bad) trailers you have seen?

2. Certain colloquial words and phrases are common to certain geographical areas. For instance, in some parts of the United States, a carbonated beverage is "pop," while in others, it is called "soda." What are some other conversational words or phrases you're aware of that vary from location to location?

3. Crass comedies—love them or hate them? "Gross-out" movies have become increasingly popular in recent years, with tasteless gags, toilet humor, etc. given center stage. Do you enjoy these movies, or do you find them too tasteless and not funny at all? Explain.

4. The oldest child, the middle child, the youngest child—each position in the family has its special prerogatives, to which the other family members give tacit consent. Write about the privileges that seem to automatically accompany each of these positions. Feel free to use hyperbole—exaggeration for comic effect.

5. Write about a time you needed to make an important decision. Do you feel you were discerning as you went about the process of making that decision, or do you think you could have been more perceptive? Looking back at the decision itself, do you feel now it was a judicious one? Or do you wish you had made another choice?

Chapter 23 (When Is a Treatment Therapy?)

1. "Alternative medicine" is a large category that includes such things as massage, acupuncture, herbal remedies, and meditation—all practices that some people believe to be **therapeutic**, even **potent**, while others dismiss as **spurious** and a waste of money. Have you had any experience with alternative medicine? What is your opinion?

2. What is the most **rigorous** physical activity you have ever participated in? How did you feel during and after that challenging experience?

3. Would a person looking at your bedroom conclude that you were an orderly, organized person, or a person who lives in a **haphazard** way? Would you **assent** to this conclusion, or would you disagree? Explain.

4. Think of a time when you and a friend or family member went through a rough patch in your relationship. Write about what either of you did to try to **ameliorate** the situation. Did those efforts to improve it work?

5. When you think of the qualities you would like in a romantic partner, certain physical qualities probably come to mind. But what are the **intangible** qualities you would look for in a partner? Write about a few of those non-physical qualities and why they are important to you.

Chapter 24 (Hawks and Doves)

1. Pit bulls are dogs that many people have strong feelings about. Some claim that they are too **volatile** to be safe around people; that you can never trust pit bulls not to suddenly become **pugnacious**. Others say that if they are not raised to be fighters, they are as gentle as any other dog. What's your opinion? Why do you feel as you do?

2. When most people witness an **altercation** between people on the street, their tendency is to ignore it, look **impassive**, and keep on going. But are there circumstances that would cause you to stop and get involved in the argument or maybe even try to **placate** the people involved? What would you have to observe in order to make you stop?

3. Have you ever been conned? Have you fallen victim to the **guile** of a person trying to get money through trickery and lies? Explain what happened.

4. Many movies are memorable because of an unforgettable villain—a truly evil character who sends chills up your spine. Who is a **malevolent** movie villain that you will always remember? Write about this character, including, in your description, examples of his or her wickedness.

5. Think about a time when you changed your plans in **deference** to the wishes of someone you cared about. Write about that occasion and why you yielded to the other's wishes.

Chapter 25 (New Year's Resolutions)

1. A weather-related **phenomenon** can be beautiful, terrifying, or awe-inspiring. This kind of event includes, for example, northern lights, tornadoes, hurricanes, or tidal waves. What is a weather-related phenomenon that you have observed? How did you respond to the experience?

2. When you're very upset about something—angry or sad or worried—what are some techniques you know can help you feel more **serene**? Do you need to achieve **catharsis** by, for instance, yelling or crying? Or can other techniques, such as talking to a friend or listening to music, soothe you?

3. "Déjà vu," a French expression meaning "already seen," is a sensation most people are familiar with. It's a brief, **ephemeral** feeling that you have witnessed or experienced a new situation before. Have you ever experienced déjà vu? What do you think could possibly explain it?

4. OK, this time you're really going to do it—make a **resolution** that you keep! Write, either humorously or seriously, about resolutions you have made and broken. Then write about one thing you're determined to do and *know* you can succeed at.

5. We've all done it—we've blurted out something we shouldn't have said and then wished we could **retract** it. Write a paragraph about a time you said something you later wanted to take back. Explain what **induced** you to say the unwise thing in the first place. Did you do anything afterward to **rectify** the situation?

Chapter 26 (Weird Facts)

1. What is a food that you have a strong **aversion** to? Have you tried to overcome your dislike of it, or are you **intractable** in your insistence that you hate it and that is that?

2. How would you describe your musical tastes? Do you like only a narrow category of music, or are your tastes **eclectic**, ranging across many categories? Explain.

3. When you have trouble sleeping, what are some remedies you have tried? Which ones would you recommend for their **soporific** effect?

4. What kind of dogs are your favorites? Are you drawn to good-sized **hardy** dogs that can spend lots of time outdoors playing roughly, or do you prefer more delicate, **diminutive** dogs that spend most of their time in the house? Which do you think make better pets? Write about the kind of dog that you would want to share your home and your life. (Alternatively, write about what kind of cat you prefer, choosing, perhaps, between purebred cats and cats that are "free to a good home.")

5. If you had a difficult decision to make about your future, which one of your friends or relatives would you go to for advice? Write a paragraph about that person and why you consider him or her more **astute** than average.

Chapter 27 (The Scholar)

1. There's an old saying that you should never discuss religion or politics at dinner. Certainly these are two topics that many people cannot talk about without **fervor**. What topic do you find hard to discuss without getting excited and emotional? Why do you think this topic **engenders** such feelings in you?

2. Especially in this era of celebrity magazines and gossip websites, there are certain people who seem famous simply for being famous—that is, no one is quite sure *why* they are well-known. Who are some current examples of famous people whose **renown** is hard to understand? Can you think of reasons why they might have become famous?

3. Imagine that you have the power to change one aspect of your school that you consider old-fashioned or outdated. It could be a rule, a class, or a physical aspect of the school. What is that one **archaic** aspect that you would change, and how would you change it?

4. Who is a quiet, little-known person you know whom you admire—perhaps one who has achieved success through **painstaking** efforts? Write an explanation of why you consider this modest person **laudable**. Give examples that show why he or she is deserving of praise.

5. Some people, even if they don't have a lot of formal education, just seem to know a lot about many subjects. Write about an **erudite** person that you know. What are some topics this person is knowledgeable about? Does the person seem **pompous** about his or her range of knowledge, or is he or she humble?

Chapter 28 (A Case of Depression)

1. It's late summer, and your garden is overflowing with produce. You have a **profusion** of tomatoes, zucchini, cucumbers, and peppers. What are some dishes you would make using some or all of those ingredients? How else could you put the extra homegrown vegetables to good use?

2. Some people actually like snakes. Others are **resigned** to dealing with them with **equanimity**, even if they don't much like snakes. Still others respond to the thought of being anywhere near a snake with terror. Which category do you belong in? Explain.

3. Certain reality shows—for example, *The Dog Whisperer, Nanny 911*, and *Super Nanny*—let us watch experts dealing with other people's badly behaved pets and children. Why do you think such shows are popular? Why might people enjoy watching other people's **recalcitrant** dogs and kids? Can you **surmise** anything about either the people appearing on the shows or the people tuning in?

4. You and your best friend (or significant other) have had a huge argument. This person, so important in your life, has been completely unreasonable, and you are not at all sure you can ever forgive him or her. Then there is a knock on the door. It's the UPS driver delivering a package from your best friend (or significant other). What could be in the package that would completely **mollify** you and help the two of you get back together? Write a description of the package and its contents.

5. Write about two people you know—one a lively, **convivial** person, and the other a low-energy, **listless** person. Describe how you imagine the two would interact at a party.

Chapter 29 (Scientific Discoveries)

1. There are some entertainers and athletes who are so enormously talented that they seem to be in a category all their own. Who, in your opinion, is an entertainer or athlete whose talents are truly **prodigious**? Give evidence that supports your choice.

2. Most of us are **biased** against certain kinds of movies. We'll say, for instance, that we don't like war movies or scary movies with **nefarious** villains. What is a category of movie (or, if you prefer, of TV show) that you're prejudiced against? Why do you dislike it so much? Also, can you think of any movie or show in that category that is an **anomaly**—one you like despite its subject matter?

3. When you feel the symptoms of an **incipient** cold coming on, what do you do? Are there any home remedies that you think can prevent or shorten the illness, especially if you use them right away, when the cold hasn't fully developed? What has been your experience with these cures?

4. When have you had to change your mind? Write about a time you initially disliked something—a job, a class, a person—but learned to **temper** your dislike as time went on. What caused you to soften your attitude?

5. Who is a person whom you have mixed feelings about—you can't quite decide if you like him or her? Write about your relationship with the person and what causes you to feel this **ambivalence**.

Chapter 30 (Saint Francis of Assisi)

1. Many people **deprecate** today's movies for being too violent. Are you disturbed by what you consider needless, **gratuitous** violence in films? Or do you think the violence in movies serves a purpose? Explain.

2. Imagine that for the next month, you will be required to live the extremely **ascetic** life of a strict monk. You will have just enough food to live on, no treats or desserts, and no electronic entertainment of any kind. Your only furniture will be a hard-backed chair and a bed. In addition, you aren't allowed to talk to anyone. Could you look at the month as a valuably **didactic** experience? If so, what has it taught you? Or would such an experience just drive you crazy?

3. Fill in the blank: "I may be flawed in some areas, but when it comes to _____, I am **unimpeachable**." Explain, either seriously or humorously, why you think you are without fault in this area.

4. What examples of **tawdry** clothing, makeup, jewelry, etc., do you observe on a daily basis? Write a description of some of the tasteless fashion choices you see around you.

5. Few people ever get to hear their own **eulogy**. Here is your chance to do so. Write a brief tribute to yourself, as if you had already died. Include the things you hope would be said about you at your own funeral.

D. Word List